Career Lines
and Careers

The Entry into Careers Series

Luther B. Otto, Series Editor
Boys Town Center
Boys Town, Nebraska

Career Lines and Careers

Volume III: Entry into Careers Series

Kenneth I. Spenner
Luther B. Otto
Vaughn R.A. Call
Boys Town Center

LexingtonBooks
D.C. Heath and Company
Lexington, Massachusetts
Toronto

Library of Congress Cataloging in Publication Data

Spenner, Kenneth I.
 Career lines and careers.

 (Entry into careers series; v. 3)
 Bibliography: p.
 Includes indexes.
 1. Occupations. 2. Vocational guidance. I. Otto, Luther B.
II. Call, Vaughn R.A. III. Title. IV. Series.
HF5381.S732   331.7'02   82-47855
ISBN 0-669-03645-5   AACR2

Published simultaneously in Canada

Printed in the United States of America

International Standard Book Number: 0-669-03645-5

Library of Congress Catalog Card Number: 82-47855

To

Patrick
Christopher
Nathan
Timothy
Stephen
Jonathan
Patrick
Angie
Theresa
Sherie
Carol

Contents

List of Figures

List of Tables

Preface and Acknowledgments

Careers play a central role in the lives of many people in industrial societies. The same topic is among the scholarly endeavors of several disciplines, including economics, sociology, and vocational psychology. This book addresses careers differently from most conventional approaches. We introduce and promote the idea of career line. The concept has roots in several fields, most notably in sociology in the works of White (1970) and Spilerman (1977). We build on Spilerman's ideas, thus forming the agenda for the book. We acknowledge the intellectual debt to Spilerman yet absolve him of responsibility for our treatment of the concept.

Our reading of contemporary views on careers revealed two different approaches: one that depended on individual-level explanations for career outcomes and one that depended on structural-level explanations. Career line is a bridging concept that links individual and structural explanations for the work-role outcomes embodied in careers. Some of our analyses concentrate on the structural side of career lines: their nature and properties, empirical variations, and possible formative influences on career lines such as economic segmentation and the technical organization of work. Other analyses reflect individual-level explanations, as employment biographies take shape from the personal resources that people bring to the labor market and from the opportunity regimes engendered in career lines. As a result, several audiences may be able to speak to the proper limits of our ideas, including economists (human capital, economic segmentation, and job search), sociologists (status attainment, labor markets, occupations, careers, and the life course), vocational psychologists (career-development theories and life stages), and educators (transferable skills).

This book is a product of the Career Development Program at the Boys Town Center. The program has the dual goals of generating new and useful knowledge and disseminating it in service to youth and families. The Center provides a continuing base of support for these activities. No institutional endorsement should be inferred, however.

The book is the third volume in the Entry into Careers series. Volume I provided a detailed design statement for the larger program of research. Volume II detailed the theory and method we used to locate 98.1 percent of Career Development Study participants twelve years after high school.

We acknowledge the help of several people: Aage Sørensen, Rachel Rosenfeld, Robert Althauser, Alan Bayer, and Dennis Hogan for reactions to the manuscript; David Chapin and John Hartman for software design; Ruth Rabalais, Jim Peterson, and Kevin Leicht for programming, coding, and clerical assistance; Sandy Wendel for copy editing and manuscript preparation; Mary Pat Roy, Marilyn Pittillo, and Dorothy Runte for word-processing services; and the Computing and Library Service Divisions of the Boys Town Center for their services.

Career Lines
and Careers

1 Introduction

Career is an everyday concept. Conventional wisdom tells you that a career is something you possess. You either have a good one, a mixed or checkered one, or one that is a dead end. You evaluate going to school, being female, or taking a new job as good or bad for your career. In school, you explore varieties of careers and prepare for them. Then you enter a career, perhaps changing from one to another on encountering a midlife crisis or change of circumstances. Yet some people are judged to have never had a career after forty years of work.

American culture reflects an individual ideology, and conventional wisdom about careers mirrors this. You are judged by the degree of success you demonstrate in your career: first, whether you have one and second, if you have one, then how you are doing. Those who do not have a career have failed. Something went wrong with the way they prepared or how they performed. If you do have a career, then you can be ahead in it, behind in it, or on track. There is a blueprint for progression. The blueprint has a clock that ticks as you age. If you have invested sufficiently in human capital, then your career will yield a significant return on the investment with the passage of time. Further, if you manage the one you have by arranging and sequencing life's pieces into the proper mosaic, then you can determine your career destiny. Such is the conventional wisdom.

Our approach to careers differs from conventional wisdom. Rather than studying what makes those who have a *career* different from those who do not have one, we prefer to think of careers in nonevaluative terms. Everyone has a career simply by virtue of the jobs that he or she has held.

Careers are individual-level phenomena. We seek to understand the variation in all careers by promoting a new concept: *career line.* By career line we mean the determinable regularities in job sequences that people follow over time. A career line is a sequence of age-graded jobs that is common to a portion of the labor force. Career line is a structural-level concept as distinct from career, which is an individual-level concept. We provided a larger theoretical backdrop for these concepts in the initial book in this series (Otto, Call, and Spenner 1981).

This book is a study of career lines and how they shape careers. We have several objectives. First, we want to show how the concept of career line builds on contemporary approaches yet goes beyond them. We describe the

1

elementary properties of career lines and pursue one measure of a large number of career lines for the American economy. A second objective is to conduct an initial examination of how career lines are rooted in labor markets and the organization of work. How are career lines formed and maintained? Third, we provide a gender comparison of career entry and the early career achievements with a conventional analytical model that leaves the effect of structure as it might be found in career lines unspecified. We use this baseline model for later comparison. Finally, we seek to show that a dynamic perspective that includes career lines and focuses on change in work-role outcomes over time adds understanding and explanatory power to the baseline model.

Several major premises underlie this book. Career lines are distinctively structural and have meaningful conceptual dimensions. Career lines can be measured and exhibit meaningful patterns of variation. Career lines define normative patterns of work-role entry, exit, rates of progression and job change, and work-role outcomes such as status, earnings, and other job rewards. Career lines have their origins in labor markets, firms, and the structure of work.

Careers are not merely a matter of personal choice or achievement. Rather, employment biographies are in part structured by preexisting career lines and the regimes of opportunity that they contain. Conventional models of careers that explain work-role outcomes only in terms of personal resources provide an incomplete view of work careers. Dynamic models that incorporate the logic of career lines and explain change in work-role outcomes over time offer a more realistic view of careers. The premises form the agenda for this book.

In this chapter we review conventional approaches to careers. This includes the historical context of career studies and several contemporary approaches. Our approach builds on previous studies. The ideas of career line and career are not new. We use the two concepts—career line and career—in concert to explain how people's employment biographies are shaped by the social structure and by a person's own attributes.

Conventional Views of Careers

Scholarly treatments of career reflect many of the themes contained in conventional wisdom. Several disciplines have studied careers, including vocational and industrial psychology, economics, and sociology. The various disciplinary approaches constitute views of what careers are and how they operate. The approaches have characteristic strengths and weaknesses that inform the concept of career line.

Career as Personal Preferencè and Life Stage

Two themes predominate in psychological studies (Super 1957; Holland 1973; and Roe 1957). The first is the trait-factor assumption, which says that jobs and careers are environments that reflect personality and interest differences of people. Before entry into the labor force, people's personality and self-concept more or less match occupational environments. Occupational choice, job satisfaction, and career progression are related to the match between personal and occupational characteristics. Personality-environment "fit" motivates individual behavior and accounts for the variation in careers among people. As discussed in this literature, career typically is a matter of personal choice or underlying personality predispositions.

The second theme in psychological studies of career is the notion of life stage. Through aging and social definitions, people pass through developmental stages. As part of development, vocational concerns and behaviors change. Super's (1963) stages of vocational development are typical: crystallization (ages 14-18), specification (ages 18-21), implementation (ages 21-24), stabilization (ages 25-35), and consolidation (ages 35 and up). The stages are nonreversible and immutable: People pass through them without turning back and move through the stages at the prescribed ages more often than not. Levinson (1978) offers a contemporary version of the life-stage theme. The underlying notion is that the stages are preprogrammed and are part of the biological and social aging of people.

In summary, psychological approaches emphasize the elements of choice and personal development in careers. By comparison, a career-line perspective suggests that choices occur within the limits imposed by normative patterns of job movement. While elements of personality may manifest in occupational aspirations and career choice, these processes are subject to the effects of background and other social influences. While workers may fit their personalities to jobs, there is substantial evidence that jobs and careers shape personalities (Kohn and Schooler 1973, 1978; Miller et al. 1979).

The notions surrounding life stages are empirical issues for which there is little data from large samples. By way of informing the concept of career lines, life-stage approaches suggest attention to the possibility that age-graded patterns in job changes may generate evidence of life stages in the population, or patterns of change in other life domains may be reflected in the age variations in career lines. Yet, life-stage approaches with few stages, little conceptualization of the stages, and no account given to variation in stage passage and timing do not appear to capture accurately the life course complexity of heterogeneous samples of people (for example, see Hogan 1981; see also, Rush, Peacock, and Milkovich 1980). Continuous, rather than discrete, concepts for timing offer greater promise.

Career as Orderly Progression
and Individual Achievement

Several areas of sociological and economic study offer two alternate views of careers: as an orderly progression of jobs and as individual achievement. The studies conveniently group into two periods: early (before the mid-1960s) and recent (mid-1960s to mid-1970s). The first group illustrates the view of careers as an orderly progression of jobs. The second group illustrates the view of careers as individual achievement.

During the early period, the investigation of careers consisted of case studies of a single occupation or industry, and an occasional study attempted more comprehensive treatment of the career concept. The case studies (for example, Hall 1948; Janowitz 1960) offered insight into the social world of occupations. They did little to describe the differences among careers or to offer analytical treatment to the larger relationships that cause occupation-level variation. A few studies ventured beyond the single occupation. For example, Lipset and Bendix (1952a, 1952b) and Lipset and Malm (1954) highlighted the variety of jobs that a sample of Oakland men held over their employment histories.

Form and Miller (1949) postulated *initial, trial,* and *stable* work periods as developmental phases in the occupational career. The initial period referenced jobs held during the pursuit of formal education. The trial phase indexed job or firm switches within a three-year period. The stable phase captured employment episodes that were longer than three years in the same job or firm.

The phases are life stages in the sense noted earlier, but for Form and Miller, the career stages were reversible. Workers could move back and forth from one stage to another. Indeed, many workers in their sample did. The research showed that secure careers, those in a stable phase, were associated with advantaged backgrounds and with white-collar, skilled, and supervisor occupations. Insecure careers—those oscillating to the trial phase—were associated with manual and unskilled positions and disadvantaged backgrounds. Form and Miller were among the first to call attention to career as a concept in its own right. Further, they produced a simple typology that classified types of work histories and then related the types to external variables.

Several years later, Wilensky (1960, 1961) called attention to the social consequences of the orderly work career. Although his sample showed that comparatively few men had an orderly progression of jobs with increasing prestige, such an ideal work history enhances social participation and may be strategic for social order. Also, the first large-scale studies of occupational mobility began during this period (Palmer 1954). In summary, studies from the early period introduced a concept of career and established precedent for investigating the social causes and consequences of careers.

The recent period features the investigation of ideas from economics about how individuals attain education, occupation, and income (Blau and Duncan 1967). The status-attainment paradigm took formal years of schooling, levels of occupational status, and income at a single point as the phenomena to be explained. Achievement and careers occurred in the context of the socioeconomic life cycle and comprised successive linkages between family background, ability, school performance, the transition from school to work, and the establishment of one's own family.

Human-capital theory (Becker 1975) provided the logic for the translation of individual endowments (ability, schooling, health) into returns in the marketplace (status and earnings). The human-capital and status-attainment traditions demonstrated how attributes of people and their backgrounds generate schooling, occupational, and income attainments at different points in the life course. The traditions have been cumulative and contain numerous extensions and elaborations.

With few exceptions, career was a weak concept in these studies. The term was frequently used but only in reference to a period in the life cycle ("the early career," "mid-career") or to an unspecified progression of jobs. Age and change were implicit features of the socioeconomic life cycle, not explicitedly developed features of employment histories. Occasionally, the socioeconomic career was more explicitly studied: assessments of the causal chains in occupational status for jobs at successive ages of men (Featherman 1971, 1973; Kelley 1973a, 1973b). But the unit of analysis in this research was the individual. Occupational career meant continuity in status or earnings levels while other career outcomes were ignored.

Social structure played a distant role in these groups of studies. There was no explicit conceptualization of how social structures and institutional arrangements might shape job histories. Only select points, such as first job or current job, in job histories were most often the subject of study. What one obtained by way of career outcomes was still fundamentally seen as a matter of personal factors. In human-capital theory, workers were rewarded in the career according to their productivity (Mincer 1974). Productivity changed when the worker acquired new human capital such as schooling or experience.

The traditions that view careers as orderly progression and individual achievement inform our career-line perspective in two ways. First, generic groups of occupations may facilitate distinct types of employment histories. Perhaps each type contains different forms and levels of progression—some built around skill progression, others around increasing seniority, and others may contain no progression. Second, the studies suggest that a career-line perspective attend to the socioeconomic life cycle and the larger framework of intergenerational transmission of inequality. To these perspectives, a career-line approach can give a more prominent explanatory role to social structure, afford more comprehensive coverage of the labor force, and treat more explicitly the dynamic variation in careers as it is shaped by career lines.

Careers as Labor Markets

In the 1960s and 1970s scholarly interest in radical and structural perspectives on social inequality reemerged. They offered a different view of careers: as labor market phenomena. Where status attainment and human capital viewed social inequality as differences among people in endowments and returns to endowments, radical perspectives shifted the focus to the larger structural mechanisms that might cause inequality among positions. The dual labor market hypothesis illustrates that difference (Doeringer and Piore 1971).

Jobs fall in one of two labor markets. Doeringer and Piore defined an internal labor market as an administrative unit that can occur within a single firm or can span establishments, such as craft or trade unions and professional associations. Administrative rules and procedures determine the price and allocation of labor for jobs. Internal labor markets contain good jobs, stable employment, and promotion hierarchies. External labor markets price and allocate labor to jobs on the basis of direct economic relationships such as competition. External market jobs are lower in quality, offer few advancement opportunities, and are not insulated from competition as are jobs in internal markets. The economic segmentation implied by market sectors emerges from larger changes in the economy that differentiate large, concentrated, capital-intensive firms from smaller, less capital-intensive ones (Reich, Gordon, and Edwards 1973). But consensus is lacking on this point. In certain versions of the thesis, mobility chains are a defining characteristic of market sectors (Piore 1975; Althauser and Kalleberg 1981a).

The rise of radical perspectives was important. Careers were not merely a matter of individual achievement. The studies recognized the existence of preprogrammed lines of job mobility. Depending on a person's location in the job structure, career opportunities were set and beyond the realm of personal control. Further, the positional inequality found in careers flowed from the larger organization of firms, occupations, industries, sectors, the economy, and society.

Substantial disagreement exists on the conceptualization and measurement of sectors and labor markets (Baron and Bielby 1980). The state of evidence on the operation of sectors as they shape career outcomes is in an early stage of development and is equivocal (Kalleberg and Sørensen 1979). Many of the applications of radical and structuralist ideas ignore the role of personal factors and competing neoclassical explanations (Cain 1976; Baron and Bielby 1980).

Career line is neither a well-developed concept in this literature nor is there sizable empirical evidence on the operation of lines of job progression. As for other views of careers, this tradition provided little empirical work on the dynamics of careers within or across sectors and labor markets. The ways in which promotion hierarchies might combine with personal resources to shape careers is, at best, implicit in the theories. Finally, this literature typically deals with change in jobs and careers in very general qualitative terms rather than in explicit, falsifiable statements.

Yet radical and structural literatures provide a young but important legacy for studying how social structure shapes careers. The research tradition offers an important source of hypotheses about how career lines are formed and maintained. In turn, a career-line perspective offers a concept that bridges the larger structures in the society and economy with the micro-reality of jobs in people's employment biographies.

The Next Steps

Past and contemporary research identifies important components of an expanded treatment of career lines and careers. The career-line concept received its most formal development in a paper by Spilerman (1977). Spilerman distinguished a career, or person's job biography, from structurally formed career lines or the age-graded sequences of jobs through which significant numbers of workers move. As we shall see, several other writers use concepts very similar to career line. But Spilerman defined the concept in a way that bridges social structure and the person. Employment biographies were acted out on the stages called career lines.

Spilerman's work provided a conceptual beginning. He did not report measurement of a large number of career lines in the economy necessary to study their properties and effects. Spilerman's work set an important agenda, one that defines the objectives and chapters of this book. The first item is a more extensive measurement of career lines and description of their properties. The second asks how career lines are formed by larger social structures and institutional arrangements. The third asks how people mesh with career lines. We know from other research traditions—notably status-attainment and human-capital—that people's attributes powerfully affect work-role outcomes. Yet how do personal resources combine with career lines to shape people's job histories and the work outcomes that they experience over time?

In summary, our study is one of career lines and careers. Our primary objective is to advance the concepts in a way that builds on the strengths of earlier approaches and addresses some of the weaknesses. We develop the concept of career line—its properties and possible origins. The work proceeds under one measurement strategy for career lines. Next, we jointly consider career lines and careers. Compared to baseline explanations that explain work outcomes only in terms of personal resources, we examine a dynamic model that incorporates the concept of career line. These analyses rest on a different analytical strategy and data set. Taken together, the dual strategies offer more varied evidence against which to judge the worth of a career-line perspective.

Organization of the Book

Chapter 2 continues the introduction to the study with review of data bases. The 1970 Census Public Use Samples form one basis for estimating career lines. The Career Development Study sample forms another, but in the context of the personal resources men and women bring to the labor market.

The next several chapters deal with career lines as estimated from the census data. Chapter 3 identifies conceptual properties of career lines. What are the basic ways that career lines vary? We illustrate the conceptual properties with one measure of career lines. In chapter 4, we describe the variation in elementary properties for a comprehensive set of career lines for the economy. We examine the variation by the major occupation group in which career lines have their origin and destination and by the gender composition of career lines. The chapter is descriptive and establishes the workability of the concept and one set of operations.

Chapter 5 retreats to several literatures in search of hypotheses about the determinants of career-line features. What causes variation in career lines? In Spilerman's (1977) terms, how are career lines rooted in labor-market organization? The hypotheses—gleaned from neoclassical and segmentation perspectives—suggest the skill level of the career line along with its economic sector location should be important determinants of career-line features. We examine evidence that bears on the hypotheses.

The final chapters of the book examine career and career lines in tandem, focusing on the explanation of work-role outcomes. Chapter 6 introduces models that explain career outcomes in terms of personal resources. Chapter 7 examines models that expand the baseline explanation to include the effect of career lines.

Chapter 8 summarizes the findings and conclusions. We reflect on some implications of our work and discuss several directions for future research.

2

Data Sources

This study relies on two data sources: the Public Use Samples from the 1970 Census of Population and the Career Development Study sample. We provided background on each data set in volume I of the series (Otto, Call, and Spenner 1981). Here we review the details pertinent to the analyses in this volume. For the census data we provide information on the sample definition, job categories, and the measurement of career lines. For the Career Development Study data we provide an overview of the time 1 and time 2 data designs and present information on demographic comparisons and nonresponse bias for the data set.

The data requirements for the study center on the concepts, career line and career, and two corresponding data bases. Because career lines reference sequences of jobs that occur with regularity, we sought data that permitted the measurement of a large number of statistically frequent, age-specific job transitions. We lacked the ideal data—that is, job histories from a very large sample over the life course—so we settled on synthetic cohort analyses of census data as an approximation. Second, careers reference the employment biographies of workers. The study of career entry required knowledge of event histories of jobs and other life course activities during the first decade of labor-force participation from a heterogeneous sample of men and women. We collected the Career Development Study data for this purpose.

Census Sample

The 1970 census data offered a cross section of people in their current jobs. The cross-sectional data contained a longitudinal piece of information: the detailed occupation and industry of the job a person held in 1965. The five-year job transition information, when grouped for workers of different ages, permitted a synthetic approximation of career lines. Each age group provided a snapshot of detailed job transitions. Under the assumptions of a synthetic cohort, the consecutive snapshots were linked to provide coverage of job transitions over the work portion of the life course (Spilerman 1977). Estimation of a large number of career lines for detailed job categories necessitated the large census sample.

We used the combined 3 percent neighborhood, county, and state Public Use Samples (N $\cong$ 3.3 million; U.S. Bureau of the Census 1972). The target population included persons age 23 to 62 in 1970 or age 18 to 57 in 1965, and persons who reported a codable occupation and industry in 1965 and 1970 (N $\cong$ 1.874 million). The age range corresponds to the earliest age of post-high school labor-force entry and an age intermediate to early and mandatory retirement. We did not restrict the analysis by race, gender, region of the country, or hours worked per week. Instead, we measured these characteristics for members of career-line categories (for example, sex composition or average hours worked per week).

We grouped the sample into 8 five-year age cohorts accomplishing the match to the 1965 to 1970 quinquennium for the synthetic cohort. The basic components of career lines are jobs, operationally defined as detailed 1970 census occupation-industry categories (U.S. Bureau of the Census 1971; see appendix A). The categories we use capture a mixture of occupation and industry variation, but they do not tap the variation in career lines as it might be organized within firms or labor markets in one or more firms. This is an important limitation because variations in career lines that depend on firm changes but involve staying in the same occupation and industry are not captured with the census data.

We linked the age-specific job transitions for each job category using branching criteria. Branching criteria are decision rules that designate a job transition from the ith origin category to the jth destination category for the kth age group as a career line. Our experimentation led us to joint decision criteria in terms of transition probabilities ($P_{ijk} \geq .04$) and transition frequencies ($f_{ijk} \geq$ ten persons). A job transition meeting both criteria was designated a career line. For example, when calculated for the youngest age cohort, the 1970 career-line destination for a 1965 origin became the origin category for the next oldest cohort, and probabilities were again calculated, designating career-line transitions. The process was repeated for all 8 age cohorts and 384 job categories.[1] We refer to these estimates as *origin career lines*.

The branching criteria are a compromise between more relaxed rules that designate a larger number of career lines and stricter rules that reduce the number of career lines to the number of job categories. We also computed career-line sets for each 1970 destination job category, which we refer to as *destination career lines*. We constructed the two forms of career lines (origin and destination) identically, except that in the case of destination lines the transition probabilities are calculated with the 1970 age-specific category frequency as the denominator. The origin career lines use the 1965 age-specific category frequency as the term in the denominator of the transition probability. The origin career lines display where persons are likely to go, given location in an age-specific origin category. The destination career lines display the paths that people followed in order to reach an age-specific destination category. We use both forms of career lines in our analyses because they speak to different substantive questions.

Figure 2-1 provides an example of career lines for electric-power linemen and cablemen. Each job transition that exceeds the branching criteria is indexed with a transition probability (P_{ijk}) and a transition frequency (f_{ijk}). For example, 112 of 180 or 62 percent of 18- to 22-year-old cablemen and linemen in 1965 report the same job category in 1970. The other sixty-eight linemen and cablemen in 1965 reported forty-six different jobs in 1970. None of these transitions exceeds the branching criteria, so the job transitions are not displayed. The transition frequency (112) refers to the number of people who report the same job in 1965 and 1970. For successive age cohorts, the percentage who report being a lineman and cableman in 1965 and 1970 increases to over 80 percent for workers in their late forties and early fifties. Under synthetic cohort assumptions, we treat the eight successive job transitions as an approximation to the career line of being and staying an electric-power lineman and cableman. Thus a career line taken over the working lifetime is any unique path from left to right in the display.

There are two other career lines in figure 2-1. Both involve the transition to foremen in a transportation, communication, and utilities industry. One career line traces workers involved in line and cable work for fifteen years who then move to the foremen category and stay there for the remainder of their working lifetimes. Thus, 15 of 361 33- to 37-year-old linemen and cablemen in 1965 (4 percent) report being foremen in a related industry in 1970. Given this transition, we display the job-transition information for the foremen category in order to follow the career line. The third career line is identical except that the transition to foremen occurs five years later during the late thirties and early forties. We refer to the three career lines emanating from the linemen and cablemen position as the career-line set for electric-power linemen and cablemen.

Electric-power linemen and cablemen make other transitions, but these do not exceed the branching criteria. The focus on frequent transitions makes career lines distinctively structural. A job transition is a career line because it occurs with regularity. Frequency of transitions differentiates a career line from a piece or segment of a few people's career histories. A career line is structural because the more frequent transitions are embedded in the very organization of work, of industries, and of firms. Further, they are embedded in people's expectations and job behaviors.

The use of a synthetic cohort to estimate career lines involves several methodological issues (see Otto, Call, and Spenner 1981, pp. 29-35).[2] Most important, a synthetic cohort requires some strong assumptions. For example, we assume that the entire effect of workers' prior job histories as they might influence their 1970 job is translated through their 1965 job. We assume that young workers face the same mobility regime that older workers faced on entering the labor force, and younger workers will face a regime in the future that is equivalent to the one encountered by older

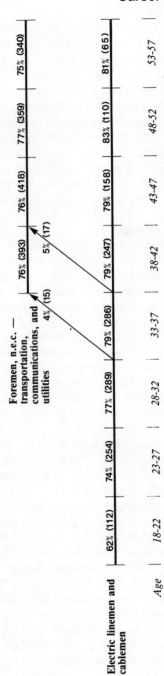

Figure 2-1. Career-Line Outflow Display: Electric-Power Linemen and Cablemen

workers today. Effectively, we assume that the economy and the occupational structure are in a steady state over time. This is obviously not true as
mobility regimes evolve over time, albeit slowly (Featherman and Hauser
1978). Further, cross-sectional cohorts have different sizes, rates of labor-
force participation, and death rates that are fallible substitutions for a true
cohort over its history (Duncan 1966). Elsewhere, we crudely estimated that
there was a 5 to 10 percent distortion in the transition probabilities caused
by violations of these assumptions (Otto, Call, and Spenner 1981). The distortion levels may be higher. The findings from analyses of the synthetic
cohort clearly await replication with more suitable data and assumptions.

The transition probabilities reflect two sources of variability in the occupational structure: the marginal distribution of workers to jobs and the
underlying mobility regime. The former is subject to more change historic-
ally, while the latter may have been quite constant in recent times (Featherman and Hauser 1978). The transition probabilities for career lines reflect
both the underlying mobility regime and growth or decline in the size of job
(and age) categories across cohorts. We chose not to attempt adjustments
for marginal change in the size of job categories for analyses in this book
because we consider marginal change to be a meaningful generator of
career-line patterns, not a confounding effect. The cost of this strategy is
that we cannot separate the effect of mobility regime from marginal
changes in inferences about career lines. For example, if a career line shows
an increased propensity to remain in the same job across successive cohorts,
then this may reflect a pattern in the underlying mobility regime and/or a
change in the age, job, or age-job distributions of workers between 1965
and 1970. Finally, we assume reliable measurement of contemporaneous
and retrospective reports of occupation and industry. Other research suggests that this is a reasonable assumption (Featherman and Hauser 1977).

For several analyses, we use variables such as median earnings and sex
composition measured for workers in each job category, based on census
data. In each case, we use the same target population that was used for
career lines. We describe these variables where they occur. Additionally,
some analyses require measures of job characteristics such as routinization,
complexity of work, or skill level. These measures rely on information in
the *Dictionary of Occupational Titles* (U.S. Department of Labor 1965) estimated for census occupation-industry categories. We describe the job
characteristic measures in later chapters.

In summary, our estimation strategy for career lines is a pragmatic one
that requires some strong assumptions. We proceed with the career-line estimation, recognizing, according to Blau and Duncan (1967, p. 183), that the
synthetic cohort is a fiction that is difficult to maintain with complete con-
sistency.

Career Development Study Sample

The data requirements for the joint study of career entry and career lines include a sample that references a heterogeneous population of men and women, with longitudinal information from adolescence and personal histories for work, family, and education through at least the first decade of labor-force participation. Our data source is the Career Development Study sample, which represents extensive panel data on men and women who were first studied as juniors and seniors in high school in 1965 and 1966 ($N = 6,729$). We resurveyed the same respondents in 1979 when they were 28 to 31 years old. Otto, Call, and Spenner (1981; Call, Otto, and Spenner 1982) provide complete design information, including sample design, time 1 survey procedures and instrumentation, the time 2 follow-up study procedures and instrumentation, and selected demographic comparisons. We summarize the information here.

The original investigators at Washington State University defined the population to consist of juniors and seniors in public high schools in the state of Washington during the 1965-1966 academic year. They drew a stratified sample of schools and administered an in-school questionnaire. We conservatively estimate that at least 86 percent of the target sample completed the questionnaire. The nonrespondents included a small number of students who refused and who were absent on the day of questionnaire administration. We refer to the group that completed the questionnaires as the 1966 sample. It includes persons who dropped out of high school after the date of survey. The original questionnaires gathered considerable background and social psychological information.

In 1979 we successfully relocated 98.1 percent of the original sample and completed telephone interviews with 86.9 percent (5,850 interviews). Excluding those who were deceased or institutionalized or who were foreign-exchange students in 1966, the time 2 telephone interview response represents 88.9 percent of the original eligible respondents.

The concept behind the time 2 data collection was that of "event history" (Hannan and Tuma 1979; Tuma, Hannan, and Groeneveld 1979). An event history records the start, duration, and endpoint of all episodes in a sequence. For example, in our data the event history for jobs contains the starting date, ending date, and other information about each job in a person's work history since leaving high school. The larger data requirements meant gathering event histories for education, family, military, and work domains since respondents left high school.[3]

We gathered the event histories with month as the smallest unit of time. For example, in the event history for schooling, we gathered a record of every formal and nonformal educational experience since high school, with greater detail for full-time episodes. The information included dates of attendance, interruptions, degrees, majors, and the name and location of the school. In the work history, we gathered detailed information for each full-time job and more limited information for spells of unemployment, work disability, part-time jobs, or periods of not working. Respondents held from zero to twenty-two different full-time jobs since leaving high school. For each full-time job, we gathered information such as occupation, industry, major activities and duties, firm or employer, class of worker, hours worked per week, promotions, salary, start and stop dates, and reasons for leaving the job. We coded all jobs in 1970 census occupation-industry categories (U.S. Bureau of the Census 1971).[4] For the Career Development Study sample, we report on the measurement of particular variables where they occur.

We made demographic comparisons of Career Development Study data to other state and national data. We found substantial similarities and a few differences. In social background, measured by father's occupation and education, the sample was very similar to comparably aged males in the state of Washington and the nation. If anything, sample members had slightly more advantaged socioeconomic origins and achievements at age 30, compared to other large samples of similar type. The only sizable difference was in racial composition. Only 2 percent of sample members were nonwhite compared to 4 percent of the state population and 12 percent of the nation in 1970.

Demographic comparisons aside, we report data on potential nonresponse bias in the 1979 follow-up data. With longitudinal data we can partially evaluate the seriousness of the problem by comparing sample statistics from 1966 for groups of respondents and nonrespondents in 1979.

Table 2-1 reports univariate statistics for selected variables in the 1966 sample for 1979 respondents and nonrespondents. The table also contains variable descriptions and metrics. The variables circumscribe the social background and high school academic performance and plans of respondents. We compare means and standard deviations and provide tests of significance for the difference between 1979 respondents and nonrespondents. The column labeled "error" is the difference between estimates in the 1966 sample and 1979 follow-up. The column labeled "bias" reports the error differences as a percentage of the 1966 sample standard deviation.

For example, the estimated mean and standard deviation for father's occupational status (Duncan SEI scale) are 44.14 and 25.36, respectively. The mean father's status for 1979 respondents is slightly above this at 44.29. The mean for 1979 nonrespondents is about one point below the 1966 sample mean at 43.10. The estimates of standard deviation are about equal across all groups. Neither mean nor standard deviation differences are significant when formally tested. The 1979 respondent mean overstates the 1966 mean by 0.15 of one scale point (error), or about one-half of 1 percent

Table 2-1
Descriptive Statistics for Select Variables in the 1966 Sample and 1979 Follow-Up

Variable	1966 Sample	1979 Respondents	1979 Nonrespondents	Error[f]	Bias	Test of Difference
Father's occupational status (Duncan scale)						
Mean	44.14	44.29	43.10	-0.15	-0.59	NS
Standard deviation	25.36	25.33	25.47	0.03	0.12	NS
Father's education[a]						
Mean	3.22	3.24	3.13	-0.02	-1.34	NS
Standard deviation	1.49	1.49	1.49	0.00	0.00	NS
Mother's education[a]						
Mean	3.18	3.21	3.04	-0.03	-2.63	**
Standard deviation	1.14	1.15	1.12	-0.01	-0.88	NS
Mother's employment (percent)						
Mean	54	55	46	-0.01	-2.00	NS
Standard deviation	50	50	50	0.00	0.00	NS
Parents' income[b]						
Mean	6.70	6.70	6.64	0.00	0.00	NS
Standard deviation	1.96	1.96	1.96	0.00	0.00	NS
Rural origin (percent)						
Mean	35	35	33	0.00	0.00	NS
Standard deviation	48	48	47	0.00	0.00	NS
Intact family (percent)						
Mean	85	85	80	0.00	0.00	*
Standard deviation	36	35	40	0.01	2.78	***
Number of siblings						
Mean	2.73	2.71	2.85	0.02	1.11	*
Standard deviation	1.81	1.79	1.94	0.02	1.11	*
Mental ability[c]						
Mean	48.88	48.88	48.78	0.00	0.00	NS
Standard deviation	8.31	8.30	8.53	0.01	0.00	NS

Grade point average[d]						
Mean	2.58	2.59	2.43	−0.01	−1.56	NS
Standard deviation	.64	.64	.67	0.00	0.00	NS
Parent encouragement to college (percent)						
Mean	80	81	76	−0.01	−2.50	***
Standard deviation	40	40	43	0.00	0.00	**
Friends with college plans (percent)						
Mean	63	64	53	−0.01	−2.08	***
Standard deviation	48	48	50	0.00	0.00	NS
College plans (percent)						
Mean	75	76	65	−0.01	−2.27	***
Standard deviation	44	43	48	0.01	2.27	***
Occupational aspirations (Duncan scale)						
Mean	56.63	57.10	53.20	−0.47	−2.09	***
Standard deviation	22.52	22.22	24.38	0.30	1.33	NS
N[e]	6,729	5,850	879			

*.01 ≤ P ≤ .05.

**.001 ≤ P < .01.

***P < .001.

NS = p > .05.

[a]Parental education metrics: 1 = eighth grade or less, 2 = some high school but not a graduate, 3 = high school but not a graduate, 4 = some college but not a graduate, 5 = college graduate, 6 = more than four years of college.

[b]Parental income metric: 1 = under $2,000; 2 = $2,000-$2,999; 3 = $3,000-$3,999; 4 = $4,000-$4,999; 5 = $5,000-$5,999; 6 = $6,000-$7,499; 7 = $7,500-$9,999; 8 = $10,000-$14,999, 9 = $15,000 or over.

[c]Washington Pre-College Test, average of verbal and quantitative scores. See chapter 6, table 6-1, note b, for further description.

[d]Overall grade point average for the high school years, where: A = 4.0, B = 3.0, C = 2.0, D = 1.0, and F = 0.0.

[e]Several variables were measured only for subgroups of the 1966 sample: parental income (one-sixth of the original sample) and friends with college plans (one-half of the original sample). In addition, each variable excludes a small number of cases with missing values.

[f]See text for definitions of error and bias.

of the standard deviation of father's occupational status in 1966 (bias = −0.59). In short, the difference is trivial for the case of father's occupational status.

The error and bias are very small across all of the variables in table 2-1. Although some of the differences are statistically significant under formal test, in no case is the bias even as much as 3 percent of the standard deviation for the variable in the 1966 sample. Some of the larger differences occur for college plans and occupational aspirations. Yet, even here the bias in inferences based on the 1979 responses is very small. From the 1966 sample, 75 percent of students planned to go to college and aspired to occupations with an average Duncan score of 56.63. The inferences are off by just over 2 percent if we use the 1979 respondents to make the same judgments. We conclude that 76 percent of students planned to attend college and aspired to occupations with an average Duncan score of 57.10. The nonrespondents as a group are different from respondents (65 percent plan to attend college; the mean of status aspirations is 53.20). In general, nonrespondents came from less advantaged backgrounds and have lower aspirations; but the number of nonrespondents is sufficiently small such that inferences based on respondents are not seriously distorted.

In summary, an initial look at nonresponse bias suggests that it is quite small. We assume this is the case for other variables in the data set, which is not an unreasonable assumption for many areas of study. Further, we assume that the effects of nonresponse bias are small as well for multivariate relationships. This assumption is less certain but still a reasonable one for this area of study (see, for example, Sewell and Hauser 1975).

Summary

The data requirements for the study center on the concepts for career line and career. By definition, career lines index frequent job transitions in the economy. To estimate career lines for a large number of job categories requires an extraordinary number of cases with information about job transitions. Using census data is one of the few available data sources if we choose to move beyond the domain of a single firm. The limitations of the census data include the very large data manipulation tasks and strong assumptions that are required to approximate time (age) in job histories. Thus the measures of career lines are synthetic approximations. We use them to judge the initial worth of a concept and welcome the refinements that future work will yield.

The detailed career histories of people are an equally valid way to inform the study of career lines. Typical data sets do not permit accurate estimation of a large number of career lines for detailed job categories, but other inferences about the interplay of careers and career lines are possible. The Career Development Study provides career histories for the first decade of labor-force experience. The event histories contained in the data measure the timing of all job moves. They permit more explicit consideration of time and change as features of careers and career lines. In conjunction with other event histories such as schooling, we can start untangling the ways that background and personal resources shape careers compared with the effects of structure found in career lines. Our initial comparisons of the Career Development Study data to other data sets, and the comparisons for nonresponse bias, offer some confidence in the data.

Notes

1. The full set of origin career line sets is graphically displayed in Otto, Spenner, and Call (1980).

2. For a commentary on the synthetic cohort strategy, consult Blau and Duncan (1967, pp. 177-188), Eckaus (1973, pp. 66-79), Mayer (1972), Spilerman (1977), Wells (1978), and Telesky (1979).

3. In addition to the time 2 telephone interview, we obtained mail-questionnaire data from 84 percent of respondents interviewed by telephone (73.1 percent of the 1966 sample). By mail questionnaire we gathered detailed attitudinal information on work and sex-role orientations and several other concepts, as well as further descriptive information on current job, marriage and family relations, and leisure-time activities. We were authorized by 72.7 percent of the 1966 sample to obtain their high school transcripts, from which we secured measures of several variables. We also used a reduced-form mail questionnaire to gather information on respondents who did not participate in the telephone interview ($N = 113$). The respondents who answered by mail are not part of the working sample in this book.

4. For information on the census method of occupation measurement and the reliability of retrospective reports of occupation, consult Featherman and Hauser (1977, pp. 51-80) and Bielby, Hauser, and Featherman (1977). Our coding reliability on a random sample of independently coded jobs was 93.7 percent, which compares favorably with established census procedures.

3 Conceptual Properties of Career Lines

Career line is a new concept that has not yet been used in any comprehensive fashion. Is the concept reasonable? Does it offer some explanatory advantage for the understanding of work histories and social inequality? A logical step in the development of the concept would be to elucidate the properties of career lines. We define an initial set of five elementary properties. We then illustrate the properties with a measure of career lines based on a synthetic cohort.

Jobs are the units that compose career lines. We conceptualize jobs as work roles or positions that have requirements for entry, as a set of routines that characterize the content of the role, and as rewards for role incumbency and performance. Career lines reference the determinable regularities in job sequences that people follow over time. The concept assumes that job movements and stabilities are patterned. These normative patterns of job change set expectations for significant numbers of workers over their employment histories. Career lines have identifiable, work-related consequences—requirements, routines, and rewards—for their incumbents. Additionally, empirical regularities describe entry and exit from career lines through a limited number of age-graded jobs and employment statuses. Career lines are nested in firms, occupations, industries, labor markets, and regions of the country. We assume a finite number of occupations, industries, and types of firms; hence, a finite but large number of career lines subsume a large portion of labor-force careers.

The concept is simple. It bridges social structure and the individual. It permits attention to age-related variations in job holding and change (Otto, Call, and Spenner 1981).

In identifying elementary properties of career lines, we distinguish among the following:

1. career-line features, which are the proper domain for elementary properties.
2. proximal causes of career-line features such as characteristics of labor markets or firms.
3. consequences that might flow from career-line features such as discrimination or shunting of a class of workers to a group of career lines.
4. features of individual work histories or careers such as a worker's earnings history.

Further, we distinguish between elementary and derived properties of career lines. A derived property is one that can be defined in terms of one or more elementary properties. Piore (1975) made a similar distinction in his discussion of characteristics of labor-market segments.

Research often blurs the distinction between elementary and derived properties. Many alleged properties of employment histories, such as *ordered, dead end, mobility blockage, a good career,* or *checkered-career* are not elementary properties of career lines, but rather are derived properties, proximal causes, consequences, or features of individual work histories. For example, Sofer (1970) describes the plight of British bureaucrats who experience "career disappointments" in response to "disorderly" versus "orderly" careers. At times, Sofer (1970, p. 25) alluded to "well established career routes" in the organization, consistent with the notion of career line. At other times in Sofer's discussion, career meant individual employment biography, whether upwardly mobile or not.

Order and disorder are derived properties of career lines and careers. Order in the career line can be defined as some composite of elementary properties of career lines, graded by age. Further, order in the individual career might simply be defined as job-hopping, whether or not the job-hopping sequence matches a pattern characteristic of many workers. Disorder may be the imputed psychological experience of the worker doing the hopping, rather than anything to do with the hopping per se. Alternately, order-disorder can be defined as the extent to which the career approximates the normative pattern implied in a career line for the number and timing of job changes. If a given manager is late in making a particular job transition that many of his or her counterpart managers have made by the same age, then there is some degree of disorder because the career departs from the career line.

Spilerman (1977, pp. 551, 559-565) briefly mentioned some features of career lines. They include entry portals, the number of constituent positions, availability of transfer options to alternate career lines, and the shape of returns in earnings, status, and work satisfaction. The list is a good starting point. But we think it is neither exhaustive in spanning the features of career lines nor are all of the items elementary properties. Some are derived properties. We seek a reduced, simple set of properties that offers a starting point. We propose five such properties: size, differentiation, holding power, ports of entry and exit, and role continuity.

Size

Size refers to the number of people, the sheer volume of flow of workers through a career line. A career line can be of constant size in two independent senses. Developmental time refers to age or age cohorts. Constant size over developmental time would mean an equal number of people at every age point in a career line. Historical time refers to real or calendar time (1910, for example). Constant size over historical time means either that the absolute number or relative proportion of workers in a career line compared to the total labor force remains equal across successive calendar years. It is difficult to imagine an example that equals the ideal type of constant size over developmental and historical time. Perhaps career lines for members of the clergy approach constancy over developmental time. Until recently, exit rates from such a career line were low: that is, once a member of the clergy, always a member of the clergy. But this has changed, and certainly there are historical variations in the supply and demand for clergy. Yet the relative size or portion of the labor force in clergy career lines may have been fairly constant in modern times. The point is that absolute size constancy is an ideal type rarely, if ever, equaled.

Variations in career-line size over developmental time are very common (Kaufman and Spilerman 1982). Elementary school teaching and recreation work bulge in size at younger ages; many managerial career lines crest in size during the forties and fifties of the life course. The volume need not be constant over developmental or historical time.

Variations in size over historical time are also common. New career lines that require highly trained workers show an increase in volume in younger age cohorts (for example, computer programmer); career lines that are becoming obsolete and closed off to younger workers would reveal a bulge in the volume at the older ages (for example, railroad conductor). Historical conditions might stimulate bursts in volume that are correlated with—but are not an age effect—and produce volume bubbles moving through a career line. For example, the number of elementary and secondary school teachers expanded dramatically during the 1950s and 1960s in order to accommodate the large increase in school-age children from the post-World War II baby boom. A structural feature of society—increased fertility—caused historical and developmental time variations in the size of school-teaching career lines. In historical time, there was an increase in the number of people in such lines, and in recent years, a sharp decrease occurred. In developmental time, those who were established in school teaching at the onset of the baby boom found themselves followed by an immense wave of new school teachers. Those who enter the profession of school teaching today find that they follow the same wave, albeit in reduced numbers of followers and leaders. The engineering boom that accompanied the space program during the 1960s is another example.

Size of a career line does not refer to the size of firms in which career lines are located, although the size and differences among organizational locations might cause variations in the size and other features of career lines.

Just as labor supply and demand operate as mobility suppressors or generators for jobs in the economy, the same processes should operate for career lines but perhaps in slightly different ways. If demand for workers in a certain career line declines, we might expect that size will be restricted most among workers of younger ages in the career line because older workers have more seniority and experience. In some cases, size might be expected to contribute to other structural properties of career lines such as differentiation and forms of specialization. The organizations literature contains a long tradition of research on the size of firms (Kimberly 1976), but the direct application to career lines remains to be demonstrated.

Differentiation

Differentiation refers to the number and work course location of job transitions in a career line or set of career lines. Work course is that portion of their life course people are gainfully employed in the labor force, typically from the late teens to middle sixties. Differentiation occurs along the axes of age, occupation, industry, and firm or employer. Given an age-specific job location, say early in the work course, the career line or lines that emanate from the position might contain many different positions with increasing, decreasing, or constant differentiation over the work course. Alternately, a career line may be very simple and contain but one position in a single firm over the entire work course.

Occupational specialization, unionization, and labor-market location should cause variation in career-line differentiation. Traditional craft and professional career lines (such as electrician) should have less differentiation compared to many managerial career lines that are firm- or industry-based and usually involve occupation switches. Because of size, career lines located in the public sector, particularly the federal government or in large firms and bureaucracies in the private sector, should be more differentiated than lines in small firms. A growing industry should afford more differentiation to its career lines than would a shrinking one.

For example, Rosenbaum (1979b) showed that organizational growth in a very large corporation benefited the promotion chances of many groups of workers in the firm. Grandjean (1981) found that the occupational and salary advancements of workers in the civil service were linked to organizational growth and differentiation in some federal agencies but not in others. The relationship is apparently more complex than a simple linear one.

The life course location of differentiation in career lines is just as important as the sheer level of differentiation. Age norms in our society generally suggest that job and career movement occur earlier rather than later in the life course (Neugarten and Datan 1973; see Sofer 1970, for evidence from

Great Britain). Whether cause or effect, such norms are the basis for workers' expectations and behavior. Studies of the school superintendency role (March and March 1977; Gaertner 1980) suggested a fairly small number of career lines in and out of the position, with the maximum differentiation during midlife (thirties and early forties). Before accessing the school-superintendent role, one typically must have spent some time in the system in elementary or secondary school teaching or lower-level administration. After a certain point in the work course, one tends to leave or stay permanently. Most of the mobility in the form of entry or exit from the school-superintendent role occurs during a middle fifteen-year period of the work course. Recent case studies of mobility hierarchies in several "core" firms also illustrated varying differentiation (Bielby and Baron 1980). Finally, a rich tradition of studies in organizational research might serve as a source of hypotheses about size and differentiation in career lines (Blau and Schoenherr 1971; Kimberly 1976).

Holding Power

The *holding power* of a career line refers to the probability of people continuing in the line once they have entered. Related concepts in stratification research are found in mover-stayer models (Mayer 1972) and in studies of mobility-immobility (Featherman and Hauser 1978). The probabilities vary across and within career lines. The holding power reflects two opposing forces, analogous to push and pull. A very high holding power might mean that one is locked into a career line. Exigencies of specialization, or low skill generalizability among jobs, or firm reward strategies may force a high proportion to continue in the line. Alternately, desirable work conditions and rewards may attract workers to stay in the line. Piore (1975) noted the dual forces underlying retention rates; Tuma's (1976) models of job durations conceptualized and estimated some of the push-pull factors.

One line of research that informs patterns in career-line holding power is mathematical modeling of the rates of intragenerational mobility (see Mayer 1972, for a review). The unit of analysis is not the career line nor even, typically, detailed occupation or industry. Usually, the transition probabilities among a few, highly aggregated categories are the object of modeling. A number of studies posited a mobility rate that declines exponentially with time (Sørensen 1975a; Tuma 1976). Other studies—those in the Markov tradition—predicted rates of intragenerational mobility that were independent of time (Mayer 1972). Time in this research included age, history, and duration of a job. The classic Markov prediction did not work well. Yet other studies built more history and time effects into their predictions about the rate of mobility (Rosenbaum 1979a; Chinoy 1955). The weight of evidence suggests that the rate of mobility, and by extension, career-line leaving, declines sharply with age. There is not agreement on the exact shape of the decline nor on its underlying causes.

Entry Portals

Entry portals are the age-specific jobs through which workers enter a career line. Two features of entry portals are important: the number of different entry portals and the age-width of the entry portal. The number of different entry portals is simply the number of distinct positions that grant access to a career line. Such positions may be jobs in the labor force or non-labor force statuses (for example, in the military, in school, not working). When considering all recruitment bases for a career line, it is meaningful to speak of the diffuseness-versus-concentration of recruitment origins to a line. A small number of recruitment locations per unit number of entrants to a career line reflects concentrated origins; a large number of recruitment origins per unit entrants reflects diffuse origins. Career lines should vary in the number of entry portals and diffuseness-concentration of recruitment locations.

Entry portals vary in their age-width. Some portals are narrow in age terms, affording greater access to a career line during a relatively small age range. Other portals might be very broad, granting increased access to a career line over a very wide range of ages. Labor-market location is among the important determinants of the age-width of entry portals. For example, Piore (1975) hypothesized narrow, tightly scheduled mobility chains in internal labor markets. Rosenbaum (1979b), Martin and Strauss (1959), and Chinoy (1955) suggested the existence of age plateaus in organizations, after which a precipitous decline in the rates of advancement and promotion implies age-concentrated ports of entry.

Exit Portals

The conceptualization of *exit portals* as an elementary property of career lines is isomorphic to entry portals. Exit portals are the age-specific jobs through which workers exit a career line.[1] For a career line, they might vary in number, diffuseness-concentration, and age-width.

Popular works on career change, second careers, and the cycles of job changing in people's lives point to critical ages at which *career changes* increase or assert qualitative differences in job transitions at certain ages (Levinson 1978). Note, for example, the *midlife crisis* concept. If these arguments are correct, then such age-related patterns should be evident in entry and exit portals of career lines.

The central issues for our purposes include mapping the variation in career-line entry and exit portals and identifying the causes of variation in entry and exit portals. Segmentation perspectives imply that career lines in some sectors of the economy are insulated from competition and contain tightly scheduled job changes. The argument suggests ports of entry and exit that are more concentrated in number and age-width compared to career lines in other sectors of the economy.

Role Continuity

Role continuity refers to the changes in levels of role requirements, routines, and rewards associated with jobs in a career line. Most writers restrict consideration to the status or earnings profiles associated with a sequence of positions. For career lines, such a restriction is limiting. If career lines are conceptualized as roles, then role continuity is the more fundamental concept. Status and earnings profiles are but two of many possible indicators of role continuity. Other indicators of role continuity may be important for other purposes.

Training and education credentials are indicators of role requirements for entry to a career line. Schooling levels are fairly constant after entry to a line, but the training and experience requirements likely grow for scheduled movements through some career lines. Both neoclassical (Mincer 1974) and radical perspectives (Bowles and Gintis 1976) are sources of hypotheses about changing work-role requirements as they might apply to career lines.

Continuities in role content in career lines are rarely investigated, though cross-sectional studies of job characteristics proliferate. Among the more central indicators of career-line role content are skill, authority, complexity, routinization, and closeness of supervision. Again, both radical and conservative stratification literatures offer hypotheses about what generates differences in role content.

Continuities in role rewards, particularly for earnings and status profiles, have received substantial attention for people (Sørensen 1977; Featherman 1971, 1973; Kelley 1973a, 1973b) and less attention for jobs or career lines (Eckaus 1973; Haller and Spenner 1977). The relatively flat profiles for some jobs (bad ones) and individuals (women, minorities) versus growth profiles for other jobs (good ones) and individuals (whites, males) are claimed by radical and conservative theorists in support of their respective positions. In one case, the explanation refers to differences in human capital, productivity, and returns to investments; in the other case, the same profile differences in career, or career-line, returns are caused by economic segmentation and labor-market location (for example, see Leigh 1978). Althauser and Kalleberg (1981a) defined a related concept, the "progressive development of skill or knowledge," which is an important feature of internal labor markets. But our concepts are different. Althauser and Kalleberg's concept is evaluative in defining progressive growth in role content and rewards from lower to higher levels. Our concept of role continuity is nonevaluative and assumes no upward as opposed to downward development. We simply mean the level and correlation of role components over time. In summary, role continuity means the working conditions, the routines of work, the requisites, and the rewards of work as they change over developmental time in the career line.

Thus far, we have sketched several conceptual properties of career lines. They include size, differentiation, holding power, entry and exit portals, and role continuity. The next section illustrates the properties with a measure of career lines based on a synthetic cohort. We work through several examples to illustrate measures for the new concepts and to provide an impression of the variety in career-line sets.

Examples

There are several ways to estimate career lines, each with limitations. The main options reduce to a synthetic-cohort strategy with cross-sectional data, or longitudinal job histories within or across firms. We discussed the strategies, their strengths, and limitations in chapter 2. Here we use the synthetic-cohort strategy with data from the 1970 Census Public Use Samples. Later we analyze careers and career lines with longitudinal job histories.

Measurement Definitions and Distinctions

The figures shown in the following pages provide examples of career lines based on age-specific job transitions between 1965 and 1970. Several distinctions are helpful.

Career Line. In each figure, a career line is any single path reading from left to right, including workers staying in the same job. Considering all eight age cohorts, the career-line display for accountants in accounting firms (figure 3-1) contains over fifty career lines whereas the display for tool and die makers (figure 3-4) contains one career line.

Career-Line Set. A career-line set refers to all career lines that originate in an origin position (the entire display for accountants in accounting firms in figure 3-1). Equivalently, a career-line set refers to all career lines that termi-

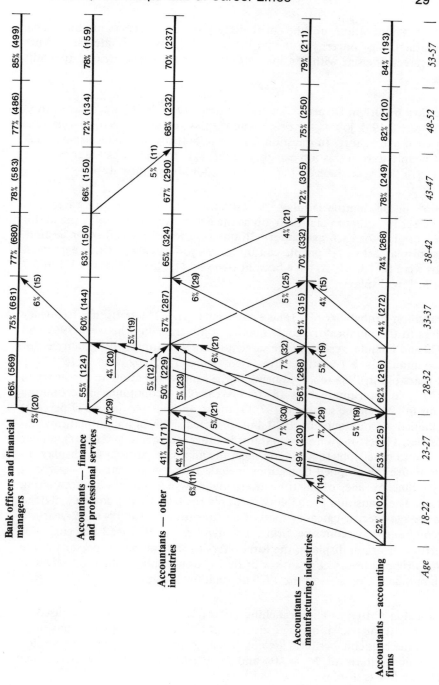

Figure 3-1. Career-Line Outflow Display: Accountants in Accounting Firms

nate in a destination job (the entire display for bookkeepers in nondurable manufacturing concerns is shown in figure 3-6). We estimate career lines and career-line sets with 384 job categories for the economy (see appendix A).

Outflow or Origin Display. An origin display refers to a career line or lines that take a 1965 job as the origin and display the major 1970 destinations for each age cohort. In question form, the outflow or origin display asks, "If people start in this job category at this age, to what jobs are they likely to move five years later?" Figures 3-1 to 3-4 are outflow displays.

Inflow or Destination Display. A destination display refers to a career line or career lines that take a 1970 job as the destination and display the major 1965 origins for each age cohort. In question form, the inflow or destination display asks, "If people end up in this job category at this age, what jobs were they likely to have been in five years earlier?" Figures 3-5 to 3-7 are inflow displays.

Transition Probability (P_{ijk}) and Frequency (f_{ijk}). The transition frequency refers to the number of people making a job transition between 1965 and 1970 and includes reporting the same job five years apart. For example, for accountants in accounting firms (see figure 3-1), 102 who were 18- to 22-years-old in 1965 reported being in the same occupation and industry in 1970. The total number of 18- to 22-year-old accountants in accounting firms in 1965 in the sample is 197. Of these, another 14 workers (7 percent) remained accountants in 1970 but reported jobs in manufacturing industries, 11 persons were accountants in other industries, and the remainder moved to other jobs that did not meet the minimum criteria for display. In this figure the graphed transitions include from 65 percent to 84 percent, depending on age, of all transitions made by accountants in accounting firms. The transition probability is simply the transition frequency divided by the age-specific category total of persons (that is, for 18- to 22-year-old accountants in accounting firms, 102 divided by 197 or 52 percent). For outflow or origin displays, the total refers to the number of persons in the 1965 origin category. For inflow or destination displays, the total refers to the number of persons in the 1970 destination category.

Branching Criteria. The branching criteria are the decision rules used to designate a job transition as an element of a career-line display. Transitions below the branching criteria are not displayed graphically. Here, we employ branching criteria of $P_{ijk} \geq .04$ and $f_{ijk} \geq 10$. Both criteria must be met before a line is displayed.

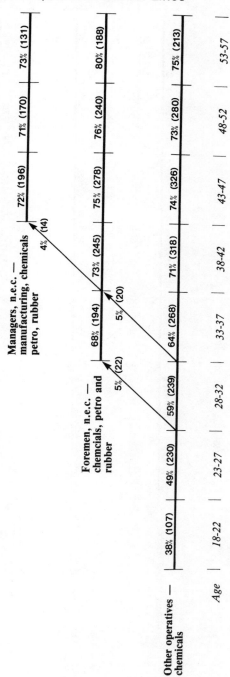

Figure 3-2. Career-Line Outflow Display: Other Operatives—Chemicals

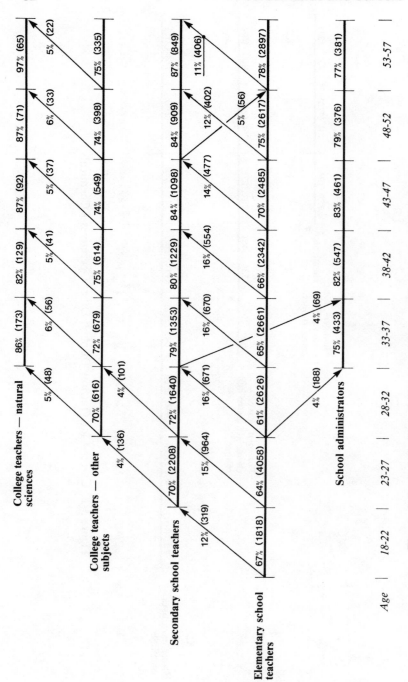

Figure 3-3. Career-Line Outflow Display: Elementary School Teachers

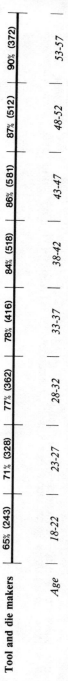

Tool and die makers	65% (243)	71% (328)	77% (362)	78% (416)	84% (518)	86% (581)	87% (512)	90% (372)
Age	18-22	23-27	28-32	33-37	38-42	43-47	48-52	53-57

Figure 3-4. Career-Line Outflow Display: Tool and Die Makers

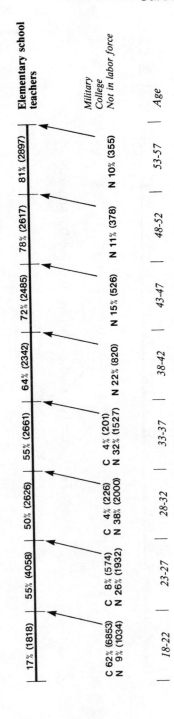

Figure 3-5. Career-Line Inflow Display: Elementary School Teachers

Note: **M** = Military; **C** = College; **N** = Not in labor force.

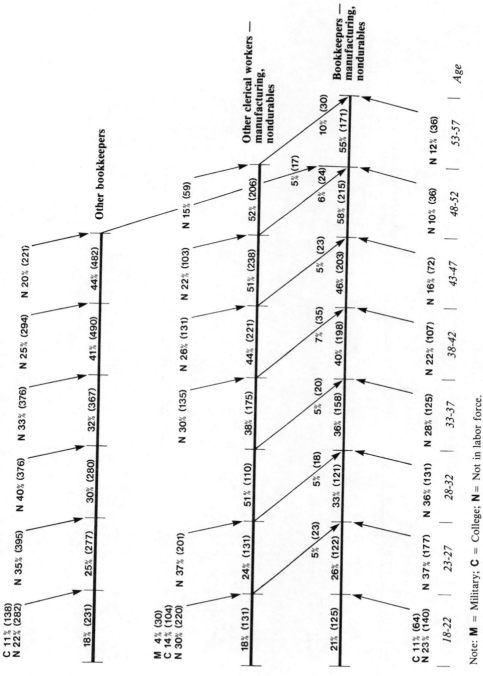

Figure 3-6: Career-Line Inflow Display: Bookkeepers—Manufacturing, Nondurables

Note: **M** = Military; **C** = College; **N** = Not in labor force.

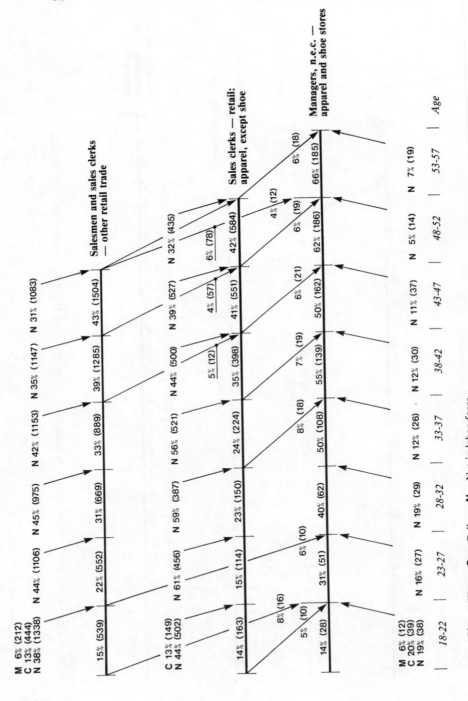

Figure 3-7: Career-Line Inflow Display: Managers, n.e.c.—Apparel and Shoe Stores

Note: **M** = Military; **C** = College; **N** = Not in labor force.

Origin Career-Line Sets (Outflow)

Figures 3-1 to 3-4 provide four examples of origin career-line sets for accountants in accounting firms, other operatives in chemical manufacturing industries, elementary school teachers, and tool and die makers, respectively. Otto, Spenner, and Call (1980) report the origin displays for all 384 categories. The figures illustrate several of the conceptual properties of career lines.[2]

We use the transition probability for staying in the same job as a measure of holding power. With the census data the measure ignores the role of staying with or leaving a firm or employer and equates holding power with staying in an occupation-industry category. This is not a statement on the unimportance of firms but an exigency of available data.

Several patterns are evident. First, career lines differ in the initial levels of holding power for the youngest cohorts in the line. About two out of three of the youngest elementary school teachers and tool and die makers report the same job in 1965 and 1970. About half of accountants in accounting firms report the same job while only 30 percent of chemical operatives report the same job between 1965 and 1970. For the accountants, 13 percent retain the accounting profession but pursue career-line options that involve industry switches. Sixty-two percent of chemical operatives leave the job and do not pursue any systematic career-line options under the branching criteria but disperse to many different jobs in the labor force.

Second, for each career line that represents staying in the same job, the holding power increases markedly with age. At the end of the work course, from 75 percent to 90 percent of incumbents in these career lines at age 53 to 57 in 1965 retain the same job category in 1970 at ages 58 to 62.[3] The pattern follows the well-known decline in job changes and increases in job duration that are correlated with age (Sørensen 1975a; Tuma 1976).

Finally, among the examples, the holding-power profiles reach their apex most rapidly for tool and die makers, less rapidly for accountants and teachers, and least rapidly for other operatives in chemical industries.

The outflow displays also illustrate the different levels of differentiation in career-line sets. Career lines for accountants in accounting firms show a large amount of differentiation, mostly industry shifts during the late twenties and early thirties but relatively little differentiation later in the work course. Career lines for elementary school teachers increase in differentiation during the first ten to fifteen years in the labor force but remain fairly constant thereafter. In contrast, other operatives in chemical industries show a slight increase in differentiation during the middle of the work course, reflecting an advancement pattern from operative to foreman to managerial positions in chemical and related industries. The career line for tool and die makers shows no differentiation over the work course.

As Althauser and Kalleberg (1981*b*) note, the outflow type of display accommodates the study of certain types of questions. Where are promotion hierarchies located in the work course, given origins in a particular job? What patterns of growth in the knowledge and skill levels attached to jobs occur in the promotion chains from origin positions? For example, for accountants in accounting firms, the mixture of career lines denotes the application of similar skills but in very different industries, from manufacturing concerns to financial institutions to all other industries. By comparison, career-line transitions for chemical operatives imply a transition from manual labor to the application of interpersonal and supervisory skills, and then a transition to managerial functions.

The career-line set for elementary school teachers illustrates the notion of ports of entry and exit. A very broad port of exit from elementary school teaching appears in the movement to secondary school teaching. For every, age, a sizable fraction of elementary school teachers (from 11 to 16 percent) makes the transition to secondary school teaching. The width of this port is at the maximum in spanning every age cohort. But the reverse transition from secondary to elementary teaching occurs for only one age cohort. In contrast, school teaching—both elementary and secondary—provides a very narrow, tightly scheduled port of entry into school administration. The transition from teaching to administration is most likely in statistical terms during the late twenties and early thirties from elementary schools, and during the early and mid-thirties in secondary schools. A similar, tightly scheduled set of transitions appears for chemical operatives if they transfer to foremen and managerial positions.

In summary, the outflow career lines provide illustrations of meaningful variations in holding power, differentiation, and ports of entry and exit. Our illustration of role continuity involves measures beyond the career-line displays that we pursue in the next chapter. Next we turn to several examples of career-line inflow displays.

Destination Career-Line Sets (Inflow)

Figures 3-5, 3-6, and 3-7 display the inflow career lines for elementary school teachers, bookkeepers in nondurable manufacturing industries, and managers of apparel and shoe stores. The inflow displays contain some additional information that was not available for outflow displays. For each age-specific destination, we display three non-labor force origins in 1965: military (M), college (C), and not in the labor force (N). These origins operate as general ports of entry to career lines. Most formal definitions of non-labor force would include military and college. The census data permit separating the three origins, and there is some conceptual advantage because each position might characterize quite different ports of entry and resources relevant to career-line entry. The display of non-labor force origins follows the regular branching criteria.

The holding power in destination displays shows sizable variations. All three base career lines contain substantial increases over the work course in holding power, more so for school teachers and less so for bookkeepers. Compared to holding-power estimates from origin displays, destination holding power is lower because the transition probability is calculated with the 1970 category frequency. The size of the labor force grew between 1965 and 1970. In addition, the destination displays include non-labor force origins (not included in the outflow displays) in the category totals. As we noted earlier, the transition probabilities reflect two effects: the underlying transition regime between jobs and the marginal distribution of people to jobs (between 1965 and 1970 or by age cohort).

The figures reveal several differentiation levels. Elementary school teaching contains no career-line differentiation in recruitment origins other than from college and not-in-the-labor-force origins. The supply of elementary school teachers is unlikely to enter teaching from other labor-force positions. In contrast, both the career-line sets for bookkeepers and managers of apparel and shoe stores contain differentiation over the work course. As might be expected, salesmen and salesclerk positions in the same or related retail industries are the major recruitment sources for managers in apparel and shoe stores. These lines of recruitment concentrate in the first ten and last fifteen years of the work course. The lines of advancement at younger ages likely reference those who move into the managerial position after a brief apprenticeship in sales positions. The latter work course transition may refer to those who are promoted into store management positions after many years in the firm or industry.

Differentiation for bookkeepers in nondurable manufacturing industries is fairly even over the work course. There are two primary recruitment sources for every age cohort: those not in the labor force and other clerical workers in similar industrial settings. Additionally, a small number of other bookkeepers move to the focal job category for the 48- to 52-year-old age cohort.

The inflow displays are best suited to examine ports of entry and other recruitment patterns because they include labor force and non-labor force origins. Teacher career lines rely on college origins (62 percent for the youngest age cohort) more than is the case in the bookkeeper or manager career lines. Non-labor force origins are major ports of entry in all three inflow displays for every age cohort. The largest percentages are for teaching, and relatively smaller percentages occur for managers. Bookkeepers are intermediate. This is an expected pattern. Elementary teachers and bookkeepers are more likely to be women, who are more likely than men to interrupt their work careers for family reasons and then return to a previously occupied career line. The other ports of entry in these inflow displays range from very broad in age terms (other clerical workers for bookkeepers and salesclerks for managers) to more narrow ports of entry (salesmen in other retail trade for managers and other bookkeepers for bookkeepers in non-durable manufacturing industries).

Figures 3-1 to 3-7 represent but seven illustrations from the total of 384 outflow displays and 384 inflow displays. They are not a systematic sample but were selected to illustrate several of the conceptual properties for career lines. In the next chapter we examine variations in the elementary properties across all inflow and outflow displays.

Summary

We identified a set of conceptual properties for career lines: size, differentiation, holding power, ports of entry and exit, and role continuity. Size refers to the volume of flow of persons through a career line. It varies over developmental and historical time. Differentiation refers to the number and work course location of job transitions in a career line or set of career lines. Holding power refers to the probability of continuing in the career line. Ports of entry and exit reference the age-specific labor force and non-labor force positions through which workers enter and exit a career line. Finally, role continuity means the changes in levels of role requirements, routines, and rewards associated with jobs in a career line.

We illustrated several of the conceptual properties with one measure of career lines based on a synthetic cohort in the 1970 census data.

Notes

1. The notions of entry and exit portal involve an implicit contradiction. If the origin from which people enter a career line is another job and if a sufficient number of transitions occur, then the job transition for entry becomes part of the focal career line, by definition. If the destination of an exit is another job and if many people make the transition, then there is an extension of the career line and not an exit. The formal definitions make greatest intuitive sense if exit and entry are to and from non-labor force statuses (such as military, not working, school), or if the reader concentrates on an occupation, industry, or firm shift within a set of career lines. Our subsequent operational definitions avoid the problem.

2. We forgo the empirical treatment of size as a conceptual property. The census data do not permit sorting out size variations in historical versus developmental time.

3. Of course, some workers may have left the job category after 1965 but returned to it in 1970.

4 Career-Line Variations

We now more systematically pursue the description of the variations in career lines to assess the face validity of our concepts and measures. We define measures for the conceptual properties of career lines. If there is face validity to the concept of career line and if the synthetic cohort measure is a reasonable approximation, then the properties should exhibit meaningful variation in several ways. First, the properties should vary systematically over the work course. Second, the properties should show meaningful patterns when grouped by the major occupation group in which the career line has its origin or destination. Third, the properties should vary if career lines are grouped by their gender composition. In Spilerman's (1977) terms, the task at hand is to elucidate and chart the properties of career lines. The task is an empirical, descriptive one.

A number of studies have used concepts related to career line. For example, Piore (1975) defined a mobility chain as the more or less regular channels through which socioeconomic movement occurs in a society. Mobility chains consisted of people holding jobs in some regular order or sequence. Piore designated the points on a mobility chain as stations, which include jobs as well as "other points of social and economic significance." Rosenbaum's (1979a, 1979b) notion of tournament mobility comes very close to the career-line concept. Rosenbaum (1979a, p. 220) investigated career mobility in a corporation, defined as the "flow of individuals along sequences of jobs." Tournament mobility casts careers as a sequence of competitions. Each competition has implications for a person's future mobility chances. Winners of competitions are permitted to compete for further upward mobility; losers of a competition are shunted to lesser competition or denied opportunities to compete for future promotions and upward mobility. Rosenbaum reported support for the model's predictions using data from two entry cohorts that remained in a single corporation for thirteen years. Rosenbaum's tournament model stressed history in the career. Present position and opportunities for career mobility depended on past successes and failures, even those of a decade earlier. White's (1970) study of vacancy chains in a religious bureaucracy, Stewman's (1975) study of a state police bureaucracy as an open system of vacancy chains, and March and March's (1977) study of turnover and recruitment to the role of school superintendent are other examples of studies of lines of job progression as system properties.

Hence, there is a tradition of investigation of concepts very similar to career line. Most of the studies deal with a single organization as the total system or with a narrowly defined feature of job histories. The restrictions permit more powerful specification and eliminate many confounding effects. Such approaches do not offer a broader picture of the heterogeneity in career lines across the economy. We pursue this larger descriptive picture, but we are aware that there is some loss of precision and some loss of control over the explanations for differences.

Measures

We use one or more empirical indicators for each conceptual property of career lines. In some cases, the indicators very closely capture the content of the concept. In other cases, the indicators offer only a very crude approximation. We use indicators calculated for both inflow and outflow displays. The actual measures involve approximations to all career lines in the economy. In some cases, the analysis uses the 384 career lines that represent staying in the same job for each age cohort. For still other indicators, the units of measurement are all age-specific job transitions that exceed the branching criteria (equivalently, the complete career-line set for each of the 384 categories). For other indicators, we calculate measures that reflect the experiences of all persons in a 1965 or 1970 job category, irrespective of whether the transition information exceeds the branching criteria. Finally, we forgo empirical consideration of the concept of size. Historical and developmental variations are completely intertwined in the census data. The data and methods required to effectively treat career-line size are beyond the scope and goals of this study.

Holding Power

As a measure of holding power, we use the percentage who stay in the same job category between 1965 and 1970, for each of the 384 job categories, for each age cohort. For origin holding power, the percentage is calculated with the 1965 category frequency. For destination holding power, the percentage is calculated with the 1970 category frequency. The range of observed values is considerable, from 8 to 97 percent for origin holding power and from 4 to 91 percent for destination holding power.

Differentiation

As an indicator of differentiation, we measure the number of job transitions that involve moving to a different job category and that exceed the branching critiera ($P_{ijk} \geq .04$, $f_{ijk} \geq 10$) for each age cohort. The units of analysis are career-line transitions originating from each of the 384 job categories. This measure depends heavily on the particular branching criteria and job categories that we use. Obviously, the measure ignores differentiation of career lines within firms or bureaucracies. It captures only select occupation and industry differentiation in career-line sets. For these reasons, the measure only roughly approximates the concept.

The observed differentiation values range from zero to four. Preliminary analyses under these branching criteria showed even less variation in differentiation when measured for inflow displays of career-line sets, so we restrict attention to the outflow measure of differentiation.

Entry and Exit Portals

To capture entry and exit portals, we measure (1) the diffuseness-concentration of destinations (exit portals) for each of the 384 age-specific origins; (2) the diffuseness-concentration of origins (entry portals) for each of the 384 age-specific destinations; and (3) the percentage who report being out of the labor force in 1965, for each 1970 age-specific destination. Diffuseness refers to the total number of different 1970 destinations per 100 persons leaving the 1965 origin category for exit portals, and the total number of different 1965 origins per 100 persons entering a 1970 destination for entry portals. The measure refers to all job transitions (whether they exceed branching criteria or not) for each of the 384 categories, for each age cohort. For this reason, the measure only minimally overlaps with the measure of differentiation, which indexes only major transitions (that is, those that exceed the branching criteria). The average correlation between differentiation and diffuseness measures is about .25. The observed values range from 11 (very concentrated) to 97 (very diffuse) for exit portals and from 5 to 88 for entry portals.

Role Continuity

Finally, we use two indicators for role continuity in career lines. First, we calculated the gender-specific median earnings for each age cohort in each job category. The measure includes all people in the job category without regard to their job category in 1965. The census question refers to earnings in 1969 from wages, salary, commissions, bonuses, or tips from all jobs. Further, we placed no constraint on hours worked per week, so the measure captures full- and part-time workers.

Second, we developed a measure of the skill distance involved in career-line moves. We conceptualize skill as the mental, interpersonal, and manipulative complexity inherent in a job (Spenner 1979).

We base the measure on several variables from the *Dictionary of Occupational Titles* (U.S. Department of Labor 1965): levels of involvement with data, people, and things, and specific vocational preparation (see appendix B). We take the four variables to circumscribe the skill level of a job. The seven-point scales for levels of involvement with data, people, and things measure the highest function in each hierarchy to which workers in a job have a significant relationship. The measure of specific vocational preparation uses a nine-point scale. It captures the amount of time required to learn techniques, acquire information, and develop a facility for average performance in a job. It includes on-the-job training, experience, and vocational and formal schooling, inasmuch as it is directly relevant to job performance.

The measure was constructed in several steps. First, estimates of the four variables were made for each career-line category (Spenner 1980). Second, the matrix of skill indicator scores by job category was orthogonalized by principal components analysis (components = 4) at no loss of information. The new scores were used to compute a skill distance matrix (384 by 384) (see Kaufman, Hodson, and Fligstein 1981, for methodological details). The result is a skill distance score for every pair of job categories. Skill distance for a career line is simply the average distance between an age-specific 1965 origin category and all of its 1970 destinations, weighted for the number of individuals making the transition to each destination.

The measure captures the similarity in skill level and scope between an origin category and all of its age-specific destinations taken together. The observed values range from zero (zero skill distance) to about 13 (maximum skill distance). For a given age cohort, if all transitions from a 1965 origin were to the same destination category or to 1970 destinations with skill scores equal to the 1965 origin, then the skill distance would be zero. The measure is new and exploratory. Baron and Bielby (1982) and Cain and Treiman (1981) discuss problems of such measures.

Empirical Variations

Table 4-1 reports the means and standard deviations for the indicators by age cohort. Across all career lines, holding power of the career line increases sharply with age, nearly doubling from the youngest to the oldest age cohort for origin holding power and more than tripling when measured for destinations. For the youngest age cohort, nearly 60 percent of people change jobs over the five-year period. In contrast, three out of four members of the

Table 4-1
Means and Standard Deviations for Select Career-Line Variables by 1970 Age Cohort

Variable	Age Cohort (1970)							
	23-27	28-32	33-37	38-42	43-47	48-52	53-57	58-62
Holding Power								
Origin	40.93	51.32	59.54	64.40	68.45	70.98	73.23	75.28
	(13.24)	(12.79)	(11.87)	(11.55)	(10.79)	(10.25)	(10.09)	(10.14)
Destination	19.42	33.88	42.09	49.58	54.50	57.97	60.95	62.41
	(8.28)	(11.24)	(14.14)	(14.88)	(13.77)	(12.91)	(11.85)	(11.14)
Differentiation	.35	.41	.44	.38	.33	.28	.27	.24
	(.72)	(.71)	(.71)	(.64)	(.63)	(.60)	(.59)	(.54)
Ports of entry and exit								
Ports of entry	37.44	36.33	34.46	33.24	33.04	37.40	30.46	22.98
	(14.58)	(13.82)	(13.66)	(13.18)	(13.35)	(15.21)	(13.35)	(9.69)
Ports of exit	59.10	57.76	58.41	57.12	55.83	57.16	60.28	63.69
	(18.98)	(16.50)	(15.88)	(15.75)	(16.15)	(16.31)	(17.16)	(17.98)
Percent entering from out of the labor force	21.00	24.05	22.68	22.35	19.17	16.36	13.79	12.75
	(13.14)	(17.32)	(16.78)	(15.13)	(12.57)	(10.35)	(8.65)	(7.58)
Role continuity								
Skill distance	3.28	2.55	2.02	1.68	1.45	1.31	1.18	1.09
	(1.32)	(1.00)	(.80)	(.69)	(.62)	(.57)	(.56)	(.55)
Median earnings (1969 dollars)								
Male	6,015	7,611	8,524	8,845	8,843	8,801	8,305	7,678
	(1,841)	(2,133)	(2,988)	(3,723)	(3,475)	(3,994)	(3,444)	(3,235)
Female	3,189	2,921	3,579	3,875	4,257	4,358	4,612	4,353
	(3,408)	(2,810)	(2,962)	(2,715)	(2,612)	(2,537)	(3,607)	(3,007)

Note: Standard deviation in parentheses.

oldest cohort report jobs in the same career-line category over the five-year period. The comparable figures for destination holding power are 80 percent and 38 percent. The variance is slightly greater for younger compared to older cohorts for origin holding power. For destination holding power, the variance increases to the middle of the work course and then declines slightly. Several possible effects underlie the trends, including age, age-correlated job durations, and marginal changes in the occupational structure.

Differentiation measured across all career-line sets shows only small variations by age cohort. Recall that the differentiation measure indexes the number of major job avenues exceeding the branching criteria for each age-specific origin. The level of differentiation increases slightly to age 33 to 37 and declines for each successive age cohort. Further, the variance in differentiation of career-line sets declines over the work course. The maximum career-line movement among job categories occurs early in the work course, but there are no massive disjunctures from one age cohort to another.

The number of ports of entry and ports of exit show no clear trend over most of the work course. The exception is a decreased number of ports of entry to career lines at the very end of the work course and an increased number of ports of exit at the end of the work course. For an average career-line category, exit portals range from 55 to 64 different destinations per 100 exits from the career line and ports of entry from 23 to 37 different origins per 100 entrants into a career line.

Diffuseness of exit portals greatly exceeds diffuseness of entry portals at every age. Entering career lines is a much more concentrated and restricted process than exiting; how to get to a particular position is more predictable than knowing where a particular position leads. Diffuseness of entry portals declines somewhat at the very end of the work course, while the diffuseness of exit portals, if anything, increases slightly for transitions at the end of the work course. The percentage entering career lines from out of the labor force ranges from 24 percent for those age 28 to 32 in 1970 (age 23-27 in 1965) to about 13 percent for the oldest age cohort. As we find later, age trends in ports of entry and exit occur if career lines are further grouped by major occupation group.

Skill distance decreases dramatically over the work course. This is not a statement about the skill level of jobs occupied by older compared to younger workers. Rather, job transitions later in the work course involve jobs less distant in skill terms (more similar) than job transitions earlier in the work course. Since the measure is weighted to reflect the frequency of transitions, the statement is about career lines. In this restricted sense, generalizability of skill increases. The variation around the mean also declines dramatically. Career-line movement later in the work course entails substantially less skill distance. Much of this trend is caused by the increased holding power of career lines over the work course. These patterns are not surprising.

Finally, the median earnings for men and women averaged across all career lines reveal well-documented patterns. The age-specific medians for men are nearly twice the corresponding values for women. The measure includes full- and part-time workers. Earnings for men and women generally increase in the work course but appear to decline for older age cohorts. The decline may be an artifact of the cross-sectional synthetic cohort (Eckaus 1973) and requires cautious interpretation for the two oldest cohorts.

To further illustrate the elementary properties, we group career lines by the major occupation group of the origin category. Figures 4-1 to 4-9 display the age-specific patterns of means for career lines with origin (or destination where applicable) categories in the major occupation groups. We employ the following seven categories:

1. professional and technical
2. managers, proprietors, and non-retail sales
3. clerical and retail sales
4. skilled workers (craft)
5. semi- and unskilled (operatives and laborers)
6. service
7. farm

These categories are simple and maximize socioeconomic differences among categories (Featherman and Hauser 1978; Sewell, Hauser, and Wolf 1980). The estimates for career lines with farm categories are based on only four career-line sets and thus are less stable than estimates for the other categories.

Holding Power

The pattern observed in the aggregate for career-line holding power (figures 4-1 and 4-2) of increases with age is widely characteristic of career lines with origins and destinations in all major occupation groups. Farm career lines are the possible exception with a flatter-than-average profile. The intercept levels of the origin profiles roughly approximate the socioeconomic differences among major occupation groups. Professional, skilled, and managers are highest; clerical and service are intermediate; and semi-skilled and farm are lowest. But the variations in slope by group appear quite minor. As others have suggested (Doeringer and Piore 1971; Spilerman 1977), occupation-based career lines such as craft and professional have holding-power profiles that are the highest and closest to one another.

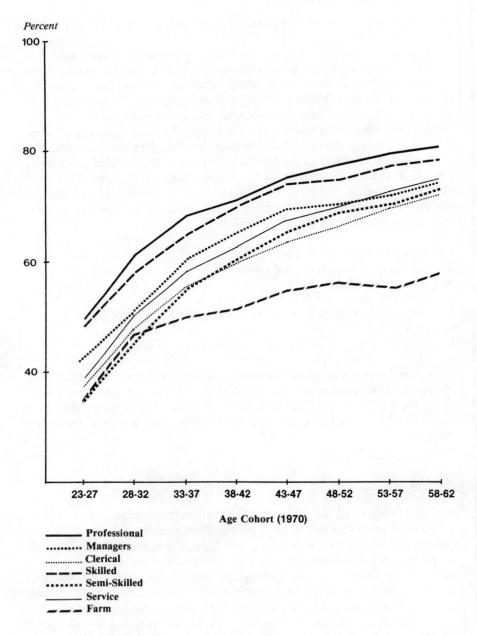

Figure 4-1. Origin Holding Power by Career-Line Major Occupation
            Group and Age Cohort

Again, these patterns are unadjusted gross levels that may reflect several underlying mechanisms such as age, job duration, differential mortality, and marginal change.

For destination holding power, several patterns are apparent (figure 4-2). First, career lines grouped by destination category are more differen-

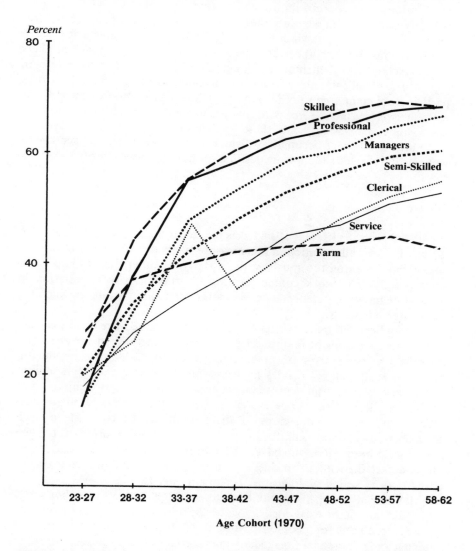

Figure 4-2. Destination Holding Power by Career-Line Major Occupation Group and Age Cohort

tiated in holding power as the work course progresses. Second, as for origin holding power, career lines with farm destinations have a much flatter profile than other occupation groups. Finally, career lines with clerical destinations show a precipitous drop from 45 to 35 percent between ages 33 to 37 and 38 to 42 in 1970 (ages 28 to 32 and 33 to 37 in 1965). The clerical and retail sales group contains more women than any other category and particularly more women who are likely to move in and out of the labor force on a part-time basis or switch between full-time and part-time status when changing jobs. Further, the ages in question span the ages of many mothers with preschool and elementary school children (Sweet 1973). Career lines in clerical and retail sales more frequently accommodate irregular labor-force participation compared to other groups of career lines. Equivalently, those with intermittent labor-force participation are shunted to this section of the labor force. Consistent with these explanations, career lines that have destinations in service occupations, which also contain a high percentage of women, have one of the lowest destination holding-power profiles.

Differentiation

Figure 4-3 reports differentiation levels for career lines by major occupation group. The overall variation in this measure is less than for other measures, so we avoid making too much of the differences other than to make two observations. The work course location of maximum differentiation in career-line movement depends on the major occupation group in which the career line has its origin.

A number of popular writers, speaking from a neo-Freudian perspective, point to periods of midlife crises or increased activity in *career changing* or *second careers* (for example, see Levinson 1978). Supposedly, the impetus for such changes resides in deep-seated biological and personality-based needs. If the argument is correct and applies to a significant number of workers, then it should be evident in the differentiation profile as age-specific increases or decreases in differentiation. In contrast to such arguments, no age shows uniformly higher or lower differentiation. If there is such a pattern, it is linked to the major occupation group of career lines—a fact difficult to reconcile with the position that job changing is based in deep-seated biological or personality needs.

Managerial career lines peak in differentiation during the early thirties and again during the early forties. No doubt this reflects the longer time investment required for people to work through lower-level positions into foremen and managerial slots. Many managerial slots are reserved for those who have accrued extensive time with a firm. Collins (1979) reports a study of employers in the San Francisco Bay area where supervisory and

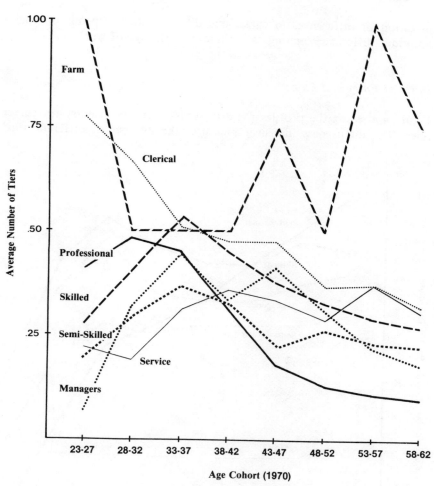

Figure 4-3. Differentiation by Career-Line Major Occupation Group and Age Cohort

managerial slots were recruited from within a firm more than any other occupational group. Before promotion from within the firm, one must have logged sufficient time to demonstrate competence, loyalty, and the other traits prerequisite to positions of higher authority and responsibility.

Professional, skilled, and semi-skilled career lines have their maximum differentiation during the first ten years of typical labor force participation. Clerical and retail sales career lines show maximum differentiation for the youngest cohort and decline for every successive cohort. Clearly, the interpretation of differences in career-line differentiation depends on socio-economic differences among career lines and the age of workers.

Ports of Entry and Exit

Figure 4-4 shows the profiles for diffuseness of ports of entry for career lines. The diffuseness indicator measures the number of different 1965

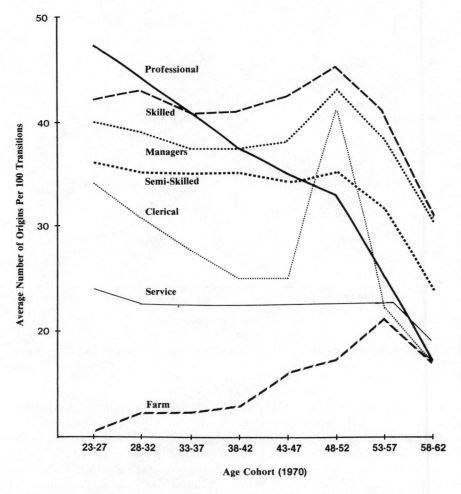

Figure 4-4. Diffuseness of Entry Portals by Career-Line Major Occupation Group and Age Cohort

origins (entry ports) per 100 entrants to a career-line category. Higher-status career lines have more ports of entry than lower status lines, more early in the work course than late. At the earliest point in the work course, professional, skilled, and managerial career lines average forty to fifty different entry ports per 100 entrants. During the same age sequence, service career lines have fewer than twenty-five entry ports.

Career lines in several occupation groups exhibit marked work course variation in the pattern of entry ports. Professional career lines have the largest number of entry ports early in the work course and the smallest number at the end of the work course compared to all other career lines. The consistent decline is congruent with the notion of increasing insulation of the career line from external labor competition over the work course (Doeringer and Piore 1971). Second, career-line destinations in clerical and retail sales show a decline in ports of entry over the work course years that typically engender childbearing and child rearing, and then a precipitous increase in the diffuseness of entry ports for the 48-to-52-year-old age cohort (ages 43-47 in 1965). Finally, career lines with destinations in managerial and skilled occupations recruit labor from more diffuse origins over more of the work course than any other group of career lines. Many managerial positions and supervisory positions are open only to those with ten or more years of experience. Further, the recruitment stock reflects a broad array of origins.

Diffuseness of ports of exit (figure 4-5) also reveals some intriguing patterns when plotted by occupation group origin of the career line. Several profiles are evident as follows:

1. U-shaped for managers, professional, and skilled (craft) career lines with more diffuse destinations early and late in the work course, and more concentration of destinations during the middle twenty years.
2. Inverted U-shaped for service career lines, with maximum diffuseness during the middle years of the life course.
3. Flat or slightly increasing over the life course for semi-skilled and farm groups.
4. S-shaped for clerical and retail sales career lines, with diffuseness of destinations increasing for the first two age cohorts, decreasing for the next two age cohorts, and increasing sharply for the final three age cohorts.

Generally, we interpret greater concentration of exit ports during the middle years of the work course (professionals, managers, skilled) as denoting more "order," while diffuseness during the middle years denotes some disorder in terms of unsystematic movements among many different jobs. We develop this argument further in the next chapter. We strongly doubt

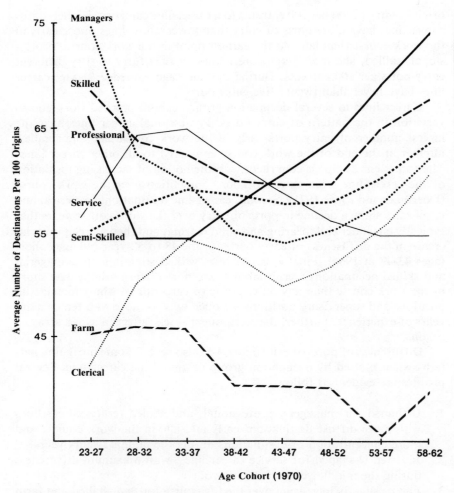

Figure 4-5. Diffuseness of Exit Portals by Career-Line Major Occupation Group and Age Cohort

whether a single explanation will account for the different patterns by major occupation group.

The percentage entering a career-line category from out of the labor force indicates several things (figure 4-6). It indicates the competition that workers in the line receive from a large pool of labor power. It indirectly shows the substitutability of one worker for another, particularly if the pool of those not at work is considered equally inexperienced with respect to the training and skill requirements of one career line compared to another. Fur-

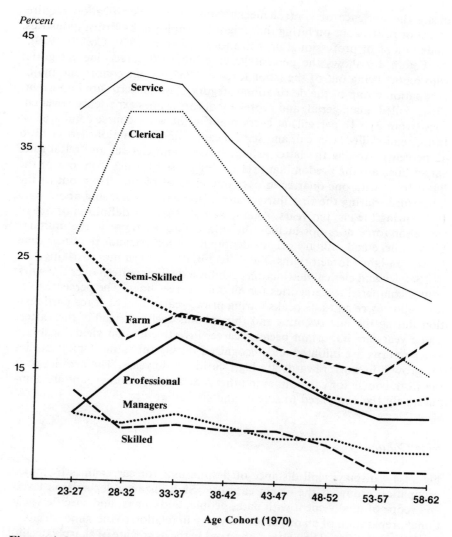

Figure 4-6. Percentage Entering from out of the Labor Force by Career-Line Major Occupation Group and Age Cohort

ther, if the percentage entering from out of the labor force is high, then the labor supply for the career line is large, and firm investment in workers is likely to be less in training and reward terms. A higher percentage connotes a more disorderly state of affairs for the career-line traveler. Finally, a low percentage entering a career line from out of the labor force might in-

dicate the presence of control mechanisms such as certification requirements or restrictions on hiring that might be employed by firms, industries,
trade unions or professional organizations (Edwards 1979; Collins 1979).

Figure 4-6 shows the percentage entering 1970 career-line categories
who report being out of the labor force in 1965, by age cohort and major
occupation group of the destination category. Two patterns are important.
First, skilled, managerial, and professional career lines experience fewer entries (from 8 to 18 percent) at every point in the work course compared to
farm, semi-skilled, clerical, and service career-line destinations (from 13 to
42 percent). Among the latter group, service, and clerical and retail sales
career lines are the predominant refuge for those entering from out of the
labor force with one-quarter to over one-third of recruits from out of the
labor force during the first thirty years of the work course and about one-
fifth during the last ten years. Again, we note that our definition of out of
the labor force does not include those in college or those in the military.
Since college and military origins denote more job-relevant resources than
other non-labor force origins, the differentials are even more striking.

Service and clerical destinations exhibit a distinct pattern over the work
course compared to categories for all other career lines. The percentage of
non-labor force entrants peaks during prime years of labor force participation during the late twenties and thirties and declines steadily thereafter.
These years are important because career investments that yield fiscal and
other returns are initiated and recognized during this time. Opportunities
for growth in work rewards are high during these years. The profiles over
the work course for career lines in other major occupation groups are comparatively flat compared to service and clerical groups.

Role Continuity

Figure 4-7 displays skill distance of destinations for career lines by major
occupation group of the origin category. Skill distance depends on levels
and scope of involvement with data, people, and things, and specific vocational preparation of an origin job category in relation to the same variables
for all destinations. The pattern observed in the aggregate of sharply declining skill distances by age cohort holds for career lines by major occupation
group except for farm lines. The slope differences from group to group appear trivial compared to the overall age trend. The more meaningful trend is
the sharp decline in skill distance over the work course, rather than differences between career lines. Again, this is not to say jobs held by older
workers require lower skill but rather that job transitions later in the work
course involve jobs that are more alike in skill terms compared to career-line
moves early in the work course.

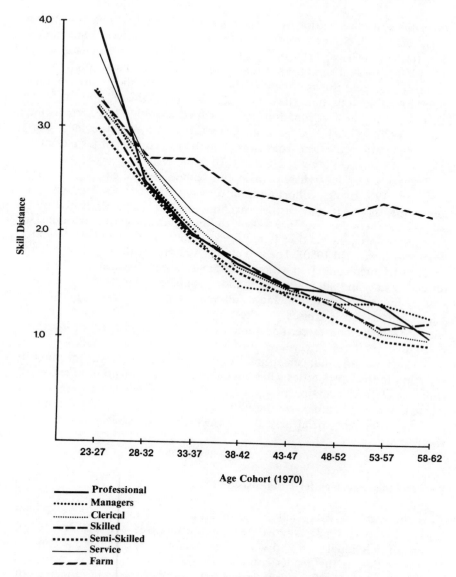

Figure 4-7. Skill Distance by Career-Line Major Occupation Group and Age Cohort

Job transitions that involve farm origins are a sharp outlier to the overall pattern. For all but the youngest two age cohorts, transitions out of farm career lines involve more skill distance to the destinations compared to career lines in other major occupation groups. There are several explanations, each of which likely contributes to the observed pattern. Most important, those who leave farm occupations disperse to a very diverse set of destinations in skill terms. Farming is quite different work compared to nonfarm jobs, and this is evident in the transitions for all but the youngest cohort. Additionally, over the course of this century the proportion of the labor force in farm occupations has declined steadily (Featherman and Hauser 1978, pp. 41-48). Between generations and, for the most part, within generations over the work course, successive cohorts of farm occupations have witnessed a net decline in their numbers.

Figures 4-8 and 4-9 display male and female median earnings, respectively, for 1969 by age cohort and major occupation group. The synthetic cohort measurement may distort earnings profiles, particularly for older cohorts as their earnings are taken to reflect the eventual earnings of younger cohorts, so caution is required (Eckaus 1973; compare Goldner 1965; and Rosenfeld 1980). The two effects we note are the markedly higher earnings for men compared with women, and the equally sizable differences for career lines in high-status occupation groups compared with low-status groups. Since the measure includes full- and part-time workers, part of the gender difference is caused by the larger number of part-time workers among women. The career-line categories are effective in capturing these well-known patterns in earnings profiles.

In sum, we find that career lines contain considerable, quite meaningful variation in their properties when investigated by age or point in the work course and by the major occupation group in which the career line is located. We later summarize the patterns in greater detail. We emphasize another prominent social axis along which the properties of career lines should vary.

Career Lines and Gender Composition

That there are stereotypically male or female jobs and careers is beyond question (Gross 1968; Angrist and Almquist 1975; McLaughlin 1978). Although individual men and women have careers, the analogous concept for career lines is the gender composition of the career line. A face-valid concept and measure for career lines should show variation in properties of career lines when gauged by their gender composition.

To this end, we classified each age-specific career line by its gender composition. We designated as female those with 75 percent or more women; as male those with 75 percent or more men; and as androgynous those with 26 percent to 74 percent men and women. Appendix A reports the gender composition group of each career-line category. Figures 4-10 to

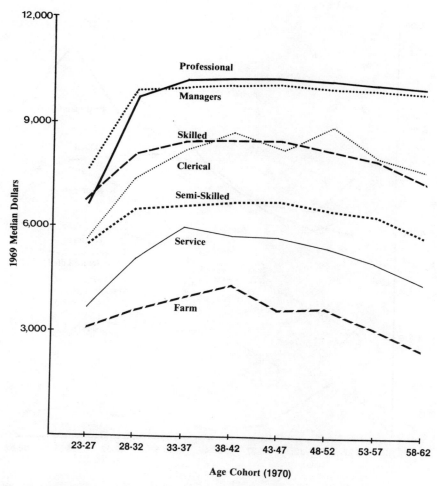

Figure 4-8. Male Median Earnings by Career-Line Major Occupation Group and Age Cohort

4-17 show the variation in properties of career lines by age cohort and gender composition of the career line. We briefly describe the differences.

As before, holding power (see figures 4-10 and 4-11) shows more variation within than between career lines. If anything, male career lines have greater holding power by five to ten percentage points. Of note, destination holding power for female career lines shows a modest drop in holding power at age 38 to 42 (33 to 37 in 1965), years of child-rearing responsibility. Differentiation (figure 4-12) is greater for female career lines—more

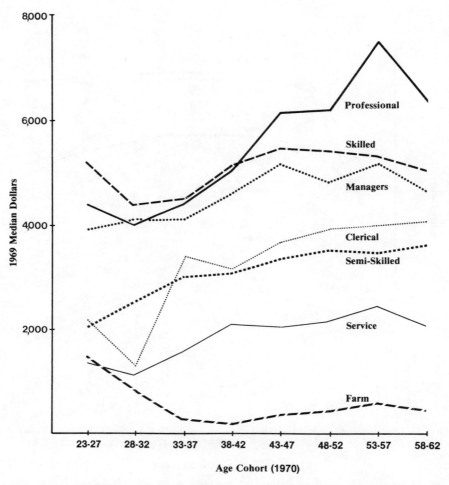

Figure 4-9. Female Median Earnings by Career-Line Major Occupation
Group and Age Cohort

early in the work course than later—compared to male and androgynous
career lines.

Ports of entry and exit and percentage entering from out of the labor
force (figures 4-13 to 4-15) show sizable variation by gender composition of
the career line. Male career lines have nearly twice as many ports of entry at
every point in the work course and from one-third to one-fifth more ports
of exit compared to female career lines. Further, male career lines have
dramatically fewer entrants from out of the labor force (5 to 10 percent)

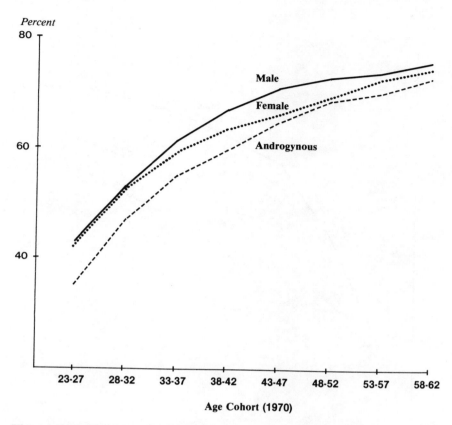

Percent

Figure 4-10. Origin Holding Power by Career-Line Gender Composition and Age Cohort

compared to androgynous (15 to 25 percent) and female career lines (20 to 50 percent). The career lines traditionally traveled by women have much more concentrated ports of entry, somewhat more concentrated ports of exit, and are dramatically more likely to accept workers entering the career line from out of the labor force. Rather than indicating flexibility or an orderly state of affairs, the concentration of entry and exit ports bespeaks career lines that contain restricted options. The pattern is consistent with the popular notion that "women have jobs while men have careers."

Skill distance (figure 4-16) reveals large declines over the work course, as was the case for major occupation groups. The profiles are approximately parallel for male, female, and androgynous career lines. Transitions in androgynous career lines entail slightly more skill distance than transi-

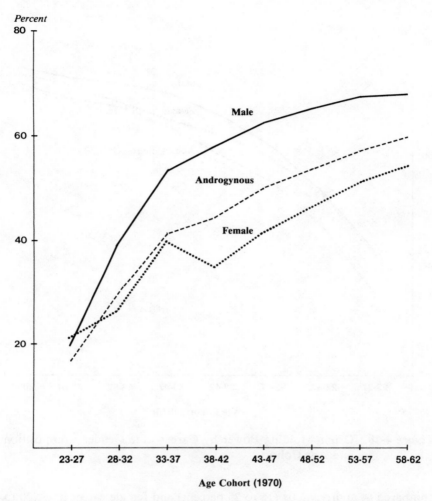

Figure 4-11. Destination Holding Power by Career-Line Gender Composition and Age Cohort

tions in male career lines, which in turn are slightly more skill distant at
every age than transitions in female career lines.

Finally, we note the sizable, indeed massive, differences between male
and female median earnings by age cohort and gender composition of the
career line (figure 4-17). Several differences are noteworthy. First, male
earnings have the characteristic convex profile over the work course: rapid
earnings growth in the first twenty years of labor-force participation. The
pattern characterizes male earnings in male, female, and androgynous

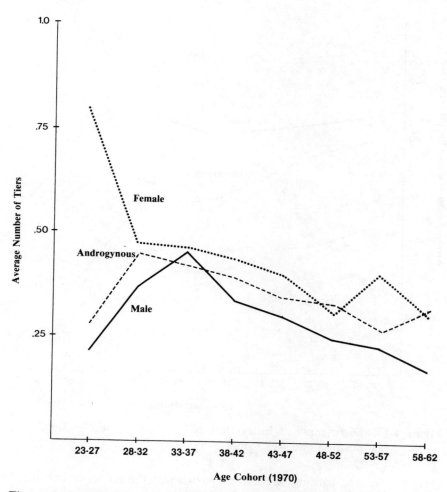

Figure 4-12.   Differentiation by Career-Line Gender Composition and Age
Cohort

career lines. Women, on the other hand, have earnings profiles with positive
slope but not the sharp growth pattern characteristic of males. The male-
female earnings difference in part reflects the large number of women who
are part-time workers.

   Second, both men and women receive an earnings boost for being in a
typically male career line compared to a female or androgynous career line.
Additionally, men—but not women—receive an earnings boost for travel-
ing an androgynous compared with a female career line. Thus, beyond the

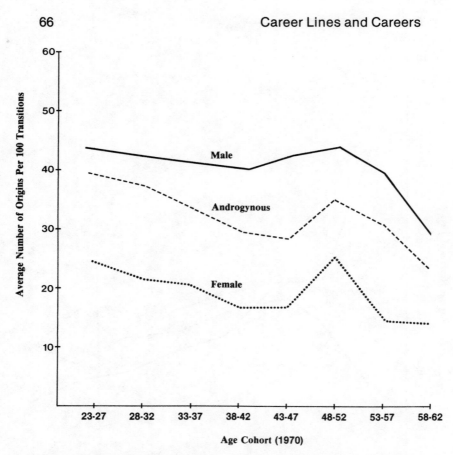

Figure 4-13. Diffuseness of Entry Portals by Career-Line Gender Composition and Age Cohort

gender difference, earnings are also associated with the gender composition
of the career-line category.

   Finally, perhaps the most dramatic demonstration of gender variation
in the pattern of earnings for career lines results from joint consideration of
all six earnings profiles. In average median 1969 dollars, even males
in stereotypically female career lines earn more by several hundred to
several thousand dollars at every step of the work course, even when compared with women in stereotypically male career lines. This comparison is the
closest point of intersection between male and female earnings. Women lose
at every step. Their starting wages are lower. The growth in women's earnings by age is less than for men's earnings, and the career lines that they
typically travel engender lower earnings than those of mixed gender composition or those traveled by males.

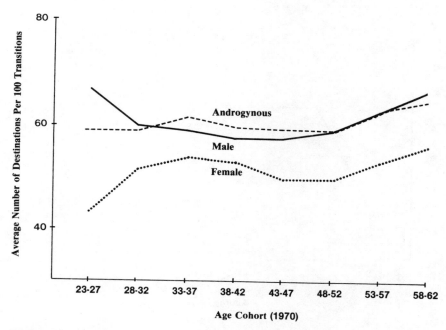

Figure 4-14. Diffuseness of Exit Portals by Career-Line Gender Composition and Age Cohort

In summary, at least three effects appear to govern role continuity in earnings over career lines. First, one's gender makes an earnings difference irrespective of career line location. Second, the characteristic growth in earnings that occurs with age may be conditioned on both gender and the gender composition of the career line. Finally, aside from gender and age, the effect of structure on earnings—gender composition of the career line— is to the advantage of a traveler of male career lines and to the disadvantage of the traveler of female career lines, irrespective of the traveler's gender.

Summary

Our goal was to describe the variation in career-line properties. The concepts for properties are a first specification. The measures are new and imply a strong set of methodological assumptions embodied in the synthetic cohort. For one elementary property—size—our analytic design is not well suited to investigate the variation. Yet, in the properties and measures we think there is evidence of meaningful variation that contributes to the face validity of the career-line concept and measure.

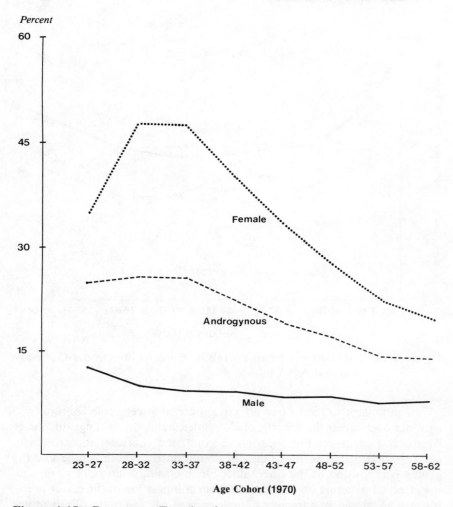

Figure 4-15. Percentage Entering from out of the Labor Force by Career-Line Gender Composition and Age Cohort

We reasoned that a face-valid concept and measures would exhibit meaningful patterns over the work course, by major occupation group of the career line, and by gender composition of the career line. We found substantial growth in the holding power of career lines over the work course. The work course also contained the expected patterns in career-line differentiation, ports of entry and exit, and in both the skill distance and earnings indicators of role continuity. When examined by major occupation group, career-line properties exhibited a number of meaningful pat-

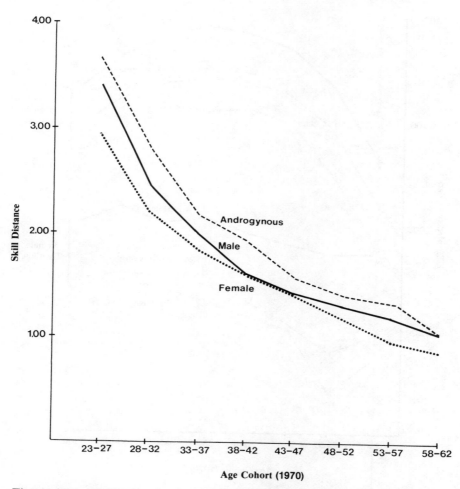

Figure 4-16. Skill Distance by Career-Line Gender Composition and Age Cohort

terns: higher-status career lines contained higher holding power, more diffuse ports of entry early in the work course, more concentrated later, more diffuse ports of exit early and late in the work course but not in the middle, less competition from those entering career lines from out of the labor force, and well-documented earnings patterns. Further, the pattern of differentiation in career lines over the work course exhibited a complex but reasonable pattern that depended on major occupation group for their shape.

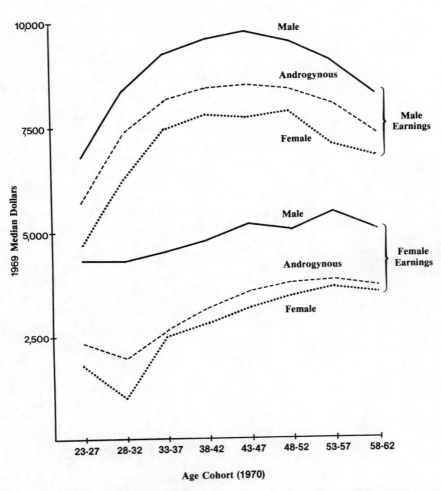

Figure 4-17. Median Earnings by Career-Line Gender Composition, Age Cohort, and Gender

Finally, we expected and found meaningful variation in career-line properties when grouped for stereotypically male, female, and androgynous career lines. Most of the variations depicted advantages for male career lines. The advantages included higher origin and destination holding power, much more diffuse ports of entry to career lines over the entire work course, more diffuse ports of exit, dramatically less competition from those entering career lines from outside the labor force, and sizable advantages in earnings. Thus, for each type of comparison that we made, the variations suggested a favorable verdict on the face validity of the career-line concept and measures.

Where we offered interpretation to the patterns of variation, our reasoning was post hoc. Nonetheless, we find evidence for the face validity of the career-line concept and measures. We find grounds to proceed, and thus, in the next chapter we examine hypotheses to explain the variation in career lines.

5

Origins of Career-Line Structure

How are career lines rooted in social and economic structure? What causes the variation that we see in the properties of career lines? We structure the analyses in demand-side rather than supply-side terms. A demand-side explanation examines career-line variation in terms of larger features of work organization, the economy, and the society. A supply-side explanation would examine the characteristics of individuals as these might explain the shape of career lines and careers. We pursue demand-side explanations for careers and career lines here. We consider supply-side explanations in chapters 6 and 7.

We draw on two literatures for hypotheses to explain career-line variation: (1) neoclassical perspectives and (2) economic segmentation and labor-market perspectives. We develop measures to test the hypotheses and present the results of the tests. Finally, we extend the findings to include the effects of unionization.

Insights from Neoclassical Theory

Several areas compose neoclassical economics, including the theory of the firm (Henderson and Quandt 1971), marginal productivity theory, and theories of labor supply such as labor-leisure choice and human-capital (Mincer 1974; Becker 1975). Kindred perspectives in sociology include status attainment (Blau and Duncan 1967; Featherman and Hauser 1978), the industrialism thesis (Kerr et al. 1964; Treiman 1970; 1977), and the functional theory of stratification (Davis and Moore 1945; Parsons 1954). None of the theories directly treats career lines as a concept or makes explicit empirical predictions about the properties or causes of career lines. Rather, the theories advance a perspective on the patterns in social and economic life and on the structure and quality of work life. We extrapolate hypotheses from that general perspective.

The theories share a common gestalt on the workings of Western industrial societies. Treiman's (1977) theory of occupational prestige typifies the view. Societies have basic needs; a division of labor with specialized occupations develops to meet the needs. Differences in access and control over scarce resources follow from differentiation. Some occupations come to have more resources, power, and privilege, and others have less. Resources include skill, authority, and property. The increases in societal size and complexity that accompany industrialization generate further differentiation. The division of labor operates in this fashion because it is efficient. Thus occupations "naturally" come to differ in their skill levels, authority, and control over economic resources.

Our extrapolation suggests that career-line structure is determined by the same processes.[1] To provide for an efficient division of labor, positions of greater "importance" and resources will get a more desirable set of career-line outcomes. This is the demand side of the neoclassical argument.

Treiman (1977) cites two processes for the translation of differences in occupational resources (that is, skill, authority, and economic control) into differences in privilege. Resources affect market position, hence the prices paid for work. Moreover, resources permit manipulation of the system to obtain valued goals and direct allocation of surplus. Occupational resources of jobs in career lines should explain some of the variation in career lines, to the extent that career-line arrangements and outcomes are valued commodities in the stratification system.

The theory of the firm offers a related argument from economics (Henderson and Quandt 1971). It assumes a free market economy, perfect competition among firms, and complete information for actors (that is, employers and employees). As in Treiman's structural theory of occupational prestige, rationality and efficiency are the engines that drive the organization of production and, in turn, the organization of work and the mobility linkages among jobs.

Each firm has a production function that expresses an optimal relationship between outputs and inputs in terms of profit and efficiency. The inputs include the generic categories of capital and labor. The labor component includes the skill mixture of jobs for production, wage levels, task differentiation, and the organization of jobs that provides for production. Firms will use a mix of skill levels and jobs that maximizes efficiency and profit in the production and provision of goods and services. If the extrapolation is correct, career lines should provide a stable supply of labor for the production tasks; they promote the operation of the production function in maximizing efficiency and profit. Career lines are among the devices that provide for meeting the technical skill levels required by organizations and more generally by the economy.

In short, the contemporary pattern and arrangement of career lines exist because they provide the levels and mixture of skills for optimal production. Other things being equal, the skill level and scope of a job should be an important determinant of the career-line outcomes attached to incumbency in the job. If neoclassical arguments are correct, greater occupational resources as indexed by high skill level should promote role continuity, a growth in holding power over the work course, "order" in career lines as indexed by differentiation, and ports of entry and exit.

For example, consider a neoclassical argument for why career-line holding power should covary with the skill level of jobs in the career lines. Since the learning of occupation and firm-specific skills entails more costs for higher skill positions, a career line that minimizes turnover is less costly to the production process and to the employer. Positions in the economy that require higher skills and offer more opportunities for on-the-job training, compared to those that require and offer less, should bear patterns of holding power that reflect positional differences (Mincer 1974; Leigh 1978). Holding-power profiles should covary positively with the skill level of jobs in career lines.

An ideal test of the neoclassical perspective would directly measure the operation of the production function and career lines in firms. Our design does not permit that. We reason that if such processes are in operation, then they should operate through the skill levels and resources of jobs. In turn, differences in resources and skill undergird patterns in the career-line structure; hence, the examination is indirect.

Insights from Segmentation Theory

In contrast to neoclassical perspectives, segmentation theories argue that considerations of efficiency, cost minimization, and profit maximization are only part of the story—perhaps not the most important part.[2] Segmentation perspectives developed in response to anomalies in the neoclassical paradigm. Labor markets appeared neither fully competitive nor fluid in response to supply and demand considerations. Certain groups in the labor force—minorities and women—seemed to fare much worse than might be expected from neoclassical predictions.

Common to segmentation perspectives is the notion that larger societal and organization forces such as the logic of capitalism, monopoly, concentration, size, and control systems in firms cause segmented units in the economy. The units include labor markets, industries, occupations, firms, and jobs. The segments differ in their operation, power, work structure and consequences, and labor-force composition.

Segmentation theory is not a single unitary perspective. There is disagreement on what it is that is segmented (for example, the economy, labor markets, firms, jobs, occupations, industries, or some combination). There is disagreement on the number of sectors (from two to sixteen) (see Kaufman, Hodson, and Fligstein 1981). There is disagreement on the causes and criteria for defining segments. Also, there is disagreement on how one goes about studying segmentation (Baron and Bielby 1980). The evidence in support of segmentation is mixed and is only beginning to accumulate. Finally, there is disagreement on the nature and consequences of segmentation (Baron and Bielby 1980).

Given the diversity of views, we have selected two arguments and have tried to maintain their letter and spirit (Piore 1975; Edwards 1979). The two positions are among the more parsimonious and among the few that make explicit predictions about career-line outcomes. If the arguments fail, then more complex versions of the thesis may prove more fruitful. Given the disagreement among segmentation writers, it makes more sense to give attention first to the versions that are simple and make explicit predictions about career lines and to later consider more complex versions that make only passing reference to career-line outcomes, if the initial analyses warrant.

Piore's Thesis

Piore's thesis is an expansion of the dual labor market hypothesis proposed by Doeringer and Piore (1971; Piore 1975). The central concept is *mobility chain.* A mobility chain refers to the jobs that people hold "in some regular order or sequence" (Piore 1975, p. 128). Points on a chain are "stations," which include jobs and "other points of social and economic significance." Mobility chains are the key defining characteristic of sectors. The mobility chains of primary sectors constitute "career ladders" with growth in earnings and status. Mobility chains in the secondary sector provide little growth in status or earnings. The concept of mobility chain is similar to that of career line. Piore also speaks of ports of entry and the subsequent access to jobs that is gained by being in a port of entry at the right time during the work course.

Piore addresses the question of why mobility chains are constructed as they are.

> The construction of mobility chains can be cast as a conventional problem of cost minimization: jobs (or, more broadly, stations) are formed into chains . . . so as to minimize the adjustment involved in movement from one station to another. . . . one would want to translate the concept of open "adjustment" into monetary costs (Piore 1975, p. 135).

But Piore rejects cost minimization as the sole factor governing the formation of mobility chains. Other factors augment the cost minimization principle. For example, mobility chains should form where the learning that occurs in the origin position can be applied in the destination position. But Piore argues, *who* gets access to the opportunity to learn in the origin position depends on prior mobility into *that* position. In the primary sectors (independent and subordinate), reinforced patterns of mobility restrict the flow of people into key positions. Piore does not agree that an open contest governs access at every stage.[3]

Piore turns to technology as the underlying determinant of types of mobility chains.[4] Adjustment in the demand for labor follows one of two paths: (1) a change in the composition of demand for the product, or (2) change in the way a product or service is produced. Production techniques and the implied organization of jobs range over a continuum. At one end, work is arranged into a series of highly specialized tasks often assigned to specific persons with execution aided by machine. For this type of production, the investment in capital equipment is high. Jobs are structured around the repetition of a specialized task. The repetitive, more automated technology defines jobs in the primary-subordinate sector.

Production is structured around a broader scope of skills and tasks at the other end of the continuum. Work is more variable, hence less subject to mechanization and automation. There is less investment in capital equipment under this production organization. Work is less routinized. Piore argues that under this technology jobs polarize into two groups: the primary-independent sector and the secondary sector. The more highly skilled jobs, with high variety and judgment in the task structure (for example, professional, managerial, and craft) define the primary-independent sector. The secondary includes unskilled jobs that involve menial work and, consistent with the technology, jobs that involve nonrepetitive but obvious judgments. In short, the repetitiveness and generality of task structure differentiates primary-subordinate from secondary and primary-independent jobs. Piore argues that jobs in the latter two sectors are obviously different from each other in skill and training levels.

Production technology determines the sector location of jobs. Implementation of production technique depends on the degree of standardization of product demand, the stability of product demand, and the certainty of product demand. Standardized products with stable and certain demand are likely to generate primary-subordinate jobs. Departures from certainty, stability, and standardization of product demand generate primary-independent and secondary jobs and mobility chains. Piore hypothesizes an explicit set of exogenous factors that differentiate jobs and their attached mobility chains into three sectors. These are important for our purposes.

Piore is not explicit on exactly what the mobility chains look like in each sector other than to insist on fundamental differences. Secondary jobs are low skill, have very diffuse recruitment patterns (particularly from out of the labor force), and portend low earnings and status growth trajectories. Unemployment, underemployment, and unstable employment are characteristic features. Primary-independent jobs possess the opposite career-line characteristics. Primary-subordinate jobs (for example, operatives and some clerical and sales jobs) are somewhere in between. Primary-independent jobs organize skills around the occupation, particularly the crafts and professions. In the case of managers, the mobility chain is built around a succession of jobs and progressive skills, often within the same firm. In the primary-subordinate, unionization is most prominent, and mobility chains typically are organized within the firm (such as, operative to foreman job transitions). We return to specific career-line predictions after reviewing Edwards's (1979) kindred ideas.

Edwards's Thesis

In *Contested Terrain: The Transformation of the Workplace in the Twentieth Century,* Edwards (1979) chronicles the historical roots of segmentation. The fundamental problem for industry has been the control of labor. The system of control in an organization involves the coordination of three components: the direction of work, the evaluation of work, and the disciplining of workers. In earlier days, a direct, *simple system of control* ruled the work place. Foremen personally gave direction, evaluated, and disciplined workers. With growth in the size of firms, unionization, vertical integration, diversification of products, and international markets for products, the control system that assured a high return on investment at low risk ran into problems.

Facing crisis, corporations imposed what Edwards labels "structural control" (1979). The work place changed such that control became embedded in the structure of work. The pace and nature of work was only nominally controlled by a foreman and primarily controlled by the tasks built into the job and the bureaucracy in which the job was located. The two new systems of control were technical control and bureaucratic control.

In *technical control,* machines are the key (Edwards 1979). As argued by neoclassicists, firms choose production strategies that maximize profit and efficiency. But, as for Piore, the choice of production technique also provides for transforming labor power into products and services. Under technical control, the design of machinery, the planned flow of work in assembly lines, piece rates, and automated systems control labor. Work is routinized. It becomes repetitive and more predictable, workers more interchangeable, and the labor force and jobs under technical control become more homogeneous.

In *bureaucratic control,* the social-organizational structure of the firm is the nexus of the control system. For jobs under bureaucratic control, the bureaucracy (that is, rules, communication channels, and lines of authority) rewards a rules orientation, dependability in work, and internalizing the goals and values of the firm (Edwards 1979). Control over labor is exercised in different ways.

Hence, firms are responsible for segmenting jobs and labor. In firms, it is easier to deal with segments of workers with the control system embedded in the structure of their work than to confront a monolithic undivided labor force. Jobs tend to fall in distinct segments because one of the three systems of control underlies each segment. The secondary market is organized by simple control, although there are exceptions (for example, Southern textile jobs under technical control or part-time academic jobs under bureaucratic control). Primary-subordinate jobs tend to occur in a technical control system (exceptions include unionized garment workers under simple control and secretarial jobs under bureaucratic control). Primary-independent jobs tend to fall under bureaucratic control (some exceptions include jobs in a small consulting firm under simple control, continuous production process technicans under technical control). In short, the type of control system structures a job and places it into a segment. The nature of work and, by hypothesis, the career-line properties and consequences flow from the nature of the control system.

Edwards (1979) provides a detailed account of jobs in the secondary, primary-subordinate, and primary-independent sectors. His account later serves as a basis for hypotheses regarding career lines and for the measurement of jobs in sectors.

The *secondary sector* includes production and nonproduction jobs. It includes many service jobs, lower-level positions in wholesale and retail trade, lower-level clerical jobs, and agricultural labor. The work involves low pay, little job security, high turnover, few prospects for advancement, and few rewards for seniority. Employment may be casual. Age or experience yield few returns. Little training or experience is required for jobs that demand few skills and, once entered, jobs at which few skills can be learned.

Edwards establishes segments to define career-line types. In demarking secondary from primary markets, he (1979, p. 171) notes, "all primary jobs share the characteristic of offering well-defined occupations, with established paths for advancement."

The *primary-subordinate sector* includes production jobs in unionized mass-production industries (for example, transportation equipment, machine and other durable-goods manufacture), unionized jobs in lower-level sales, clerical, and administrative work, and production positions in transportation, utilities, and jobs in retail and wholesale trade. Primary-subordinate jobs are much more likely to be unionized than are secondary jobs. Crucial for our later measurement of sector, compared to jobs in the primary-independent, primary-subordinate jobs are "repetitive, routinized and subject to machine pacing" (Edwards 1979, p. 172). On this key prediction, Piore and Edwards are in agreement. Primary-subordinate jobs are better paying, more stable, and more permanent than secondary jobs. Edwards states that the requisite skills can be acquired in a matter of days or weeks. Although workers have little opportunity to control their own jobs in this sector, salary and promotion provide returns to age and experience. Mobility chains tend to be firm-specific and bounded by union rules. Finally, the turnover rates for primary-subordinate jobs are hypothesized to be much lower than for secondary jobs.

The composition of the *primary-independent sector* includes professional, craft, and managerial jobs, the middle layers of corporations (for example, longer-term sales and technical and clerical positions), and much of the employment in the public sector. These jobs often require advanced schooling and educational credentials. The jobs are more secure, the employment more stable, and the pay higher when compared with other sectors. There may be professional associations and occupational standards for performance. Primary-independent jobs offer the greatest return to age and experience. The work is more complex, more challenging, and often involves initiative and self-pacing. The requisite skills may be general to an occupation rather than firm-specific; thus career ladders may imply movement between firms as well as within firms.

The sectors described by Edwards are best treated as ideal types. Both Piore and Edwards primarily speak of jobs as the unit of segmentation. They grant attention to firms and industry, but jobs are the fundamental unit. Some writers would take issue with this stance (Baron and Bielby 1980; Althauser and Kalleberg 1981a). But Piore and Edwards speak of jobs. It is their hypotheses that we examine.

Our design approximates job with census occupation-industry categories, an exigency of available data. We reason that if work and career lines are arranged as Edwards and Piore argue, then we should be able to detect some meaningful signal of segmentation for the 384 career-line categories.

General Hypotheses

This section derives general hypotheses for the career-line implications of occupational resources as embodied in skill levels and in the sector location of jobs. The hypotheses represent a first attempt to specify how career lines are rooted in the economy and labor-market organization. Our goal is not to test neoclassical and segmentation theories for that should be done with much more detailed analytical and measurement designs (see Leigh 1978; Kalleberg, Wallace, and Althauser 1981). Rather, our goal is to examine whether career-line properties covary with simple variables taken to measure neoclassical and segmentation sources of variation.

Holding Power

As job resources (skill level and scope) increase, holding power should increase. The linkage to neoclassical theory is straightforward. Turnover in more skilled positions is more costly to the firm in terms of efficiency and retraining. The pattern should be evident in both inflow (for a career-line destination, those present in the same position five years earlier) and the outflow displays (for a career-line origin, those who report the same destination five years later).

The patterns of holding power by sector should also differ. Holding power should be greatest for primary-independent positions, intermediate for primary-subordinate positions, and lowest for secondary sector positions. Segmentation theory would make this prediction because career lines in the primary-independent sector are organized around a bureaucratic control system that encourages loyalty and longevity to the firm or profession. Further, secondary career lines under a simple control system promote a higher substitutability of one worker for another and hence, will have the lowest holding power. A similar pattern should hold for career lines having their destinations in each of the respective sectors.

Differentiation, Ports of Entry, and Exit

Differentiation captures the number of major job paths to and from a career-line position, indexed by location in the work course. Both theoretical perspectives suggest a more orderly state of affairs for high-skill compared with low-skill positions or for primary compared to secondary career lines. From a neoclassical perspective, an orderly career line is more likely for more skilled positions because it provides a stable supply and mixture of labor, which are more scarce and costly resources for skilled than unskilled positions. From a segmentation perspective, primary-independent career lines are more orderly because they are insulated from market competition, and orderly career lines may be a form of reward in bureaucracies.

But what constitutes order? One possibility is to gauge the definition of order against points in the work course and the normative levels of role responsibility associated with work, schooling, and family domains of life (Hogan 1981). Consider three periods. During the early period of the work course—say the first five to ten years—formal schooling is typically completed, and job search and change behaviors are likely to be at their peak. The responsibilities of family formation, child rearing, and home ownership may be undertaken but do not reach their peak in terms of physical and work-security demands. In age terms this period spans the later teens and much of the twenties.

Following the early period, role responsibilities increase due to marriages that are formed or dissolved, offspring that are reared at increasing expense, or the greater physical demands of home ownership. For the sake of argument, consider this period the late twenties, thirties, and forties in age terms for most persons.

Finally, during the last period there is typically a lessening of the role demands. Children have left the nest. The mortgage is retired or more manageable. Finances are not as tight, and some of the demands associated with career may have eased. In other words, role responsibilities over the work course are inverted-U or inverted-J shaped: lowest at the beginning, then greater for a twenty-year period or so, and perhaps declining at the end.

What pattern in a career line would best accommodate the role-responsibility curve? The pattern should grant the greatest security in earnings growth during the years of high responsibility. The pattern should offer well-scheduled, predictable transitions during or prior to the same years. Finally, the pattern should restrict any instability or insecurity to the extremes (early or late) and concentrate security during the larger portion of intervening years.

A career-line set that has equal differentiation at every point in the work course does not schedule transitions for one period versus another.[5] This pattern should be more characteristic of lower-skill and secondary positions. Primary-sector and higher-skill career lines should show a U- or J-shaped pattern in differentiation over the work course.

A similar argument can be made for the diffuseness of ports of entry and exit. A J- or U-shaped profile for diffuseness of entry and exit denotes mobility involving movement to or from different positions that is scheduled to a portion of the work course in which it is most affordable. A horizontal profile of diffuseness denotes no such scheduling in the career line. The diffuseness of ports of entry and exit to a career line does not change over the work course. Defined in this way, order means more predictable scheduling of movement. It is the predictable work course scheduling that is a valued commodity to the career-line traveler.

For secondary and low-skill positions and career lines, the number of different positions that serve as ports of entry and exit should remain constant over the work course. Low skill level denotes an interchangeability of labor. Firms have little reason to protect their investment by attaching valued rewards to the career line. The segmentation perspective predicts that primary positions, and by our reasoning, career lines, enjoy some degree of insulation from external competition, given passage through the port of entry. Primary career lines should show evidence of insulation: relatively more ports of entry early in the work course, then a decline in the number of positions that grant access to the line for four or five successive cohorts, and perhaps an increase at the last stage of the work course. Further, primary career lines should have more concentrated ports of entry consistent with the notion of insulation from competition.

In summary, we expect skill level and sector to govern the level of order in the career line. Order is narrowly defined in terms of career-line differentiation, ports of entry, and exit. The changing role responsibilities over the work course provide the criterion. A more orderly pattern has differentiation restricted to one portion of the work course and more concentrated career-line origins and destinations during the middle years of the work course. Disorder means equal career-line differentiation over the work course and diffuseness of career-line origins and destinations that are (1) high for low-skill and secondary positions compared to high-skill and primary-sector positions, and (2) ungraded with respect to age in the work course.

Role Continuity

Both neoclassical and segmentation perspectives make their strongest predictions about the role continuity in career lines. Role continuity refers to the work role requisites, routines, and rewards as they change over the work course. Continuity includes the pattern of means for a role characteristic over the work course (for example, earnings) and the correlation among successive levels of a characteristic over the work course. We concentrate on two indicators of role continuity: (1) the skill distance between a career-line origin job and all of the age-specific destinations, and (2) gender-specific, age-specific median earnings.

The concept of role continuity does not assume any progression or growth. Explicitly, the denotation is that of sequence without an implicit evaluative connotation of progress or development (compare Althauser and Kalleberg 1981a). One could study progression in role components such as skill, but that would be a *subset* of phenomena defined by the concept. For our present purpose, the continuous low-grade mixture of skills that characterizes the career line of dishwasher is a form of role continuity no less than the earnings progression of professional career lines.

Neoclassical arguments regularly explain age-earnings profiles in human capital terms (Mincer 1974). The demand-side argument says that high-skill positions yield a steeper earnings profile because the higher reward secures stable, quality labor power for the firm. The segmentation prediction also suggests slope differences in earnings profiles by sector. The primary-independent and, to a lesser extent, the primary-subordinate sectors yield returns to age while the secondary sector does not.

Skill distance refers to the mixture of data, people, and things skills in a career-line origin category, relative to the mixtures of data, people, and things skills in the job destinations of those in the origin category. Low skill distance means very comparable mixtures of involvement with data, people, and things for origin compared to destination; high skill distance implies a very different mixture of the three skills. We define skill generalizability to mean low skill distance.[6] Skill distance can be a desirable or undesirable commodity. Small distance may imply high specialization as in some high-skill jobs. Conversely, when measured for job transitions of lower skill, low skill distance may reflect a desperate employment situation: The origin job involves a low-grade mixture of skills and, in turn, destination positions reflect the same low-grade mixture of skills.

In general, transitions among jobs that are very different in skill terms are inefficient and costly in retraining. Job transitions that involve related skills are more efficient from a neoclassical perspective. Thus, career-line transitions for highly skilled jobs should involve less skill distance, or more skill similarity. On balance, we expect a negative relationship between skill level and skill distance. From a segmentation perspective, career lines in the secondary should involve little relationship between the skill requirements of successive jobs, thus high average skill distance. On the other hand, career lines in the primary-independent involve transitions with a close articulation of skills from one job to another, hence, on average, less skill distance. Career-line locations in the primary-independent and primary-subordinate should suppress the skill distance of job transitions compared to career lines in the secondary.

Measures

Skill Level

We conceptualize skill as the level and scope of mental, interpersonal, and manipulative complexity inherent in a job. We use the concept of skill to capture the sources of variation that are important in neoclassical perspectives. For measures we use the variables from the *Dictionary of Occupational Titles* for involvement with data, people, and things. Appendix B reports the original measurement scales. The crucial component is complexity of the job. As a concept, skill is rarely defined, and most often its meaning is assumed obvious. In many treatments it is the worker who is more or less skilled, not the job (see Becker 1975). As a result, skill measures pertain to a person's formal schooling or on-the-job training. This strategy confounds credential with performance and substitutes an indirect indicator of complex work for a direct measure.

The focus on complexity of role performance is consistent with more rigorous concepts of skill and work in the literature (Kohn 1977; Coser 1975; Field 1980; Baron and Bielby 1982). For example, Field delineates three components in the skill level of a job: the span of the job (the number of identifiable discrete tasks to be mastered), the difficulty of each task, and the extent to which the job requires judgment in response to a changing environment.

We recognize that involvement with data, people, and things constitutes one component of a larger relationship between job and technology. The three primary measures of skill level correlate well with related criterion variables in validity studies (Spenner 1977, 1980). The distributions of data, people, and things variables in their original metrics are skewed. We employ dichotomous variables (0 = low) to alleviate the problem. Finally, we treat the three indicators as three separate but correlated measures.

Sector

Two important predictions from Piore (1975) and Edwards (1979) form the basis for the measurement of sectors. Both writers concur that primary-subordinate employment is fundamentally distinguished from other sectors in the scope, repetitiveness, and machine-paced nature of jobs. Each theorist identifies numerous other correlates and consequences of sectors, yet repetitiveness and task scope derive directly from demand technology considerations for Piore and are central defining characteristics of a technical control system for Edwards. Both writers also concur that the remaining jobs—those that are nonrepetitive, not as extensively machine-paced, and of greater task scope—are readily placed in sectors by their overall skill and training levels. Our placement of jobs, hence career lines, in sectors parallels the two predictions.

First, we measured the degree of repetitiveness of work for each of the 384 job categories with the repetitiveness indicator from the *Dictionary of Occupational Titles* (U.S. Department of Labor 1965). Appendix B reports the actual measure. Spenner (1980) provides details of the measurement of repetitiveness for job categories. The scores range from 0.00 (low) to 1.00. The mean for all jobs is 0.30 (standard deviation = 0.34).

After some experimentation, we placed career-line categories that were more than one standard deviation above the repetitiveness mean into the primary-subordinate sector.[7] The remaining career-line categories were then allocated to the primary-independent sector or the secondary sector on the basis of the specific vocational preparation score for the category. Specific vocational preparation (SVP) indexes the total training (vocational, formal education, and on-the-job) time required to learn the techniques, information, and facilities required for an average performance on the job (see appendix B). Jobs with SVP levels from short demonstration to up to six months were placed in the secondary. Jobs with SVP levels of six months or greater were placed in the primary-independent sector.

With this classification, the average SVP scores by sector are 6.68 for the primary-independent (about two years of training), 3.55 for the primary-subordinate, and 3.80 for the secondary (from thirty days to three months of training). As expected, jobs in the primary-independent sector involve much more training than do jobs in the other sectors. Jobs in the primary-subordinate under this classification are not different in training terms from jobs in the secondary sector. Many segmentation writers suggest secondary jobs should be lower in training than primary-subordinate jobs (Rumberger and Carnoy 1980). We decided to retain this classification because the use of training to define primary-subordinate jobs would violate the hypotheses of Piore and Edwards. Both writers argue that primary-subordinate jobs are distinguished on the basis of the repetitive nature of work. Our measurement scheme allows for this. The sector measure that we use may be weak in discriminating secondary from primary-subordinate jobs, but that then is a problem of the Piore and Edwards specifications. Other classification systems and subsequent research may provide more effective measurement criteria.

The classification of jobs and career-line origin categories provides reasonable face validity (see appendix A). Nearly all professionals, managers, upper-level sales, and many craft jobs fall in the primary-independent sector. The primary-subordinate sector compromises largely clerical and operative jobs. The secondary includes retail sales jobs, lower-level clerical positions, some service jobs, operative positions, and some laborers. In short, job placement is consistent with the compositional description given by Edwards (1979, pp. 167-178). The classification places 49.6 percent of the labor force in the primary-independent sector, 25.1 percent in the primary-subordinate sector, and 25.3 percent in the secondary sector. The measurement is not ad hoc in allocating jobs to sectors but is analytically consistent in placing jobs in sectors on the basis of two independently measured and theoretically derived technical features of work.

Table 5-1 further illustrates the differences among sectors in select work and labor-force-composition variables. In skill terms, the primary-independent sector involves the most complex work with data and people. Both primary sectors involve more complex work with things compared with the secondary; but the secondary sector involves more complex work with people than the primary-subordinate sector and, in overall complexity and socioeconomic status, is slightly higher than the primary-subordinate sector. Yet both sectors are considerably below the primary-independent sector in overall complexity and status. As predicted, the primary-independent sector is considerably more male, white, better educated, and likely to involve variety, freedom from close supervision, and control over work compared to jobs in the primary-subordinate and the secondary sectors. As specified by Piore (1975) and Edwards (1979), the primary-subordinate sector is most different from the primary-independent sector and the secondary sector in levels of unionization (38 percent versus about 20 percent) and the variety and repetitiveness in work. In sum, the mean comparisons suggest the sectors are fairly close to what Edwards (1979) and Piore (1975) described.

We use the following regression equation to capture the impact of positional skill level and sector location:

$$Y_{ij} = b_0 + b_1 \text{DATA} + b_2 \text{PEOPLE} + b_3 \text{THING} + b_4 \text{PR-INDEP} + b_5 \text{PR-SUB} + e_{ij}$$

where Y_{ij} is the ith career line property for the jth age cohort ($j = 1\text{-}8$); DATA, PEOPLE, and THING are skill levels measured with dichotomous variables (1 = high); PR-INDEP is a dichotomous variable scored 1 if a career-line job category falls in the primary-independent sector; and PR-SUB is a dichotomous variable scored 1 if a career-line job category falls in the primary-subordinate sector. For the latter two variables, job location in the secondary sector is the left-out category. Hence, coefficients refer to the effect of being in the primary-independent or primary-subordinate compared to the secondary sector. The units of analysis are the 384 job categories. With the age-specific job transitions to and from these categories, we are effectively studying career lines with their origins or destinations in one of the categories. This is only an approximation to a full operational measure of career lines. The advantage is analytical tractability; the disadvantage is loss of some information.

Our goal is to examine whether career-line properties covary with structural sources of variation identified from neoclassical and segmentation perspectives. The variables for levels of involvement with data, people, and things measure a technical feature of work—the skill level and scope of jobs. Skill level and scope are important from a neoclassical perspective because they indicate the importance of a position to the production process in a firm; the scarcity of personnel to fill more- versus less-skilled positions; and the actual and/or perceived productivity, resources, and power of incumbents of positions (Thurow 1975). We take the dichotomous variables for sector location of jobs in career lines to capture the simple additive effects of segmentation on career line properties. We include both sets of variables in the equation in order to examine the net patterns of covariation. Fligstein, Hicks, and Morgan (1982) used a similar equation to examine the sector and task complexity determinants of personal income. A more refined analysis would expand the measures of sector and task structure and examine interactions within sectors. We rely on the simple additive model because it is consistent with our purpose of providing an initial demonstration of patterns of covariation in career-line properties with sources of structural variation.

Table 5-1
Means of Career-Line Variables by Sector

Variable	Primary-Independent	Primary-Subordinate	Secondary	P	Between Sum of Squares/Total Sum of Squares
Complexity-data	2.35	6.54	5.40	***	57
Complexity-people	6.10	7.70	7.10	***	16
Complexity-things	5.12	5.27	6.57	***	5
Overall complexity	13.91	3.60	7.45	***	44
Variety of work	.52	.10	.46	***	31
Work under special instruction	.03	.53	.37	***	52
Control over work	.35	.02	.04	***	25
Sex composition	72	56	51	***	7
Race composition	94	86	85	***	23
Median years education	12.38	10.05	10.71	***	25
Unionization level	19.64	37.90	20.19	***	12
Overall socioeconomic status	52.60	22.82	29.26	***	36
Holding power-origin					
Age 23-27	46.84	34.71	32.96	***	24
Age 28-32	57.22	44.82	43.14	***	26
Age 33-37	64.41	54.32	52.49	***	21
Age 38-42	68.70	60.18	57.64	***	18
Age 43-47	72.48	65.11	61.23	***	19
Age 48-52	74.43	68.13	64.80	***	15
Age 53-57	76.38	71.06	67.01	***	14
Age 58-62	78.31	72.78	69.85	***	12
Holding power-destination					
Age 23-27	19.56	20.49	17.58	NS	1
Age 28-32	37.44	30.70	27.92	***	13
Age 33-37	52.19	41.86	39.41	***	16
Age 38-42	55.34	43.98	40.51	***	19
Age 43-47	59.88	49.90	45.07	***	20
Age 48-52	63.07	53.80	48.77	***	21
Age 53-57	65.71	56.91	52.52	***	22
Age 58-62	66.90	58.83	54.19	***	22
Differentiation					
Age 23-27	.37	.27	.41	NS	0
Age 28-32	.45	.33	.41	NS	0
Age 33-37	.46	.36	.47	NS	0
Age 38-42	.35	.33	.50	NS	1
Age 43-47	.31	.28	.48	NS	1
Age 48-52	.24	.26	.45	*	2
Age 53-57	.21	.26	.47	**	3
Age 58-62	.18	.25	.38	*	2
Diffuseness-entry portals					
Age 23-27	40.87	34.15	31.86	***	7
Age 28-32	39.72	33.44	30.36	***	8
Age 33-37	37.37	32.39	28.80	***	6
Age 38-42	35.84	31.11	28.51	***	5
Age 43-47	35.75	30.59	28.50	***	5
Age 48-52	39.20	35.47	34.81	*	2
Age 53-57	32.17	28.65	27.95	*	2
Age 58-62	24.35	21.55	20.95	**	3

Table 5-1 *(continued)*

Variable	Primary-Independent	Primary-Subordinate	Secondary	P	Between Sum of Squares/Total Sum of Squares
Diffuseness-exit portals					
Age 23-27	65.05	51.94	52.24	***	12
Age 28-32	58.92	55.90	56.92	NS	1
Age 33-37	58.35	58.46	58.54	NS	0
Age 38-42	57.44	57.39	55.87	NS	0
Age 43-47	57.34	56.58	53.00	NS	1
Age 48-52	59.04	56.66	52.49	*	2
Age 53-57	63.33	59.04	53.08	***	5
Age 58-62	67.05	62.79	55.15	***	6
Percent entering from out of the labor force					
Age 23-27	14.01	29.01	28.53	***	32
Age 28-32	17.33	28.62	32.40	***	15
Age 33-37	16.61	25.39	31.96	***	14
Age 38-42	17.26	23.97	29.37	***	11
Age 43-47	15.37	20.14	24.43	***	9
Age 48-52	13.14	16.42	21.45	***	10
Age 53-57	10.65	14.05	18.72	***	14
Age 58-62	9.63	14.06	17.35	***	17
Skill distance					
Age 23-27	3.34	3.13	3.53	NS	1
Age 28-32	2.42	2.54	2.95	***	4
Age 33-37	1.93	2.01	2.31	**	3
Age 38-42	1.62	1.64	1.94	**	3
Age 43-47	1.41	1.38	1.70	***	4
Age 48-52	1.31	1.21	1.45	**	2
Age 53-57	1.21	1.04	1.28	**	3
Age 58-62	1.13	.96	1.14	*	2
Male earnings					
Age 23-27	6,772	5,314	4,771	***	22
Age 28-32	8,627	6,458	6,238	***	28
Age 33-37	9,902	6,878	6,757	***	26
Age 38-42	10,456	6,868	6,850	***	23
Age 43-47	10,475	6,927	6,705	***	27
Age 48-52	10,475	6,838	6,609	***	22
Age 53-57	9,846	6,458	6,337	***	25
Age 58-62	9,206	5,952	5,587	***	28
Female earnings					
Age 23-27	4,254	2,047	1,675	***	12
Age 28-32	3,787	2,211	1,382	***	13
Age 33-37	4,278	2,904	2,472	***	7
Age 38-42	4,729	3,229	2,285	***	14
Age 43-47	5,323	3,320	2,706	***	19
Age 48-52	5,231	3,531	2,955	***	15
Age 53-57	5,700	3,582	2,861	***	12
Age 58-62	5,096	3,771	2,996	***	8

*$.01 \leq P \leq .05$.

**$.001 \leq P < .01$.

***$P < .001$.

NS = $P > .05$.

Results

Holding Power

Both sector and skill variables affect holding power (table 5-2). The variance explained by sector and skill variables ranges from 13 to 36 percent. For skill, the effect is primarily that of complex work with things: About 3 to 6 percent more workers stay in jobs with complex work with things, and from 4 to 11 percent more originate in the same job in the case of career-line destinations involving more complex work with things. Complex work with data shows little effect on holding power in these equations with the exception of one age cohort, and there the effect is in the expected direction. Complex work with people does not affect origin holding power; it slightly decreases destination holding power for younger age cohorts and slightly increases destination holding power for the oldest two age cohorts.

The largest effect on holding power is for career-line transitions in the primary-independent versus secondary sector. With one exception, primary-independent career lines retain from 7 to 12 percent more workers in the same job over a five-year period compared to secondary-sector career lines. Insofar as holding power captures employment stability and job security, this important prediction of segmentation theory is supported. The effects are sizable as they represent a full standard deviation of the holding-power distribution for many of the age cohorts. As expected, career lines in the primary-subordinate are intermediate to career lines in the secondary and primary-independent sectors in levels of holding power. The effect is statistically significant for only one age cohort, but the coefficients are of appropriate direction for all other age cohorts and nearly of equal size. In sum, sector and skill hypotheses receive support for their effects on holding power.

Differentiation

The differentiation of career-line sets, measured by the number of transitions that exceed the branching criteria, responds to neither the skill level nor the sector location of the career line (table 5-3). No more than 7 percent—typically 2 or 3 percent of the variance in differentiation—is a function of the skill level and sector location of a career line. If differentiation captures the relative presence of major job avenues departing from a position, then the number of such avenues is only trivially a function of skill level and sector location of the origin position. For the youngest age cohort, complex work with data adds an average of one-half major job avenue,

Table 5-2
Regression Results for Holding Power, Skill, and Sector Variables
(N = 384)

Dependent Variable	Independent Variable						Contrast (P-Value)		
	Data	People	Things	Primary-Independent	Primary-Subordinate	R^2	Overall	Sector	Skill
Holding power									
Origin:									
Age 23-27	3.28	.17	5.94***	11.21***	.91	.277	***	***	**
Age 28-32	2.10	.72	4.73***	12.04***	.95	.287	***	***	***
Age 33-37	1.15	1.73	4.56***	10.19***	1.17	.234	***	***	**
Age 38-42	.81	2.58	5.56***	9.17***	1.72	.214	***	***	**
Age 43-47	.38	2.28	4.94***	9.68***	2.98	.221	***	***	**
Age 48-52	-.37	2.33	4.47***	8.54***	2.43	.185	***	***	**
Age 53-57	-.25	1.93	3.55**	8.44***	3.34*	.159	***	***	*
Age 58-62	-.21	1.87	2.86**	7.66***	2.43	.133	***	***	**
Destination:									
Age 23-27	.08	-3.22**	4.31***	1.80	.86	.156	***	NS	***
Age 28-32	-.16	-3.78**	8.74***	8.77***	.83	.362	***	***	***
Age 33-37	7.28***	-2.38	8.19***	8.05***	1.10	.256	***	***	***
Age 38-42	.62	-.99	11.72***	12.61***	.17	.347	***	***	***
Age 43-47	.86	.99	11.46***	12.07***	1.73	.347	***	***	***
Age 48-52	.80	2.08	11.03***	11.46***	2.32	.350	***	***	***
Age 53-57	1.87	2.84*	10.55***	9.75***	2.28	.351	***	***	***
Age 58-62	.78	3.05*	8.24***	10.20***	3.02	.311	***	***	***

Note: All coefficients are metric (unstandardized).

$.05 \geq P > .01$.

$** .001 \leq P \leq .01$.

$*** P < .001$.

NS $= P > .05$.

Table 5-3
Regression Results for Differentiation, Skill, and Sector Variables
(N = 384)

| | Independent Variable | | | | | | Contrast (P-Value) | | |
	Data	People	Things	Primary-Independent	Primary-Subordinate	R^2	Overall	Sector	Skill
Dependent Variable									
Differentiation									
Age 23-27	.41***	-.34****	-.22**	-.14	-.06	.077	***	NS	***
Age 28-32	.19	-.14	-.14	-.00	-.03	.024	NS	NS	NS
Age 33-37	.22	-.14	-.04	-.09	-.09	.019	NS	NS	NS
Age 38-42	.11	-.13	-.07	-.16	-.16	.018	NS	NS	NS
Age 43-47	.14	-.12	-.09	-.20	-.17	.025	NS	NS	NS
Age 48-52	.04	-.15	-.12	-.19	-.19*	.030	*	*	NS
Age 53-57	.10	-.19*	-.10	-.26**	-.20*	.044	**	*	***
Age 58-62	.06	-.14	-.07	-.19*	-.14	.029	*	*	NS

Note: All coefficients are metric (unstandardized).

*.05 ≥ P > .01.

**.001 ≤ P ≤ .01.

***P < .001.

NS = P > .05.

while complex interpersonal and manipulative jobs have a fraction fewer major job avenues. But it is not clear how one would predict this pattern from neoclassical theory nor why the effect disappears for all other age cohorts.

Sector has little effect on differentiation other than slightly depressing the number of major job avenues for both primary sectors compared to the secondary sector for older age cohorts. More important, there is no apparent order (inverted U- or J-shaped) pattern in the differentiation in career lines that might be caused by skill level and sector.

In short, the regression equations suggest that differentiation in career lines may not be closely tied to sources of variation identified from neoclassical and segmentation prediction. Perhaps our operational measure of differentiation is problematic. Under our branching criteria of $P_{ij} \geq .04$ and $f_{ij} \geq 10$, nearly half ($N = 187$) of all career-line sets have no job destination that exceeds the criteria for any age cohort. A more sensitive measure of differentiation might lead to a different conclusion.

Ports of Entry and Exit

The regressions for ports of entry and exit (table 5-4) reveal mixed support for both skill and sector predictions. First, both sector and skill variables, with an exception or two, make statistically significant contributions to the prediction of the number of entry and exit ports. Second, the contribution to explained variance is generally quite small. Third, the pattern of effects is at times consistent with expectation; at other times, it is not. We discuss percentage entering from out of the labor force later as these results more consistently support the general hypotheses.

Complex work with data generally suppresses the number of ports of entry and exit. Since level of involvement with data measures technical specialization, a neoclassical perspective suggests that comparatively fewer career-line transitions should occur for complex data jobs because of the high cost of retraining and readjustment. The effects of complex interpersonal work, though small, are consistent with the definition of order: Interpersonally skilled jobs have more ports of exit very early in the work course and allow more points of entry late in the work course.

Contrary to expectation, complex machine and tool work is associated with more ports of entry. Equally puzzling, career-line categories in the primary-independent sector average more ports of entry compared with secondary positions (from 2 to 8 or more per 100 job transits). Further, the pattern does not square with our expectation for order in the diffuseness-concentration of ports. We expected primary-sector career lines, compared with the secondary sector, to contain some degree of insulation indicated by

Table 5-4
Regression Results for Ports of Entry and Exit, Skill, and Sector Variables
(N = 384)

Dependent Variable	Independent Variable					R^2	Contrast (P-Value)		
	Data	People	Things	Primary-Independent	Primary-Subordinate		Overall	Sector	Skill
Ports of entry (number of origins)									
Age 23-27	4.37	-2.81	3.90*	6.56**	1.37	.103	***	*	*
Age 28-32	1.25	-2.77	3.55*	8.57***	1.55	.112	***	**	*
Age 33-37	-1.16	-1.84	4.60**	8.65***	1.41	.112	***	***	**
Age 38-42	-2.59	-1.57	5.75**	7.90***	-.18	.133	***	***	**
Age 43-47	-1.65	-2.13	6.15***	7.41***	-.68	.139	***	***	***
Age 48-52	3.91*	-2.26	2.69	2.33	.20	.034	*	NS	*
Age 53-57	-5.22*	1.82	7.34***	5.25*	-2.27	.123	***	**	***
Age 58-62	-4.60**	3.24*	5.14**	4.24**	-1.21	.120	***	**	***
Ports of exit (number of destinations)									
Age 23-27	-8.21**	9.80***	8.56***	13.72***	-2.25	.190	***	***	***
Age 28-32	-8.66***	4.68*	3.69	4.90	-2.99	.056	***	*	**
Age 33-37	-9.94***	3.67	1.36	3.97	-1.90	.051	***	NS	**
Age 38-42	-9.06***	2.22	.85	5.65*	-.31	.044	**	*	**
Age 43-47	-8.82***	2.52	1.85	8.06**	1.58	.051	**	**	**
Age 48-52	-7.64**	2.42	2.44	9.53***	2.20	.059	***	**	**
Age 53-57	-6.06*	3.21	3.66	12.03***	4.16	.080	***	***	***
Age 58-62	-2.22	2.85	4.10	11.69***	6.50**	.075	***	**	NS
Percent entering from out of the labor force									
Age 23-27	-5.50**	-3.17*	-6.22***	-10.18***	.03	.359	***	***	**
Age 28-32	3.08	-3.45	-10.38***	-14.94***	-2.02	.229	***	***	***
Age 33-37	-.43	-2.62	-10.49***	-13.31***	-5.22*	.213	***	***	***
Age 38-42	3.74	-2.74	-9.53***	-12.93***	-4.24	.213	***	***	***
Age 43-47	2.92	-3.30*	-8.13***	-9.46***	-3.63	.188	***	***	***
Age 48-52	1.96	-3.55**	-7.63***	-8.17***	-4.85**	.222	***	***	***
Age 53-57	-.71	-1.73	-6.33***	-6.97***	-4.78***	.242	***	***	***
Age 58-62	-1.87	-2.72**	-5.45***	-5.69***	-3.50**	.256	***	***	***

Note: All coefficients are metric (unstandardized).

*. $.05 \geq P > .01$.
**. $.001 \leq P \leq .01$.
***$P < .001$.
NS = $P > .05$.

a fewer number of entry ports. Perhaps our measurement is too crude, but if it is not, the important segmentation prediction for restricted entry ports to primary career lines is not supported.

For ports of exit, primary-independent location also increases the number of destinations, but the pattern is consistent with the concept of order in the career line. Very early and very late in the work course, primary-independent lines offer from eleven to nearly fourteen additional and different destination jobs compared to career lines located in the secondary sector. We interpret this as flexibility during low-cost portions of the work course. During the middle period of the work course, the effect is not significant or is much reduced, indicating more restricted access compared with other portions of the work course.

The patterns of entry from out of the labor force are very consistent with predictions from each perspective. For the youngest age cohort, complex work with data lowers the expected percentage of entrants from out of the labor force by 5.5 percent, complex work with people by about 3 percent, and complex work with machines and tools by over 6 percent. Level of involvement with things shows sizable effects for every age cohort; level of involvement with people has an effect for several of the older cohorts; and level of involvement with data lowers the percentage only for the youngest cohort. In short, complex work, especially with things rather than data or people, restricts access to the career line for those who might enter from out of the labor force. The effects are stronger early in the work course.

Career-line location in primary sectors substantially suppresses the percentage entering the line from outside of the labor force. For the primary-independent sector, the effect is strongest during the first half of the work course—from 10 to 15 percent—and somewhat less during the second half—from about 5 to 9 percent. Compared with secondary career lines, primary-subordinate lines average from 2 to 5 percent fewer entries from outside of the labor force for all but the youngest age cohort. On the criterion of entry from out of the labor force, primary-subordinate career lines are intermediate to primary-independent and secondary career lines, consistent with the expectation from segmentation theory.

In sum, the predictions are supported for entry from out of the labor force. Both sector and the skill demands of the job assure some level of insulation from the competition of potential workers who were not in the labor force five years prior. In this important respect, career lines requiring complex skills and located in the primary-independent resemble a restricted-access highway. The combined effect for some ages restricts the flow into the line by as much as 25 percent compared to less complex work in the secondary sector. In probability terms, one is more likely to enter insulated lines through other ports, such as college or other jobs.

Role Continuity

In general, we expected a closer articulation (that is, less skill distance) of skill level and scope in more skilled and primary-independent career-line transitions. The skill distance of career-line transitions (table 5-5) is only weakly related to skill level but is modestly related to sector location. The average skill distance of job transitions in the primary-independent is slightly less than in the secondary by one-third to one-quarter of a standard deviation. We interpret reduced skill distance as indicative of a closer task articulation of one job with another. Our concept and measure do not distinguish between progressive development or decline in skill level but measure only the average distance of transitions in skill terms. The notion of progression may prove fruitful in distinguishing one type of career line from another, but in our description of all career lines we use the more general concept (see Althauser and Kalleberg 1981*a*, for a concept that includes progression). The reduced skill distance of primary-independent, career-line transitions holds for those in the age cohorts for 28 to 47 in 1970, consistent with a pattern of order. Primary-subordinate job transitions also involve more continuity (less distance in skill terms) than secondary transitions at all ages except the youngest.

In contrast to neoclassical reasoning, high-skill jobs do not enjoy any less skill adjustment in job transitions compared with low-skill jobs. Sector clearly explains skill distance in career-line transitions better than skill level per se. Yet, sector and skill combined never explain more than 5 percent of the variance in this feature of role continuity.

Table 5-5 also reports sector and skill effects on male and female median earnings. The effects are sizable, in the predicted direction, but are of differing importance for male compared with female earnings.[8] We discuss median earnings separately by gender.

Males receive a sizable dollar return to complex work with data, a sizable though smaller return for complex work with people, and a return for complex work with things but only during the early period of the work course. The return for complex work with data grows from $967 at entry to nearly $2,000 during the late forties and early fifties and is still nearly $1,600 for the oldest age cohort. A similar situation occurs for complex work with people: Early in the work course, the return is in the neighborhood of $700, and during the last twenty-five years of work, the return ranges from $1,200 to $1,400.

Sector location of the career line yields equally sizable earnings returns for men. The return for being in a career line located in the primary-independent versus secondary sector, controlling for skill level, ranges from $1,284 for the youngest age cohort to $2,641 for those age 48 to 52 in 1970.

Primary-subordinate location also yields an earnings return, from over $600 during the early work course to $1,000 or more during the later work course compared to secondary career lines. Thus, sector and skill make an earnings difference for men. Middle-aged males doing complex work with people and data in a primary-independent career line can expect from $5,000 to $6,000 more in median earnings (1969 dollars) than their counterparts in the secondary who do less complex work in mental and interpersonal terms.

The sector and skill effects for women's earnings reveal many differences and a few similarities compared to men. Women also experience an earnings return in career lines that deal with complex data work, but the return averages only about 60 percent of what males get for the same type of work. The curvilinear pattern of returns that held for men also roughly holds true for women's earnings. Women receive no return for complex work with people (where men did) but do receive a modest return to complex machine and tool work (where men did not) that ranges from several hundred to over $1,400, conditional on age.

Women receive a sizable return for career-line location in the primary-independent, compared with the secondary, sector, as was the case for male earnings. Unlike for males, there is not a clear age trend for women. The return varies from over $1,000 to nearly $2,200. Women receive more of an economic premium than men for primary-sector employment early in the work course but substantially less later in the work course. This latter difference may be a pure age rather than point-in-the-work-course effect. Older women in the primary-independent sector are more likely to be in traditional women's professions (for example, nursing and teaching) and young women perhaps less so. Traditionally female professions of women are less well paid than traditionally male professions, and both sets of professions fall in the primary-independent. This difference may contribute to the lower coefficients of determination for female, compared with male, earnings. Gender differences in occupational composition may also explain the sex difference in returns to complex work with people.

For women, the career lines that involve complex work with people include the teaching and social-work professions. For men, complex work with people more likely means upper-level sales and managerial career lines. At the individual level of analysis, gender differences in access to and returns from authority are well documented (Wolf and Fligstein 1979; Kluegel 1978). Career-line differences in access to authority by gender, where higher authority yields an earnings return, may explain some of the gender difference. Finally, women receive lower earnings in primary-subordinate career lines (compared with the secondary) than men. The effect is statistically significant at conventional levels only for those age 38 to 42.

Table 5-5
Regression Results for Role Continuity, Skill, and Sector Variables
(N = 384)

Dependent Variable	Independent Variable					R²	Contrast (P-Value)		
	Data	People	Things	Primary-Independent	Primary-Subordinate		Overall	Sector	Skill
Skill Distance									
Age 23-27	−.28	.22	−.35*	−.02	−.31	.031	*	NS	*
Age 28-32	−.10	.02	−.12	−.46**	−.39*	.044	**	**	NS
Age 33-37	−.08	−.06	−.11	−.30*	−.30*	.035	**	*	NS
Age 38-42	−.08	−.10	−.11	−.24*	−.31**	.038	**	**	NS
Age 43-47	−.12	−.03	−.08	−.21*	−.32***	.042	**	**	NS
Age 48-52	−.05	.01	−.06	−.11	−.23*	.022	NS	*	NS
Age 53-57	−.06	.04	.01	−.05	−.25**	.027	*	*	NS
Age 58-62	−.06	.09	.08	−.01	−.20*	.024	NS	NS	NS
Median Earnings									
Male									
Age 23-27	967***	385	834***	1,284***	618*	.267	***	***	***
Age 28-32	1,527***	709**	489*	1,386***	612*	.365	***	***	***
Age 33-37	1,883***	728*	−64	2,052***	767*	.346	***	***	***
Age 38-42	1,779***	1,405***	−24	2,431***	800	.309	***	***	***
Age 43-47	1,918***	1,198***	−73	2,572***	999*	.359	***	***	***
Age 48-52	1,967***	1,351**	−226	2,641***	1,097*	.298	***	***	***
Age 53-57	1,859***	1,203**	−110	2,346***	896*	.334	***	***	***
Age 58-62	1,598***	1,374***	−112	2,558***	1,123**	.373	***	***	***
Female									
Age 23-27	406	5	1,143**	2,182***	127	.145	***	***	*
Age 28-32	742	101	1,403***	1,755***	607	.173	***	**	**
Age 33-37	1,325**	−243	911**	1,010**	408	.104	***	NS	*
Age 38-42	1,059**	−383	691*	1,849***	887*	.164	***	***	.
Age 43-47	1,692***	131	1,179***	1,466***	680	.246	***	**	***
Age 48-52	1,414***	−314	717*	1,483***	615	.193	***	**	**

Age 53-57	1,663***	185	1,258**	1,726**	780	.149	***	**	*
Age 58-62	1,037*	−375	338	1,580***	823	.098	***	**	NS

Note: All coefficients are metric (unstandardized).

* $.05 \geq P > .01$.

** $.001 \leq P \leq .01$.

*** $P < .001$.

NS $= P > .05$.

Summary

Career lines might be rooted in social and economic structure in several ways. We sought demand-side explanations for career-line variation from neoclassical and segmentation perspectives. From a neoclassical perspective, we reasoned that the pattern and arrangement of career lines reflect a differential provision of skill levels and mixtures for optimal production. Hence, the occupational resources measured by skill level should be an important determinant of career-line outcomes attached to incumbency in the job. Segmentation perspectives suggest that jobs and career lines are located in sectors. Sectors form because of larger control imperatives in the economy. We view the hypotheses and results as a first effort. The design is limited as the measures of sector and differentiation are fallible approximations; we have no data on within-firm variations. We use only one set of branching criteria, and the results depend on the assumption of the synthetic cohort.

In general, the properties of career lines are related to sources of variation defined by neoclassical and segmentation perspectives. In some cases, the equations explain 35 to 40 percent of the variance in an outcome variable; in other cases, the amount explained is below 5 or 10 percent. The skill effects are strongest for holding power (things), ports of entry (not in the labor force, for data, people, and things), and role continuity indexed by earnings. The skill variables are less powerful in explaining career-line differentiation, ports of entry (particularly for complex work with things), and skill distance.

The predictions for sector effects fare about as well or slightly better. Location in the primary-independent makes a bigger difference than location in the primary-subordinate when comparing both with the secondary sector. Sector has the expected effects for holding power, ports of exit, entrance from out of the labor force, skill distance, and earnings. In some cases, the effects are very small and specific to a single age cohort. Sector predictions failed most surprisingly in the case of ports of entry: We expected primary-independent career lines to have more concentrated ports of entry, consistent with the notion of insulation. The estimates show primary-independent career lines with more diffuse ports of entry, controlling for skill level.

Both skill and sector effects are largest for career-line properties of holding power, entrance from out of the labor force, and one aspect of role continuity (median earnings). The effects are much smaller for other features of career lines such as differentiation and skill distance.

Career lines are embedded in larger forms of labor-market and social organization. The data suggest career lines are formed partly in response to the manipulative, interpersonal, and mental complexity inherent in work.

Theoretically, we argue that complexity levels in jobs are formed according to the logic of least cost and efficient production. Career lines, in turn, form and structure job movements to provide the mixtures of complex labor required by firms in the economy.

The data also suggest that career lines are formed and maintained in sectors of the labor market. The sector location of a career line shapes some of its features. Finally, the results suggest there are other unspecified features of firms and social organization that form and maintain career lines, variables not captured in our initial examination of neoclassical and segmentation sources of variation.

Extension: Unionization

Numerous writers view unionization as a feature of social organization that defines the rules of job transition for many workers (Freedman 1976; Baron and Bielby 1980; Spilerman 1977). Both Piore (1975) and Edwards (1979) cite the effects of unions on wage rates, rules of retention, layoffs, seniority, and promotions within production enterprises. Yet both Piore and Edwards argue that unions are secondary rather than fundamental components of demand-side interpretations.

In contrast to Piore's and Edwards's views, we entertain the following hypothesis: The effects of skill and sector are spurious because of the level of unionization of jobs in career lines. To test the hypothesis, we reestimated the equation with a term added for the percentage unionized in each career-line category. Our estimates of unionization for job categories are based on data presented by Freeman and Medoff (1979). The measure indexes the extent of union membership for the private sector only.

We briefly summarize the results without tabular presentation. Unionization has no effect on differentiation at any age. It affects only one age cohort for origin holding power (small positive), one age cohort for ports of entry (small positive), and one age cohort for skill distance (small negative). For males and females, the unionization level makes a small but significant positive contribution to earnings for the youngest two age cohorts. The skill and sector effects are unaltered. For destination holding power, unionization slightly increases the percentage with the same origin job, for older cohorts only. The effects of skill and sector variables are only trivially altered. For these career-line properties, unionization has little effect. When the contribution is statistically significant, the increment to explained variance never exceeds 3 percent.

The unionization level in jobs does make a difference for career-line ports of exit and the percentage entering the career line from out of the labor force. Our original conclusions about the effects of skill and sector are largely unaltered when the effects of unionization are taken into account.

For ports of exit, unionization increases the diffuseness of exit portals for every age cohort. Ostensibly, union workers can move more readily to a larger number of different jobs. The increase explains from 4 to 15 percent more variance, depending on age cohort. The effect of unionization is at the expense of skill variables—particularly complex work with data—where some of the previous effects are reduced to statistical insignificance. The importance of sector is undiminished.

High levels of unionization result in a lower percentage of entrants from out of the labor force for all age cohorts. The conclusions about sector and skill are unchanged. If anything, skill variables exert a greater impact when level of unionization is controlled.

Thus, unionization tends to insulate a career line from the competition of those out of the labor force. For those in the labor force, high levels of unionization are associated with higher destination holding power for older ages, more diffuse ports of exit at all ages, and higher earnings at select ages. Other effects of unionization are equivocal. More important, our original conclusions about the effects of skill and sector are largely unaltered.

Notes

1. In a footnote, Treiman (1977, p. 17) notes the parallel of his argument to the functional theory of stratification (that is, occupations are rewarded in relation to their functional importance to society). He argues that the demand for an occupation determines reward, and demand is more economic than social. Demand may or may not reflect the functional importance. For our purposes, both demand and nondemand forces that (1) are caused by efficiency considerations, and (2) generate work career outcomes are under the same theoretical umbrella.

2. For review and critique see: Kerr (1954); Averitt (1968); Doeringer and Piore (1971); Piore (1975); Bibb and Form (1977); Cain (1976); Rosenberg (1975); Hodson (1978); Beck, Horan, and Tolbert (1978); Tolbert, Horan, and Beck, (1980); Rumberger and Carnoy (1980); Kaufman, Hodson, and Fligstein (1981); Wallace and Kalleberg (1981); Kalleberg and Sørensen (1979); Edwards (1979); Baron and Bielby (1980); and Berg (1981).

3. Rosenbaum (1979a) presents a similar idea in his tournament model of organizational mobility.

4. Piore treats technology and social class as underlying determinants of mobility chains. The demand-side cause is technology. Work and jobs are ultimately rooted in production technologies that require different forms of labor. On the supply-side, social class subcultures supply labor to the different market segments and maintain work values that correspond to the different segments, so Piore argues. Our interest is in testing the demand-side argument.

5. Spilerman (1977) incorporates intransitive job moves into his definition of an orderly career line. For two positions, continuous back-and-forth movement between them connotes some disorder (and lack of differentiation) in the implied career lines.

6. Other definitions of generalizability might focus on taking a set of skills and applying them in very different environments. This is more appropriate for supply-side studies wherein people possess skills, and jobs are merely the environs in which they are acted out. Our measure and concept is of the skill demands of the job.

7. The results are quite comparable for sector placement of jobs, if we use a measure of task variety (situations involving a variety of duties often characterized by frequent change) in place of repetitiveness ($r = 0.6$).

8. The findings for earnings are unaltered if the equation includes a variable for average number of hours worked per week.

6

A Baseline Model for Career Outcomes

As career lines describe the structure of roads in the labor force, so careers are the record of people's journeys over the network of roads. Careers are employment biographies. In earlier chapters, we made inferences about career lines and their properties directly from one operational measure of career lines. We found face validity for the concept, reasons to expect real gender differences in work histories, and some meaningful skill and sector differences in career-line patterns. We now shift the analysis from career lines to careers.

We directly examine career histories, using equations that explain career outcomes in individual terms. The measures are on an individual level, and the implied processes are explained as psychological and social-psychological phenomena. We treat the analyses as a baseline explanation for career outcomes. This type of individual-level explanation is consistent with the way much contemporary research approaches career outcomes.

The motivation for this section comes from the larger agenda for the investigation of career lines Spilerman (1977) proposed. How are individual careers shaped by personal resources and career lines? Specifically, how do career lines define the role returns that workers receive to their personal resources (schooling, for example). In this chapter and in chapter 7, we narrow the focus to the concept of role continuity—in particular, socioeconomic status and several related measures. In this chapter, we estimate a baseline model for individual career outcomes. The baseline model ignores career lines. In chapter 7, we consider a dynamic model that takes career lines into account. Throughout, we pay particular attention to gender differences and returns to schooling, in anticipation of how career lines might structure both of these.

We begin our study of careers by validating the well-known status-attainment model. The status-attainment paradigm embodies an established theory and method to explain individual occupational achievement. The analyses serves several purposes.

First, the validation establishes the Career Development Study data set, offering parameter estimates to compare with a standard set of equations. Second, the validation establishes a baseline for the reasoning and analyses in chapter 7. The status-attainment model takes occupational status at two points in the work course as the outcome variables. Social background and personal resources are the independent variables. Career outcomes are explained in individual terms. The analyses leave career-line concepts (that is, inertia or trajectory and ports of entry) undeveloped.

Finally, the analyses provide an independent validation of the status-attainment model from a new data set. Our data set provides a new time point for analyzing the status-attainment process. The Career Development Study provides the first comprehensive status-attainment sample of a population from the Pacific Northwest. With high school juniors and seniors from 1966 and 1967, the sample is about ten years younger than the cohorts of high school students from the late 1950s, on which much of the status-attainment tradition was built. The sample should reflect the social malaise of the 1960s and Vietnam era. The respondents were of high school and college age during that period of campus unrest (1963-1971) and were of prime draft age during the Vietnam conflict. Nearly half of the male respondents were in the military service, and about half served directly in the Vietnam conflict. Career Development Study respondents were surveyed in 1979, about thirteen years after leaving high school. The sample is comparable to many status-attainment data sets (Otto and Haller 1979). We expect some differences between our study and status-attainment studies conducted on samples from the 1950s because of historical changes during the 1960s and 1970s.

The Status-Attainment Framework

A central notion of the status-attainment paradigm is the "socioeconomic life cycle" (Duncan, Featherman, and Duncan 1972). Persons come to occupy multiple competitive roles over the life course, namely scholastic and occupational roles. The roles are fundamentally differentiated by socioeconomic levels. The achievement of persons in roles has socioeconomic antecedents in social background (that is, the occupational and educational achievements of parents) and socioeconomic consequences (that is, the effect of schooling on jobs, of earlier jobs on later jobs, and of both on earnings). Stratification occurs within and across generations, is multidimensional in the Weberian sense, and is a process that takes place over the life course.

The version of the status-attainment model that we use is given in figure 6-1.[1] It is very close to the specification reported by Sewell, Hauser, and Wolf (1980). This model is an elaboration of the Blau and Duncan model (1967) of occupational achievement and the Wisconsin model (Sewell, Haller, and Portes 1969) that includes several additional background, social-psychological, and school-performance variables. Discussions of the history and evidence for the model are referenced in footnote 1.

We concentrate on the early career portion of the status-attainment model, that is, the successive linkages between schooling and first job and

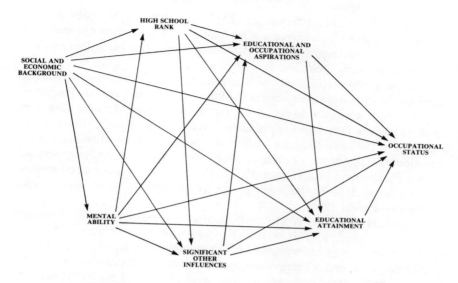

Figure 6-1. Model of the Status-Attainment Process

between first job and current job. These relationships reflect a typical approach to career in attainment studies. Further, we concentrate on gender differences in these relationships. In a review of recent status attainment research and in our own estimates, we seek a baseline picture of how men and women initiate their careers.

The elaboration of the model for samples of women is relatively recent.[2] Women are concentrated in different jobs and sectors of the labor force compared with men. For example, approximately 40 percent of women would have to change jobs in order to have the same occupational distribution as men (Tyree and Treas 1974). Women's patterns of labor-force participation and earnings returns from work are quite different from the patterns of men. The initial studies that compared occupational achievement between sexes reported small differences. The average status differences in jobs was small; the total effect of schooling on occupational status was similar for men and women. But most of the early studies focused on occupational status for a single arbitrary point in the work course (Marini 1980). *Career* differences were not the subject of examination.

More recent work reveals important differences between the sexes in occupational achievement. For example, Sewell, Hauser, and Wolf (1980), using a sample of 1957 high school graduates from the state of Wisconsin, found men achieved levels of formal schooling that were an average of about one year beyond the average for women. The first jobs of women were some 6 status points (Duncan SEI) higher than the first jobs of men, but at reinterview eighteen years after high school, the status of men's current jobs exceeded women's current job status by 5 points. In fact, women lost status between their first and current jobs.

Marini (1980) replicated the status difference in first-to-current job (men gain more status than women during the early work course) but found that first jobs are equal in status for men and women. Marini's data were from 1957-1958 high school graduates in ten Illinois schools, who were resurveyed in 1973 and 1974. In studies that permit such conclusions, the occupational status of men increases sizably over the work course (Sørensen 1975a; Featherman and Hauser 1978). The occupational status of women appears constant over the work course (Rosenfeld 1979) or grows more slowly (Rosenfeld 1980).

Sewell, Hauser, and Wolf (1980) reported the most profound difference between men and women was in their occupational locations. Women tended to be located in the middle of the occupational structure in clerical, retail sales, and service occupations and were likely to remain there between their first and current occupations. Men were distributed across the occupational structure, including the upper (managerial and professional) and lower ranks (farm and laborer). Further, men were more likely to experience upward intragenerational status shifts between first and current occupation. Women who never married or who were childless had occupational distributions that were more like those of men. Women who had children had occupational distributions that were the most different from men.

In many respects, the Sewell, Hauser, and Wolf (1980) estimates for this version of the status-attainment model (figure 6-1) were similar for men compared with women. Yet there were some important gender differences in the early career portion of the model. Occupational achievement contained a complex interaction in the direct and indirect effects of education for men compared to women. Paradoxically, the *total* effect of educational achievement on current occupational status was about equal for men and women. But the Wisconsin data showed that the similarity stops there. For men, the effect of education on current job was largely through first job: Men received a large return to schooling in their first job which, in turn, was translated into status gains in the effect of first job on current job. The greater continuity that men experienced in their job histories was evident in the larger causal linkage between first and current job.

For women, more of the effect of education on current occupational status was direct, whereas the link between first and current jobs was weaker than was the case for men. Further, this pattern was accentuated for women with children. Sewell, Hauser, and Wolf (1980) pointed to a greater likelihood of continuous employment for men, with the status of each successive job more dependent on the status of the previous job, and less so on the direct effect of education. Women, on the other hand, with a greater likelihood of discontinuous employment histories, particularly women with children, gained less from previous job status and relied more on original educational credentials in changing jobs or returning to the labor force.

Marini (1980) found some of the same results for the effects of schooling on occupational status. She found the total effect of education on current occupational status about equal for men and women and the effect of education on first job status greater for men than for women. Unlike the Wisconsin study, Marini's data showed the effect of education on current job status was *greater* for men than for women. Further, the effect of first job on current job status was *greater for women than men*. Both studies, which are representative of the status-attainment tradition, ignore the role of structure as it might occur in career lines.

The larger hypotheses about school-to-work transitions and job linkages in work careers are important. We validate the status-attainment model in this chapter and extend further consideration to the hypotheses in the next chapter. For the moment, we leave career-line concepts implicit in the linkage between first and current job, following the status-attainment tradition.

Data and Measures

Table 6-1 describes each variable in the status-attainment model. Where possible, we scaled and coded variables to approximate typical status-attainment measures (Otto and Haller 1979; Sewell, Hauser, and Wolf 1980).[3]

Our definition of the working sample included male and female respondents in the 1979 follow-up who were employed in civilian jobs in 1979, or in the five years preceding the survey. Respondents in military service in 1979 were excluded. Table 6-2 summarizes the different sources of sample attrition for men and women. The 1979 response rate was 87 percent of the wave 1 sample. An additional 3.5 percent of men (largely in the military) and 20.6 percent of women (largely not having worked in the past five years) are not used, leaving a working sample of 2,754 men (80.7 percent of wave 1) and 2,294 women (69.1 percent of wave 1). In chapter 2, we discussed the possible sources of bias in the wave 2 respondent subpopulation.[4]

In summary, our analyses to date lead us to believe that results based on this working sample are characteristic of the total sample and that our results are generalizable to the larger population of similar age in the state of Washington.

Table 6-1
Variable Labels, Sources, and Descriptions for the Status-Attainment Model

Symbol	Variable Name	Source[a]	Description
PINC	Parental income	1966 parent interview	1 = under $2,000; 2 = $2,000-2,999; 3 = $3,000-3,999; 4 = $4,000-4,999; 5 = $5,000-5,999; 6 = $6,000-7,499; 7 = $7,500-9,999; 8 = $10,000-14,999; 9 = $15,000 or over.
FOCC	Occupational status of father (or other head of household)	1979 survey (1966 student questionnaire)	During respondent's (R's) junior year of high school; Duncan SEI value of detailed census occupation.
FED	Education of father	1966 student questionnaire	1 = eighth grade or less, 2 = some high school but not a graduate, 3 = high school graduate, 4 = some college but not a graduate, 5 = college graduate, 6 = more than four years of college.
MED	Education of mother	1966 student questionnaire	Same as father's education.
MEMP	Mother's employment	1979 survey (1966 student questionnaire)	Scored 1 if R's mother was employed full- or part-time during R's junior year of high school; scored 0 otherwise.
RUR	Rural origin	1966 student questionnaire	Scored 1 if R lived in a place of fewer than 2,500 persons; scored 0 otherwise.
INT	Intact family	1966 student questionnaire	Scored 1 if R's mother and father were both alive and living together; scored 0 otherwise.
SIBS	Number of siblings	1966 student questionnaire	Number of living brothers and sisters.
MA	Mental ability	Washington Pre-College Testing Program (high school transcript)[b]	Average of verbal and quantitative composite score; test typically taken during fall of senior year.
GPA	Grade point average	High school transcript	Overall grade point average for high school years, where A = 4.0, B = 3.0, C = 2.0, D = 1.0, and F = 0.0.
PAR	Parental encouragement	1966 parent interview (1966 student questionnaire)	Scored 1 if parent reported college (junior or regular four year) as the highest level of education that they would like their son or daughter to obtain; scored 0 otherwise (where parent interview data not available, scored 1 if R reported most or all of family members expected younger members of the family to get all of the education they can; scored 0 otherwise).

FRND	Friends' college plans	1966 student questionnaire[c]	Scored 1 if R reported most or all of close friends were planning to attend college; scored 0 otherwise.
EASP	College plans	1966 student questionnaire	Scored 1 if the highest level of education R thought he/she "would actually be able to get" included attending junior college or a regular college or university; scored 0 otherwise.
OASP	Occupational aspirations	1966 student questionnaire	Duncan SEI value of occupation R realistically expected to have as his/her life's work.
ED	Educational attainment	1979 survey	Years of regular (not vocational, technical, business or nursing) schooling completed (that is, twelve years for high school graduate, sixteen years for college graduate, up to twenty years for doctoral degree recipient).
FJOB	Occupational status of first job	1979 survey	Duncan SEI value of detailed census occupation, first full-time civilian job held after completing the highest grade of regular schooling.
CJOB	Occupational status of current (or last) job	1979 survey	Duncan SEI value of detailed census occupation held at the survey date or of last occupation held within the preceding five years.

[a]If data were missing, they were obtained from the source given in parentheses.

[b]Slightly over half of subsample respondents took the Washington Pre-College Test (very similar to ACT and SAT). This group reflects those contemplating college. For remaining respondents, we searched their high school transcript for an eligible test score closest in time to fall of the senior year of high school. Eligible tests, in order, were: National Merit Scholastic Qualifying Test, Scholastic Aptitude Test, Preliminary Scholastic Aptitude Test, Iowa Tests of Educational Development, Otis IQ, California Test of Mental Maturity, Differential Aptitude Test, National Educational Development Test, Kuhlman-Anderson IQ, Lorge-Thorndike IQ and Henman-Nelson IQ. The vast majority of selections (88 percent) were for grade 9 or higher. The remaining selections were from grades 7 and 8. We always used the average composite score for verbal and quantitative or the raw IQ score. A z-score was calculated for each test score using the distribution of all respondents who took the test. The z-score was then used to construct a WPCT analog score, using the mean and standard deviation from the WPCT distribution for the linear transformation. An original WPCT or WPCT analog score is available for 75 percent of analysis subsample respondents.

[c]Available only for a randomly selected half of the sample.

Table 6-2
Sources of Nonresponse and Sample Selection in the Career Development Study by Gender

	Men (Percent) (N = 3,411)		Women (Percent) (N = 3,318)	
Nonrespondents in 1979	15.8		10.3	
Deceased		2.5		0.9
Not found		2.3		2.2
No telephone contact (disabled or institutionalized, no or unpublished telephone number, not in United States).		7.8		4.8
Refused		3.2		2.4
Respondents in 1979	84.2		89.7	
Ineligible (in military or no civilian job in past five years)		3.5		20.6
Analysis sample		80.7		69.1
Total	100.0	100.0	100.0	100.0

Results for Men and Women

Descriptive Differences

Table 6-3 reports the means and standard deviations for status-attainment variables. It provides a statistical portrait of the sample. The social backgrounds of men and women are nearly identical. The average parental income is about $7,500. The average level of parent education is in the interval that designates some college. Over one-half of the respondents report that their mother worked, about one-third were living in a small town or on a farm during the high school years, from 14 to 16 percent were in a nonintact family, and respondents averaged from two to three siblings.

Women have a slightly better grade point average (GPA) than do males. Means for significant-other variables show parents encourage four out of five students to attend college, slightly more for males than for females, and an average of two-thirds of respondents report that most of their best friends plan to attend college. These levels of encouragement are much higher than the levels reported in previous status-attainment studies. For example, Sewell, Hauser, and Wolf (1980, p. 557) found 60 percent of the parents of men and 47 percent of women's parents encouraged college attendance compared with 84 percent for Career Development Study men and 79 percent for women. We suspect that our figures are not inflated since over 70 percent of the men and nearly 65 percent of the women actually attended a college or university.

Table 6-3
Means and Standard Deviations of Status-Attainment Variables by Gender

Variable	Men (N = 2,754)		Women (N = 2,294)	
	Mean	SD	Mean	SD
Parental income	6.75	1.88	6.67	2.17
Father's occupation	44.31	25.53	45.54	25.14
Father's education	3.27	1.50	3.29	1.49
Mother's education	3.25	1.14	3.23	1.17
Mother's employment	.54	.50	.58	.49
Rural background	.34	.47	.34	.47
Intact family	.86	.34	.84	.37
Number of siblings	2.68	1.78	2.71	1.80
Mental ability	49.14	8.61	48.91	7.95
Grade point average	2.46	.64	2.70	.61
Parental encouragement	.84	.37	.79	.41
Friends' college plans	.65	.48	.66	.48
Educational aspirations	.80	.40	.74	.44
Occupational aspirations	60.95	25.01	54.79	19.16
Educational attainment	14.68	2.13	14.11	1.97
First job status	39.11	25.65	46.53	20.10
Current job status	46.87	24.64	50.25	19.82

The dramatic rise in parental expectation levels for college attendance between the mid-1950s and mid-1960s parallels the substantial increase in higher-education enrollment over the same period (Norwood 1979). The trend in actual and encouraged education levels foreshadows subsequent results from the regression analyses: Parents' influence on college plans and occupational aspirations and achievements is generally weaker than reported in other studies but perhaps for an ironic reason. Dramatically larger numbers of parents of adolescents in the 1960s encouraged their offspring to attend college. Because the vast portion of parents did so, having a parent who encouraged college attendance did not differentiate as well those who aspired and achieved high levels of schooling and occupational status from those who did not.

A similar state of affairs occurs for friends' college plans. For both men and women, more best friends plan to attend college than was reported in other studies. The change is not as large compared with parental encouragement, so the efficacy of friends as significant others is not diluted, if our reasoning is correct.

More men plan to attend college than women (80 percent versus 74 percent). Men aspire to higher-status occupations than women by 6 points on the Duncan scale. Both men and women exceed an average of fourteen years of formal schooling, with men having half a year more than women. This is consistent with national trends and is somewhat higher than reported levels for samples of high school students from the 1950s (Otto and Haller 1979).

In occupational achievement, women enter the labor force in jobs that are about 7 status points higher than men. This is consistent with previous research (Sewell, Hauser, and Wolf 1980; Rosenfeld 1980). By age 30, men have gained 7.75 status points in their current jobs. Career Development Study women gained 3.35 status points from first to current job.[5]

Thus far, we have described our sample members and their early career achievements. Although men and women in the sample grew up in comparable social backgrounds and are nearly equal in test score performance in high school, they differ in academic performance, levels of schooling and job aspirations, eventual educational attainment, and the status of their first and current jobs. We now obtain estimates for a baseline model with the structural equations in figure 6-1.

Differences in the Status-Attainment Process

The correlations that form the basis for parameter estimates appear in table 6-4. We compare the process of status attainment for men and women up to age 30, concentrating on adult achievement outcomes (education, first job, and current job status).

For the status-attainment model as it pertains to ability, grades, significant-other influence, and aspirations (tables not presented), we find the processes broadly similar for men and women. Further, our results are generally similar and compare closely with those reported elsewhere in the literature (Otto and Haller 1979; Sewell, Hauser, and Wolf 1980). Ability, grades, the educational encouragement of parents, and educational aspiration formation as outcomes are more similar for men and women; friends' college plans and occupational aspirations are less similar.

In general, we find fewer and smaller gender differences than others reported, particularly for educational aspirations. We interpret the somewhat smaller gender differences in our study compared with earlier studies in terms of recent historical changes that have benefited the schooling process for women. The encouragement for and aspirations to college became common fare for high school students during the 1960s. We found schooling encouragement from others and aspirations less dependent on social background, yet just as dependent on grades for both genders compared with other studies. In this respect, our sample women were more like the men than perhaps was the case in studies of cohorts from the 1950s.

We now turn to the adult achievement portion of the model: educational attainment, first job after the completion of regular schooling, and current job (or last job) in 1979 at about 30 years of age. Tables 6-5 and 6-6 report the reduced-form equations for educational attainment, first job, and current job for men (table 6-5) and women (table 6-6). The reduced-form equations permit treatment of total, direct, and indirect effects of

Table 6-4

Correlations among Status-Attainment Variables for Women ($N = 2,294$, above Diagonal) and Men ($N = 2,754$, below Diagonal)

Variable	PINC	FOCC	FED	MED	MEMP	RUR	INT	SIBS	MA	GPA	PAR	FRND	EASP	OASP	ED	FJOB	CJOB
PINC		.283	.226	.266	-.023	-.074	.204	-.096	.095	.172	.114	.058	.215	.089	.137	.107	.060
FOCC	.340		.589	.355	-.059	-.252	.080	-.099	.241	.219	.150	.289	.239	.174	.345	.207	.194
FED	.344	.601		.474	-.030	-.237	.048	-.121	.249	.262	.177	.306	.276	.174	.378	.213	.191
MED	.254	.415	.522		.098	-.140	.053	-.149	.214	.249	.162	.267	.289	.176	.370	.211	.142
MEMP	.067	-.036	-.014	.067		.026	-.079	-.066	-.016	.001	.036	-.048	.032	.034	.040	.026	.023
RUR	-.157	-.250	-.240	-.154	.017		-.020	.083	-.131	-.024	-.010	-.206	-.162	-.071	-.153	-.108	-.100
INT	.294	.043	.017	.020	-.032	.021		-.070	.062	.080	.059	.112	.093	.048	.114	.098	.065
SIBS	-.137	-.083	-.067	-.093	-.106	.110	-.020		-.073	-.091	-.101	-.138	-.163	-.072	-.172	-.139	-.094
MA	.113	.261	.280	.263	-.028	-.117	.007	-.032		.673	.183	.202	.230	.287	.410	.263	.245
GPA	.114	.248	.299	.270	-.002	-.051	.050	-.097	.673		.223	.288	.377	.358	.536	.343	.323
PAR	.084	.116	.124	.118	.036	-.047	.056	-.051	.183	.244		.133	.258	.226	.246	.148	.118
FRND	.295	.280	.310	.246	.019	-.189	.061	-.094	.260	.330	.098		.382	.360	.399	.307	.266
EASP	.205	.263	.295	.239	.058	-.168	.061	-.132	.234	.343	.257	.382		.461	.480	.301	.231
OASP	.168	.306	.347	.256	-.028	-.202	.047	-.124	.392	.447	.226	.360	.461		.373	.303	.255
ED	.199	.340	.374	.323	.053	-.146	.077	-.139	.454	.605	.196	.381	.458	.507		.454	.407
FJOB	.148	.234	.232	.174	.071	-.098	.055	-.109	.313	.418	.132	.259	.287	.341	.576		.509
CJOB	.137	.274	.269	.211	.050	-.117	.048	-.114	.308	.402	.156	.283	.301	.332	.561	.615	

Note: See table 6-1 for explanation of variable symbols.

Table 6-5

Coefficients of Reduced-Form Equations in the Status-Attainment Model for Men (N = 2,754)

Dependent Variable	Predetermined Variable																
	PINC	FOCC	FED	MED	MEMP	RUR	INT	SIBS	MA	GPA	PAR	FRND	EASP	OASP	ED	FJOB	R^2
	(a) Regression Coefficient (SE)																
ED	.009 (.026)	.012 (.002)	.280 (.039)	.262 (.045)	.185 (.087)	-.135 (.094)	.389 (.131)	-.108 (.024)									
ED	.014 (.024)	.009 (.002)	.216 (.036)	.164 (.042)	.233 (.081)	-.077 (.087)	.388 (.122)	-.108 (.023)	.088 (.005)								
ED	.029 (.002)	.008 (.002)	.143 (.033)	.118 (.038)	.210 (.073)	-.215 (.079)	.243 (.110)	-.065 (.021)	.011 (.006)	1.646 (.078)							
ED	-.002 (.022)	.007 (.002)	.125 (.033)	.105 (.037)	.204 (.072)	-.150 (.079)	.243 (.109)	-.061 (.020)	.010 (.006)	1.508 (.079)	.235 (.098)	.615 (.083)					
ED	-.002 (.021)	.006 (.002)	.078 (.031)	.092 (.036)	.199 (.069)	-.034 (.076)	.204 (.104)	-.039 (.019)	.007 (.005)	1.274 (.077)	-.029 (.096)	.315 (.082)	.866 (.103)	.014 (.002)			
FJOB	.347 (.336)	.130 (.028)	1.989 (.502)	.851 (.573)	3.401 (1.114)	-1.056 (1.209)	3.011 (1.687)	-1.052 (.314)									
FJOB	.390 (.325)	.100 (.027)	1.424 (.488)	-.005 (.559)	3.820 (1.078)	-.548 (1.170)	3.000 (1.632)	-1.051 (.303)	.770 (.065)								
FJOB	.516 (.313)	.094 (.026)	.804 (.473)	-.396 (.539)	3.627 (1.038)	-1.726 (1.130)	1.770 (1.574)	-.686 (.294)	.111 (.081)	14.034 (1.108)							
FJOB	.267 (.317)	.088 (.026)	.656 (.472)	-.505 (.537)	3.580 (1.034)	-1.191 (1.132)	1.771 (1.568)	-.655 (.292)	.107 (.081)	12.927 (1.136)	1.737 (1.414)	5.008 (1.196)					
FJOB	.275 (.314)	.077 (.026)	.307 (.470)	-.586 (.532)	3.628 (1.026)	-.335 (1.127)	1.493 (1.552)	-.494 (.290)	.075 (.081)	11.229 (1.151)	-.071 (1.428)	2.939 (1.227)	4.835 (1.530)	.124 (.025)			
FJOB	.289 (.290)	.045 (.024)	-.144 (.434)	-1.117 (.491)	2.476 (.948)	-.136 (1.040)	.313 (1.433)	-.270 (.268)	.034 (.075)	3.872 (1.131)	.098 (1.317)	1.118 (1.136)	-.167 (1.436)	.041 (.024)	5.776 (.307)		
CJOB	-.112 (.319)	.152 (.026)	2.182 (.476)	1.358 (.543)	2.307 (1.057)	-1.479 (1.146)	2.963 (1.600)	-1.090 (.298)									
CJOB	-.075 (.310)	.125 (.026)	1.688 (.465)	.609 (.533)	2.673 (1.028)	-1.035 (1.115)	2.954 (1.555)	-1.089 (.289)	.673 (.062)								

CJOB	.034	.120	1.151	.271	2.507	−2.054	1.889	−.774	.103	12.140							
	(.301)	(.025)	(.454)	(.517)	(.996)	(1.085)	(1.510)	(.282)	(.078)	(1.063)							
CJOB	−.277	.112	.964	.124	2.428	−1.381	1.835	−.730	.100	10.629	3.445	6.157					
	(.303)	(.025)	(.451)	(.513)	(.988)	(1.082)	(1.499)	(.279)	(.078)	(1.085)	(1.351)	(1.143)					
CJOB	−.282	.103	.684	.046	2.397	−.691	1.604	−.595	.081	9.222	1.855	4.353	5.278	.085			
	(.301)	(.025)	(.450)	(.510)	(.983)	(1.080)	(1.488)	(.278)	(.078)	(1.103)	(1.369)	(1.176)	(1.467)	(.024)			
CJOB	−.270	.074	.281	−.428	1.369	−.513	.552	−.396	.044	2.660	2.005	2.728	.817	.011	5.152		
	(.281)	(.023)	(.421)	(.476)	(.919)	(1.008)	(1.389)	(.260)	(.072)	(1.097)	(1.277)	(1.101)	(1.392)	(.023)	(.298)		
CJOB	−.388	.056	.340	.028	.359	−.457	.424	−.286	.030	1.080	1.966	2.272	.885	−.006	2.794	.408	
	(.255)	(.021)	(.382)	(.433)	(.835)	(.915)	(1.261)	(.236)	(.066)	(.998)	(1.159)	(.999)	(1.263)	(.021)	(.293)	(.020)	
									(b) Path Coefficient								
ED	.008	.144*	.197*	.140*	.043*	−.030	.062*	−.090*									.194
ED	.013	.103*	.152*	.088*	.054*	−.017	.062*	−.090*	.356*								.307
ED	.026	.095*	.101*	.063*	.049*	−.048*	.039*	−.054*	.043	.493*							.433
ED	−.001	.086*	.088*	.056*	.048*	−.033	.039*	−.051*	.042	.451*	.041*	.138*					.450
ED	−.002	.068*	.055*	.049*	.047*	−.008	.033*	−.032*	.029	.381*	−.005	.071*	.161*	.169*			.499
FJOB	.025	.130*	.116*	.038	.066*	−.020	.040	−.073*									.084
FJOB	.029	.099*	.083*	−.000	.074*	−.010	.040	−.073*	.258*								.144
FJOB	.038	.094*	.047	−.018	.070*	−.032	.024	−.048*	.037	.349*							.207
FJOB	.020	.088*	.038	−.022	.070*	−.022	.024	−.045*	.036	.321*	.025	.093*					.215
FJOB	.020	.077*	.018	−.026	.070*	−.006	.020	−.034	.025	.279*	−.001	.055*	.075*	.121*			.232
FJOB	.021	.044	−.008	−.050*	.048*	−.003	.004	−.019	.011	.096*	.001	.021	−.003	.040	.479*		.347
CJOB	−.009	.157*	.133*	.063*	.047*	−.028	.041	−.079*									.108
CJOB	−.006	.130*	.103*	.028	.054*	−.020	.041	−.079*	.235*								.157
CJOB	.003	.125*	.070*	.013	.051*	−.040	.026	−.056*	.036	.314*							.208
CJOB	−.021	.117*	.059*	.006	.049*	−.027	.025	−.053*	.035	.275*	.052*	.120*					.222
CJOB	−.021	.107*	.042	.002	.048*	−.013	.022	−.043*	.028	.239*	.028	.084*	.085*	.086*			.235
CJOB	−.021	.077*	.017	−.020	.028	−.010	.008	−.029	.015	.069*	.030	.053*	.013	.011	.445*		.335
CJOB	−.030	.058*	.021	.001	.007	−.009	.006	−.021	.010	.028	.030	.044*	.014	−.006	.241*	.425*	.452

Note: See table 6-1 for explanation of variable labels.

*Coefficient significant at .05 level.

Table 6-6
Coefficients of Reduced-Form Equations in the Status-Attainment Model for Women
(N = 2,294)

Dependent Variable	Predetermined Variable																
	PINC	FOCC	FED	MED	MEMP	RUR	INT	SIBS	MA	GPA	PAR	FRND	EASP	OASP	ED	FJOB	R²
	(a) Regression Coefficient (SE)																
ED	-.028 (.022)	.012 (.002)	.222 (.040)	.365 (.045)	.134 (.092)	-.154 (.098)	.442 (.124)	-.105 (.025)									
ED	-.026 (.021)	.009 (.002)	.178 (.038)	.310 (.043)	.149 (.087)	-.083 (.093)	.381 (.118)	-.097 (.024)	.074 (.006)								
ED	-.055 (.020)	.009 (.002)	.135 (.036)	.263 (.040)	.141 (.081)	-.237 (.087)	.338 (.110)	-.085 (.022)	.014 (.007)	1.303 (.085)							
ED	-.041 (.019)	.008 (.002)	.106 (.035)	.221 (.039)	.165 (.079)	-.124 (.086)	.251 (.107)	-.068 (.022)	.015 (.006)	1.133 (.086)	.323 (.098)	.717 (.091)					
ED	-.059 (.019)	.007 (.002)	.096 (.034)	.188 (.038)	.128 (.077)	-.067 (.084)	.237 (.104)	-.053 (.021)	.016 (.006)	.906 (.085)	.176 (.096)	.497 (.090)	.874 (.104)	.009 (.002)			
FJOB	.051 (.247)	.077 (.025)	1.066 (.444)	1.933 (.500)	.953 (1.021)	-1.730 (1.091)	3.997 (1.376)	-1.034 (.281)									
FJOB	.064 (.243)	.058 (.025)	.772 (.437)	1.560 (.492)	1.059 (1.001)	-1.250 (1.071)	3.585 (1.351)	-.979 (.276)	.500 (.064)								
FJOB	-.130 (.238)	.058 (.024)	.484 (.429)	1.246 (.483)	1.005 (.979)	-2.268 (1.054)	3.300 (1.321)	-.904 (.270)	.102 (.079)	8.616 (1.027)							
FJOB	.034 (.236)	.039 (.024)	.210 (.424)	.832 (.479)	1.314 (.966)	-1.170 (1.050)	2.424 (1.306)	-.738 (.267)	.122 (.077)	7.038 (1.040)	1.540 (1.195)	7.653 (1.103)					
FJOB	-.043 (.234)	.034 (.024)	.177 (.418)	.639 (.474)	1.004 (.952)	-.914 (1.038)	2.359 (1.287)	-.671 (.263)	.103 (.077)	5.336 (1.059)	.597 (1.190)	6.187 (1.116)	3.520 (1.292)	.145 (.027)			
FJOB	.124 (.229)	.014 (.023)	-.095 (.408)	.107 (.465)	.643 (.929)	-.726 (1.011)	1.688 (1.256)	-.520 (.257)	.057 (.075)	2.772 (1.069)	.100 (1.160)	4.780 (1.098)	1.046 (1.288)	.120 (.027)	2.830 (.313)		
CJOB	-.203 (.248)	.089 (.025)	1.200 (.445)	.779 (.501)	1.138 (1.023)	-1.696 (1.093)	2.755 (1.378)	-.643 (.281)									
CJOB	-.191 (.243)	.071 (.025)	.917 (.439)	.420 (.494)	1.240 (1.004)	-1.233 (1.075)	2.357 (1.355)	-.589 (.276)	.481 (.064)								

Top section (CJOB equations, coefficient (standard error)):

−.384 (.239)	.071 (.024)	.630 (.430)	.107 (.485)	1.186 (.982)	−2.249 (1.058)	2.073 (1.325)	−.514 (.271)	.085 (.079)	8.591 (1.030)						
−.244 (.238)	.056 (.024)	.412 (.428)	−.228 (.483)	1.461 (.974)	−1.366 (1.059)	1.362 (1.318)	−.384 (.269)	.102 (.078)	7.353 (1.049)	.669 (1.205)	6.370 (1.113)				
−.277 (.238)	.051 (.024)	.403 (.425)	−.338 (.482)	1.250 (.969)	−1.251 (1.055)	1.331 (1.309)	−.352 (.268)	.083 (.078)	6.240 (1.076)	.100 (1.210)	5.465 (1.135)	1.419 (1.314)	.118 (.028)		
−.117 (.233)	.032 (.024)	.142 (.417)	−.848 (.474)	.904 (.947)	−1.071 (1.031)	.688 (1.281)	−.208 (.262)	.038 (.076)	3.785 (1.091)	−.376 (1.183)	4.118 (1.120)	−.950 (1.314)	.093 (.027)	2.710 (.319)	
−.164 (.217)	.027 (.022)	.178 (.387)	−.888 (.441)	.660 (.880)	−.796 (.958)	.049 (1.190)	−.011 (.244)	.017 (.071)	2.734 (1.015)	−.414 (1.099)	2.307 (1.047)	−1.347 (1.220)	.048 (.026)	1.638 (.305)	.379 (.025)

(b) Path Coefficient

Dep.	1	2	3	4	5	6	7	8	9	10	11	12	13	14	15	16	17	R^2
ED	−.031	.155*	.167*	.216*	.033	−.037	.083*	−.096*										.225
ED	−.029	.120*	.134*	.183*	.037	−.020	.072*	−.088*	.298*									.306
ED	−.061*	.120*	.102*	.155*	.035	−.057*	.064*	−.078*	.056*	.406*								.400
ED	−.045*	.097*	.080*	.131*	.041*	−.030	.047*	−.062*	.063*	.353*	.067*	.173*						.429
ED	−.065*	.092*	.072*	.111*	.032	−.016	.045*	−.049*	.066*	.282*	.037	.120*	.194*	.088*				.469
FJOB	.006	.096*	.079*	.112*	.023	−.041	.074*	−.093*										.086
FJOB	.007	.072*	.057	.090*	.026	−.029	.066*	−.088*	.198*									.122
FJOB	−.014	.073*	.036	.072*	.025	−.054*	.061*	−.081*	.040	.263*								.161
FJOB	.004	.049	.016	.048	.032	−.028	.045	−.066*	.048	.215*	.031	.181*						.188
FJOB	−.005	.042	.013	.037	.025	−.022	.043	−.060*	.041	.163*	.012	.146*	.077*	.139*				.213
FJOB	.013	.017	−.007	.006	.016	−.017	.031	−.047*	.023	.085*	.002	.113*	.023	.114*	.278*			.254
CJOB	−.022	.112*	.090*	.046	.028	−.041	.051*	−.058*										.058
CJOB	−.021	.090*	.069*	.025	.031	−.029	.044	−.054*	.193*									.092
CJOB	−.042	.090*	.047	.006	.030	−.054*	.039	−.047	.034	.266*								.132
CJOB	−.027	.071*	.031	−.013	.036	−.033	.025	−.035	.041	.228*	.014	.153*						.151
CJOB	−.030	.065*	.030	−.020	.031	−.030	.025	−.032	.033	.193*	.002	.131*	.031	.114*				.164
CJOB	−.013	.041	.011	−.050	.023	−.026	.013	−.019	.015	.117*	−.008	.099*	−.021	.090*				.202
CJOB	−.018	.034	.013	−.052*	.016	−.019	.001	−.001	.007	.085*	−.009	.055*	−.030	.046	.269*	.163*	.384*	.313

Note: See table 6-1 for explanation of variable labels.
*Coefficient significant at .05 level.

each variable in the model on subsequent achievement outcomes (see Alwin and Hauser 1975).

Education. In a number of ways the schooling process is similar for men and women. The total effect of social background on schooling is nearly equal. The total effects of component background variables are about equal for men and women, although maternal employment is more important for men, and the education level of the same-sex parent is more important for each gender. Father's occupation and parent education levels are the most important background variables for the schooling of both men and women and have a significant direct effect on each group's schooling levels.

Both grades and mental ability are the most powerful resources that men and women possess to obtain further schooling. This compares closely with other studies (Otto and Haller 1979; Sewell, Hauser, and Wolf 1980). A ten-point increase in mental ability (total effect) yields men a 0.88 year increase in formal schooling and yields women a 0.74 increase in formal schooling.

The vast majority of the effect of mental ability on educational attainment is through high school grades. After controlling for social background, men obtain 1.65 years of additional schooling for each letter-grade increase in high school GPA; women obtain 1.30 years of additional schooling past high school for each letter-grade increase in high school GPA. About one-quarter to one-third of the effect of grades on educational attainment is by virtue of the fact that good grades yield (1) more encouragement for college from parents, (2) friends who are more likely to be college-bound, and (3) higher educational and occupational aspirations. This holds equally for men and women. Yet the largest portion of schooling return to grades is a significant direct effect, presumably reflecting the direct generalization of study habits and skills from secondary to higher education. As others suggest (Peng, Fetters, and Kolstad 1981), there may have been grade inflation and declining test scores during the 1960s, but our data unequivocally show—mean trends aside—that the schooling return to good grades and high test scores during high school is as large as ever, compared with studies on cohorts from the 1950s (Sewell, Hauser, and Wolf 1980; Alexander, Eckland, and Griffin 1975; Otto and Haller 1979).

Both parents and peers make a difference for men's and women's educational attainment. Friends appear to be more than twice as important as parents, but again, we suspect our measure of parental encouragement and the secular change noted earlier. Both parents and peers are slightly more important for women's educational attainment than for men's. The significant gender interaction that we find is in the way that men and women use the influence of significant others in attaining education. Men incorporate most of the influence of significant others into their educational and occupational plans. Women do so only partially; rather, the plans of friends exert a significant direct effect on years of formal schooling after aspirations are controlled.

Finally, college plans are significant determinants of eventual schooling in nearly equal proportion for men and women. Further, occupational aspirations significantly affect eventual educational attainment nearly twice as much for men as for women and, in the case of both genders, more than was reported in the Wisconsin study (Sewell, Hauser, and Wolf 1980). Our respondents were more likely to link their schooling activities to their job plans, perhaps an exigency of the tighter labor markets and job competition that they face compared with members of other samples.

In summary, we find that the causes of educational attainment are similar to the sources reported in other studies: For both men and women, social background and significant others make a difference; aspirations make a bigger difference; and test scores and grades make an even larger difference. The educational-attainment process is more homogeneous for men and women than Sewell, Hauser, and Wolf (1980) reported for their Wisconsin sample. Nonetheless, we found some gender differences in the attainment of higher education: the importance of mother's education for women, the importance of mother's employment for men, men's slightly greater return from test scores and grades, women's direct reliance on interpersonal influence, and men's greater tendency to link their schooling levels and job plans.

First Job. For men and women, several features of social background have significant total effects on the status of first job: father's occupation, the education of the same-sex parent, and number of siblings. Additionally, women's initial occupational status is significantly enhanced by an intact family (through its effects on test scores, grades, and interpersonal influence). Among men, there is again an intriguing advantage of maternal employment (worth 3.4 status points), three-quarters of which remains a significant direct effect in the final equation. These effects for social background are fairly similar to those reported by Sewell, Hauser, and Wolf (1980), although first job is less determined by social background for men in our sample than in the Wisconsin study. This finding is consistent with a larger temporal trend whereby the effects of social background on occupational achievement have slowly eroded in recent years, at least for white men (Featherman and Hauser 1978, pp. 252-262).

Both men and women receive a significant status return to higher mental ability and higher grades during high school, although men get a greater return. A ten-point increase in measured ability yields 7.7 status points for men and 5.0 status points for women; an increase of one letter grade in high school grade point average yields men 14 status points and women 8.6 status points. Most of these effects are mediated by subsequent variables in the model, although grades have a significant direct effect on initial job status for both men and women. The patterns of effects for ability and grades are consistent with those reported in the literature.

The inputs of significant others and aspirations bear significant and broadly similar total effects on the first jobs of men and women. Friends are somewhat more important for women. Virtually all effects of social-psychological variables for men are mediated by their educational achievements. Women, on the other hand, retain a direct linkage among friends' college plans, occupational aspirations, and first job status after schooling is controlled.

Finally, educational attainment is the most important variable in the first-job equation and one that contains the most profound gender difference. Men receive fully twice the status return for each year of additional schooling as women (5.77 versus 2.83 status points). Wisconsin men received 7.22 status points and Wisconsin women 3.78 status points in their first jobs for each additional year of schooling. The gender difference is identical in the two studies, yet Washington men and women get about 80 percent as much status return to schooling as Wisconsin men and women. If the social reforms and changes of the 1960s and early 1970s have had an impact or made their way into the marketplace, they have not reduced the sizable difference to the advantage of men in the translation of schooling into jobs.

Current Job. Current occupational status at age 30 is determined in broadly similar ways for men and women. The components of background, orientation, and experiences that are important for men are largely the same things that are important for women's current job status. Father's occupation and education and the number of siblings have significant total effects on current status for both sexes. For men, one-third of the effect of father's status remains direct and significant at age 30. Additionally, sons but not daughters receive a significant status increment (2.3 points on the Duncan SEI scale) if their mother worked during their high school years, controlling for other background variables. Most of this effect is mediated by educational attainment and first job.

Mental ability and grades yield a statistically significant and sizable status return, mediated by grades and educational attainment for both sexes, but the return is nearly one-third larger for both variables for men. For women, a significant component of the effect of grades on current status remains direct or unmediated by prior variables in the model. Peers' college plans exert a modest total effect on current status (6.2 SEI points for men and 6.4 SEI points for women), a third of which remains direct and unmediated at age 30. We are uncertain as to the explanation for the direct effect of friends' college plans on current occupational status.

Both educational and occupational aspirations significantly affect men's current status but entirely through the effect of aspirations on educational attainment. For women, occupational aspirations but not college plans affect current job status, mediated through educational attainment and first job status.

As reported in other studies, we find important sex interactions in the effects of schooling and first job on current occupational status (Sewell, Hauser, and Wolf 1980). As was the case for initial occupational status, men get a significantly greater (almost double) total status return to schooling than women (5.2 SEI points versus 2.7 SEI points). This difference is significant and remains after all variables in the model are controlled (2.8 SEI points for men and 1.6 SEI points for women). Sewell, Hauser, and Wolf (1980) report the opposite, as the direct effect of schooling on current occupational status is over twice as large for women (2.8 SEI points) as it is for men (1.3 SEI points).

Sewell, Hauser, and Wolf (1980, p. 577) found Wisconsin men with a greater linkage between first and current jobs than Wisconsin women (each 10 points of early status advantage was worth 3.5 points of later status advantage for men but only 2.6 points of later status advantage for women). For a cohort that is ten years younger from the state of Washington, we find no significant difference between men and women in this measure of status linkage over the early work course. Men translate ten points of early status advantage into 4.1 points of current status advantage; women are slightly behind but very close, translating each 10 points of early status advantage into 3.8 points of current status advantage. Hence, Washington women from the 1960s are more like Washington men on the value of this parameter than Wisconsin women of the 1950s are like Wisconsin men. One effect of this apparent homogenization between the genders is that women as a group are modestly more able to integrate schooling past high school into their job histories.

Summary

This chapter shifted the investigation from career lines to careers. We selected the established status-attainment model as a point of departure. While the status-attainment framework provides a well-developed theoretical rationale and methodological regime for individual socioeconomic achievements, the base model leaves career-line concepts implicit. The validation of status-attainment findings for men and women served several purposes. It established a theoretical and empirical baseline for a more explicit treatment of individual careers in the next chapter. The validation provided a carefully constructed comparison point to evaluate the properties of data. Finally, it offered a new independent validation of an important research model, yet on a more recent sample from a different part of the nation.

The analyses closely followed an earlier major study in measurement and procedure (Sewell, Hauser, and Wolf 1980). We found much more similarity than difference in results between the studies for both men and women given the large number of estimates being compared. It is fair to say that men and women experience the same broad regime of status transmissions and educational attainment during early adulthood. In most respects the studies are in agreement. We consider the validation successful and find the symmetry and understandable relationships that emerge from a new data set in its first major test encouraging.

Yet we find some differences in the processes of educational and occupational achievement for men and women and for our findings and those of Sewell, Hauser, and Wolf (1980). In the Wisconsin data and our Washington data, women are in different, more segregated occupational locations than men, though this is slightly less so in the Washington cohort than in the Wisconsin cohort (tables not reported). This is true of both first and current occupational locations. As Sewell, Hauser, and Wolf found, we too find that men obtain more schooling than women and in the process of doing so are better able to translate the advantages of background, ability, grades, interpersonal support, and aspirations into years of formal schooling.

But the differences are not as pronounced for men and women in the Career Development Study. Inasmuch as our studies permit such an inference, the process of educational achievement has become more alike for men and women, largely because the women's achievement process moved closer to that of men in parameter values. We interpreted this difference between the studies—a lesser difference between the genders—in terms of recent historical changes in society, particularly in the educational arena. Among the more important trends are the increased plans to attend, encouragement for, and eventual schooling obtained, particularly for Washington compared with older cohorts. Men do not unilaterally hold the advantages in the schooling process, but on balance they do. Apparent changes have benefited women more than men, but the net advantage in obtaining and then using schooling in occupational achievement belongs to men.

The process of occupational achievement is more different than educational achievement between men and women yet not as different as in the results reported by Sewell, Hauser, and Wolf (1980). Of particular substantive importance, we find that men get a larger occupational status return to their schooling resources than women, in first and current jobs. Explicating the nature of this difference over the work course in terms of career-line effects is an issue for the following chapter. Specifically, how do the different levels of opportunity in career lines shape the returns that men and women receive to personal resources such as schooling? Ironically, although women's mean schooling levels have increased appreciably compared with older cohorts, Career Development Study women were slightly *less* able to translate their schooling into status in their first and current jobs.

A further important result shows Washington women more like Washington men when compared with the Wisconsin cohort in that they are better able to translate the status of their first jobs into current job status. Yet they are still slightly behind men. But first and current jobs tap only endpoints of career histories. The baseline models in this chapter do not explicitly consider change in role outcomes over time. Does a dynamic analysis reach different conclusions? And how do the conclusions change for other work role outcomes? Status is important, but it is only one of a number of central indicators of work outcomes. Finally, if our earlier structural interpretations are valid, access to career lines through ports of entry early in the work course should condition role outcomes, after we account for pre-labor-force resources and human-capital updates during the career. We address these issues next.

Notes

1. For base theoretical and methodological statements of the status-attainment paradigm, consult Blau and Duncan (1967), Duncan (1968), Duncan, Featherman, and Duncan (1972), Haller and Portes (1973), Sewell and Hauser (1975), Jencks, (1972, 1979) and Featherman and Hauser (1978). For replications on different samples, see Sewell and Hauser (1972), Alexander, Eckland, and Griffin (1975), Wilson and Portes (1975), Otto and Haller (1979), and Marini (1980). For synthesis, review, and critique, consult Bowles and Gintis (1976), Kerckhoff (1976), Horan (1978), Spenner and Featherman (1978), Kalleberg and Sørensen (1979), and Baron and Bielby (1980).

2. See Alexander and Eckland (1974), Hout and Morgan (1975), Treiman and Terrell (1975), McClendon (1976), Featherman and Hauser (1976), Rosenfeld (1980), Sewell, Hauser, and Wolf (1980), and Marini (1980).

3. We experimented with a measure of guidance counselor's encouragement to attend college, available for a subsample of respondents. The results were unsatisfactory, so we dropped the measure. The measure of parental encouragement is somewhat different from typical measures, as it indexes attitudes of family members toward higher education for younger members of the family. Ours is a less direct measure of communicated parental expectations.

4. The exclusion of over 20 percent of women who have not worked in the previous five years may bias structural parameters in the status-attainment model (Heckman 1979). Fligstein and Wolf (1978) find the bias mini-

mal for a similar model of occupational achievement, estimated for employed women. Reestimation of our equations using the full complement of women (less than 3 percent of sample members have never worked at a civilian job) shows very similar outcomes.

5. Marini (1980) also fails to find a status loss from first to current job for women who attended ten Illinois high schools in 1956-1957 who were resurveyed fifteen years later. The Wisconsin study reported a status loss for women between first and current job. Women from Marini's sample gained from 2 to 3 status points from first to current job while men gained over 6 points.

7

Dynamic Models for Career Outcomes

In this chapter we merge the notions of career and career line into a more comprehensive explanation of career development. The ultimate goal is a theory of how opportunities occur in career lines and how individual careers mesh with the career-line structure. The research literature and the results in this book suggest such a theory should accommodate four concerns.

First, a theory of careers and career lines should reflect *time* as a central feature of the career-development process. The explicandum is change and stability in work roles over time. A theory or analysis that explains the level of an outcome at a single point in time in the life course, such as current job status, is not sufficient to represent the concepts of career and career line.

Second, a theory of careers ideally should explain how features of social structure affect both career-line properties and, in turn, the work-role outcomes embodied in careers. That social structure affects careers is beyond question. The literatures on labor markets (Kalleberg and Sørensen 1979) and class (Wright and Perrone 1977) document the effects of structure on work opportunities. The results from chapter 5 offer corroboration that the sector location of a career line defines some of the variation in career-line properties. Yet, through what kind of process are career-line opportunities generated and then reflected in people's career histories? The answer requires a conception of social structure and positions apart from individual-level human capital. In this chapter, we pursue a more explicit statement of how opportunities arise in career lines.

Third, a theory of careers should explain how resources of workers before and after entry into the labor force combine with system opportunities in career lines to shape the career. Human-capital and status-attainment perspectives explain achievement solely in individual terms. The linkage of the individual process of achievement with system-defined opportunities remains unaddressed in most research.

Finally, a theory of careers should accommodate multiple work-role outcomes. Most of our present knowledge is based on overall indicators of work-role quality such as socioeconomic status. Sole reliance on such indicators may mask important institutional or individual differences, such as gender differences (Roos 1981). Significant career outcomes in work quality may only be partially reflected in overall measures. For example, career lines or career histories with very similar overall status profiles may differ in underlying features of role continuity such as the skill level, complexity, or variety in work.

Our strategy for merging career line and career involves several components. As a theoretical framework, we draw on Sørensen's (1977, 1979) vacancy competition model to link the structure of inequality and the opportunity in career lines with the individual process of attainment. We use a differential equation framework that explicitly studies change in work-role outcomes over time. Defined as such, the models in this chapter explicitly treat change, whereas those in the previous chapter did not. Finally, we examine several work-role outcomes (skill level and complexity of work) in addition to socioeconomic status. The empirical analyses accomplish the following:

1. Offer further evidence on the operation of career lines.
2. Inform how social structure and individual resources might plausibly combine to shape careers.
3. Provide an independent test of Sørensen's theory.

Sørensen's Vacancy Competition Model

In several recent papers, Sørensen (1977, 1979) proposed a synthesis of the structure of inequality and the process of attainment.[1] The theory has three parts:

1. A model for the structure of inequality (the distribution of possible attainments).
2. A mathematical specification of how vacancies occur and move, given the structure defined in 1.
3. A model of how changes in attainments over the career depend on structurally induced vacancy chains and personal resources.

Sørensen's model is explicit; it joins structure with individual attainment; and the model offers deductive predictions that can be falsified. We interpret a key portion of the model as reflecting the operation of career lines.

The Structure of Inequality

The unit of analysis in the theory is jobs or, more broadly, positions (Sørensen 1977, p. 967). Jobs are characterized by different rewards (that is, work-role outcomes in our terms). A job change entails a change in rewards, but the theory assumes that different people in the same job obtain the same rewards.[2] The structure of inequality refers to the distribution of jobs with respect to rewards such as status. In its present state, the theory assumes a stable distribution of jobs over time (Sørensen, 1977, p. 968). Under a continuous distribution of rewards, Sørensen identifies the exponential distribution as the function that characterizes rewards.[3] Where y is the reward level of a job, the probability density is

$$f(y) = -\beta e^{\beta y} \qquad \beta < 0 \qquad\qquad (7.1)$$

and the distribution function is

$$F(y) = Pr(y \leq y') = 1 - e^{\beta y'} \qquad\qquad (7.2)$$

The exponential distribution provides a pyramidal shape for the distribution of job rewards with the largest density at the lowest level of reward and decreasing density as y increases. The height of the pyramid is governed by the parameter β: The larger β in absolute value, the flatter the pyramid and the more evenly job rewards are distributed (Sørensen 1977, p. 968). The exponential distribution and its geometric analog have precedent as descriptions of the shape of inequality (see Sørensen 1979, p. 367). Further, empirical applications of the theory offer support for this versus other distribution assumptions. In the Sørensen model, two parameters determine the opportunity of a social system: One is β, which has been defined, and the other is the rate at which better jobs become available. This brings us to the heart of the vacancy competition model.

Vacancy Occurrence and Movement

This part of the model, though tedious, is very important, for it provides the linkage to career lines. We summarize the important results and refer the reader to Sørensen for the complete theoretical and mathematical development (Sørensen 1977).

People encounter the structure of inequality when they are in the labor force. Job vacancies occur when people leave jobs or when new job opportunities are created. Following White (1970), Sørensen defines two types of moves: "(1) moves by people from filled jobs to vacant jobs, resulting in new vacancies to be filled by others in the system or entering it and (2) moves of vacancies in the direction opposite the moves by individuals" (Sørensen 1979, p. 367). A vacancy chain might begin with a vacancy caused by a retirement or the creation of a new job. When a higher-level vacancy is filled by a person from a lower-level position, then the latter position becomes vacant, and the cycle goes on. A vacancy chain ends when a person from outside the system fills a lower-level vacancy, or the job is eliminated.

The theory requires two additional assumptions at this point: only voluntary job moves are considered, and people maximize status when they change jobs. Neither restriction is perfect, but each is reasonable. Further, assume that vacancies are not filled immediately by persons from outside the labor force, and are created and/or arrive at every reward level at a constant rate, h. Sørensen (1977, pp. 970-971) shows that the number of vacancies arriving at level y, $m(y)$ is

$$m(y) = h \int_y^\infty n(y)du \qquad (7.3)$$

where $n(y)$ denotes the number of jobs at any level, y. Verbally, equation 7.3 says that the number of vacancies arriving at y is the sum of new vacancies created at higher levels in the structure. Further, let the rate at which opportunities for better jobs arrive at job level y be designated $q(y)$, and $q(y) = m(y)n(y)$ (the rate of better job opportunities equals the number of new jobs arriving per number of jobs at any level y). But the number of jobs at any level $[n(y)]$ can be expressed as $Nf(y)$ where N is the total number of jobs in the system, and the multiplier $f(y)$ designates the fraction of jobs at level y under a given distribution of jobs as defined in equation 7.1.

If equation 7.3 is integrated (that is, the continuous analog of doing the summation of the number of jobs at each level between y and ∞), then

$$m(y) = hNe^{\beta y}. \qquad (7.4)$$

By substituting this quantity for $m(y)$ in the expression for $q(y)$, the rate of arrival of opportunities to move to better jobs, and by substitution from equation 7.1 for $n(y)$, Sørensen achieves an important result:

$$\begin{aligned} q(y) &= \frac{hNe^{\beta y}}{N(-\beta e^{\beta y})} \\ &= \frac{-h}{\beta} \end{aligned} \qquad (7.5)$$

The result is important because q measures, for an attainment level, the probability that a person at that level will realize a gain in attainment. In this sense, the expression for q is a fundamental measure of the structural opportunities available to persons. Notice that q, in turn, depends on two parameters: h, the rate at which new promotion opportunities are created, and β (from part 1), the governing parameter of the structure of inequality. (Sørensen denotes q as $-1/b$ where $b = \beta/h$. He suggests assuming $\beta = -1$, with no loss of generality. We follow his notation.) As we shall see, the parameter b is estimable in a differential equation model of the attainment process.

The linkage to career lines is straightforward. Career lines designate statistically nontrivial, age-graded job linkages. Consider a career line or career-line set that involves one or more job changes (and by assumption, changes that involve status gains, presumably the majority of job changes in career lines, but not all of them). So defined, career lines are vacancy chains. The vacancies refer to positions or age-graded slots in career lines. Not all vacancy chains are career lines, since some vacancy chains will involve trivial numbers of actual labor-force transitions. Further, not all career lines contain vacancy chains as defined by Sørensen, since some career lines depict downward mobility, staying in the same job, or nonvoluntary job moves. But for the moment, assume that career lines that involve job change operate as vacancy chains wherein incumbents of lower levels respond to job opportunities that arrive from above.

Applied to career lines, the vacancy competition model provides an explicit statement of the rates at which opportunities for better jobs arrive at positions (levels) in the career line. We use the term *vacancy occurrence* to mean opportunities for better jobs (that is, growth in job rewards). From chapter 4, we know that career lines contain substantial variation in their properties, including work-role outcomes or job rewards. From chapters 4 and 5, we know that career lines can be grouped by major institutional axes such as sector or gender, and we find differences in work-role outcomes from group to group. If career lines operate as postulated, then each career line theoretically has a b associated with it that describes vacancy occurrence and movement in the line. When estimated for groups of job histories, we might expect the parameter b to vary, reflecting the different rates of vacancy occurrence and movement that are intrinsic to the career lines of each group.

Careers of persons contain information about career lines in the economy. If career histories are grouped for people hypothesized to follow related career lines, the individual job histories offer evidence on the career lines for the group. Group-to-group differences can be interpreted as career-line differences, once the effects of personal resources on career histories have been removed. Analogously, we observe the journeys and speeds of two groups of cars, each group on a different road. We wish to make inferences about characteristics of the roads, such as speed limit, but we have no direct data. If we observe the cars in motion and adjust for the ways in which cars and drivers differ from one another, then the resulting speed differences between the groups should tell us something about the roads each travels.

We now turn to the final part of the theory: a model of the attainment process.

The Attainment Process

The important quantity q is defined such that all people at the same job reward level are exposed to the same rate of better job opportunities. Sørensen postulates that the extent to which people take advantage of opportunities for gains in job rewards depends on personal resources such as schooling, ability, and background (Sørensen 1977, pp. 971-972). Sørensen defines resources as individual characteristics relevant to a person's attainment and further assumes that resources are in place on entry into the labor market and do not change thereafter.

In contrast, human-capital theory posits that personal resources change with time in the labor force. People acquire job training, work experience, children, and marriages. In turn, reward growth occurs with changes in personal resources, as evidenced by increased productivity. Sørensen notes that no universal claim of validity can be made for either assumption (1977, p. 972).[4] Human-capital theory uses time in the labor force *as a proxy* for growth in resources. The vacancy competition model takes time in the labor force as an indicator of the length of exposure to the mobility regime (q).

Sørensen defines the attainment process in terms of the maximum level of a job reward that a person can hope to achieve [$y(m)$]. Each job shift consumes a fraction of the difference between $y(0)$ or the reward level of the entry job, and $y(m)$. With successive job shifts, one should move closer and closer to $y(m)$. It follows that the rate of voluntary job shifts and the rate of gain in rewards declines with time in the labor force, exponentially in form (Sørensen 1975a, 1977, pp. 972-973). Equation 7.6 summarizes the relationship.

$$y(t) = y(0) + \Delta y \cdot v(t) \qquad (7.6)$$

Thus, the reward level at time t, $y(t)$, equals the initial reward level, $y(0)$, plus the average gain per shift, Δy. The term, $v(t)$, or $b^{-1}(e^{bt} - 1)$, specifies the number of job shifts undertaken by time t, given the assumed exponential decline rate.

But in the vacancy competition model, $y(m)$, or the maximum possible achievement, depends not only on personal resources but on the opportunity structure. This result is theoretically important. The status-attainment model and human-capital theory postulate that career growth and change are solely matters of personal resources. Sørensen defines personal resources independent of the opportunity structure as $z = y(m)/b$, where z is a measure of total resources. By substitution and algebraic manipulation, Sørensen shows (1977, p. 973)

$$y(t) = \frac{z}{b}(e^{bt} - 1) + y(0)e^{bt}. \qquad (7.7)$$

This equation describes a career curve that grows at a declining rate, where reward level at time t depends on the opportunity structure (b) and personal resources (z). Total resources are further assumed to be a linear combination of measured resources ($c_i x_i$) such as schooling or ability and unmeasured resources (c_0).

$$z = c_0 + \sum_i c_i x_i \qquad (7.8)$$

As a final result, Sørensen shows that integrating equation 7.7 over a time interval, $t_2 - t_1$, yields

$$y(t_2) = c_0^* + b^* y(t_1) + \sum_i c_i^* x_i \qquad (7.9)$$

where $b^* = e^{b\Delta t}$, $c_i^* = c_i/b(e^{b\Delta t} - 1)$, and $\Delta t = t_2 - t_1$ (Sørensen 1979, p. 378). Equation 7.9 looks like a lagged status-attainment equation for current job where the regression coefficients correspond to the * coefficients and the x's correspond to other independent variables in the equation. While equation 7.9 may look like an ordinary regression equation encountered in longitudinal studies, the theory in the vacancy competition model goes beyond the logic and interpretation of a status-attainment equation. Further, in most studies the time interval between lagged jobs (usually first and current) contains tremendous heterogeneity across persons in the length of the interval. This prohibits efficient use of the differential equation or dynamic framework.[5]

In summary, the vacancy competition model informs a theory of careers in several ways. First, it postulates a particular shape to the distribution of job rewards in society. The first part of the model does this in specifying the structure of inequality. We take the result to apply directly to the job rewards attached to positions in career lines. Second, the theory explicitly talks about structure through the concept of vacancy chain. It says that the effect of social structure is found in the rate at which job vacancies offering growth in rewards arrive at levels in a hierarchy of positions. We argue that career lines contain vacancy chains, accomplishing a direct link between career lines and the vacancy competition model. In other words, career lines contain the vacancy occurrence rate for better jobs specified in the theory. Third, the vacancy competition model includes the effect of person as well as structure. It says that people take advantage of opportunities commensurate with their personal resources. Thus the career is a mixture of the opportunity levels in career lines and the personal resources of the career-line traveler. Finally, the model focuses on the rate of change in job rewards, and this dynamic feature is more consistent with the notion of career than studies that focus on the level of an outcome at a single point.

In the next section we develop a design for testing the vacancy competition model with the career histories of Career Development sample members. We generate predictions from the model that inform the validity of the career-line concept.

Method and Hypotheses

If career lines operate in the economy, then institutional axes around which they form should structure the opportunity levels in one genre of career lines compared with another. For example, career lines that operate in the primary-independent sector of the economy ought to have higher rates of vacancy occurrence (b) compared with career lines in the primary-subordinate or secondary sectors. Earlier chapters suggested that men and women get access to different career lines. Thus the vacancy competition model estimated separately for men and women should reveal greater vacancy occurrence for better jobs for men, along with higher maximum achievement levels [$y(m)$] and perhaps a greater return to select resources.

We use this type of logic to examine career histories within institutional sectors and career histories of men compared with women in order to test the vacancy competition model. Since career lines are composed of vacancy chains, we take the evidence as bearing on the validity of the career-line concept.

This strategy is not without precedent. The synthetic-cohort strategy used in earlier chapters takes information about individual job transitions and aggregates the information to make inferences about career lines. Sørensen (1979) estimated fundamental parameters of the model for white and black men and women with data from the 1970 Census Public Use Samples. He used 1965 and 1970 jobs as the time 1-time 2 change interval. Resources were measured in years of formal schooling, transformed to an exponential metric, consistent with the structure of inequality as specified in the theory. Job status measures were also scored in the exponential metric. The model received support. The opportunity level (b, or the rate of occurrence of better job opportunities) was greater for whites than for blacks and greater for men than for women.[6] Whites, particularly men, had higher predicted achievement levels than blacks. Finally, within race, men and women had roughly equal resources, but men received a greater return to schooling than women, particularly the effect of schooling at equilibrium ($-c_i/b$).

Rosenfeld (1980) also used a differential equation model to study growth in status and earnings for young black and white men and women. For an important reason, the results are difficult to interpret in terms of the vacancy competition model. The theory specifies that valued job resources and rewards are distributed exponentially in society. Untransformed measures of years of schooling and job status are in an arbitrary metric relative to the theory and do not meet the exponential distributional assumption. Sørensen (1979) found that the arbitrary metrics lead to the unlikely conclusion that white women and blacks have access to *higher* rates of vacancy occurrence of better jobs than white males—an incorrect result from nearly any theoretical vantage point. Sørensen (1979) estimated the model with regular and exponential metrics. The equations with the exponential metric produced the correct ordering of population subgroups on the opportunity parameter (b) and yielded much higher coefficients of determination (R^2) than the untransformed status equation. We replicate this result.

Here we operationally capture types of career lines, or equivalently, different vacancy competition regimes, by producing separate estimates of the model for men and women and for each gender within three economic sectors: primary-independent, primary-subordinate, and secondary. We measure sector identically to the procedures in chapter 5, based on the theories of Piore (1975) and Edwards (1979).

Recall that primary-subordinate jobs are first distinguished from other jobs on the basis of the repetitive nature of the work. The remaining, less repetitive jobs are then allocated to primary-independent and secondary sectors on the basis of the specific vocational preparation score for the job. Jobs that require less than six months total schooling and training time were placed in the secondary sector, while jobs requiring more than six months of training and schooling time were placed in the primary-independent sector. Primary-independent jobs include most professional, managerial, and craft occupations, along with a few sales, clerical, and service occupations. The primary-subordinate sector includes primarily clerical and operative occupations along with a few sales, laborer, and service occupations. The secondary sector encompasses select sales, clerical, operative, laborer, and service occupations.

Piore's (1975) and Edwards's (1979) ideas provide theoretical reason to expect different types of career lines by sector. In particular, the primary-independent sector compared with primary-subordinate and secondary sectors should offer better opportunities (that is, higher rates of vacancies for better jobs), higher role reward levels [$y(m)$] and greater returns to formal schooling than the other sectors. The reasons lie in the control structures that undergird each sector and the degrees of insulation that sectors provide for workers' careers once underway.

Earlier we assumed that rates of vacancy occurrence for better jobs were constant at every reward level. We now produce separate estimates of the rate for career lines traveled by men versus women and for career lines within each sector. The estimation by subgroup allows for different rates for reward levels as they are differentially distributed to each group.

Our data offer more detailed measures of personal resources and work-role outcomes compared with previous research (Sørensen 1979; Rosenfeld 1980). We expand the dependent job reward variables to include socioeconomic status, the complexity of work, and skill level of work. All three concepts are important components of work-role continuity and indicators of work inequality (Spenner 1981, 1979; Spaeth 1979; and Kohn 1977). Sørensen (1979) restricts the measurement of personal resources to formal educational attainment because of data availability. We expand measurement of the conceptual domain of personal resources to include socioeconomic and family background, ambition, ability, academic performance, formal and nonformal schooling, certification, and resource demands or contingencies (that is, military service, work disability, children, and marital status).

Additionally, we have the data to explore the effects of fixed and changing resources after entry into the labor market. We pay particular attention to two resource variables: levels of formal schooling and certification (degrees). Essentially we use the other resource variables as controls. Schooling and certification are among the most important resource variables and have generated substantial theoretical and applied interest in economics and sociology (Granovetter 1981).

Hypotheses

We offer hypotheses for several parameters and derived quantities in the vacancy competition model. The quantities are obtained from the estimation equation 7.9. The parameters of interest are calculated from the * estimates in the estimation equation.

Opportunity Level.($b = \ln b^*/\Delta t$) We expect men to have more favorable opportunity levels than women because they are more likely to occupy career lines protected by internal-labor-market arrangements (Doeringer and Piore 1971). We expect more pronounced gender differences for socioeconomic status and substantive complexity of work. Gender differences may be smaller or nonexistent for skill level and scope since our conceptualization of skill includes features of tasks that are stereotypically male (mental and manipulative) and female (interpersonal).

We expect greater opportunity levels for both genders in the primary-independent compared with the primary-subordinate and secondary sectors. The theoretical justification derives from Piore (1975) and Edwards (1979). We are less certain about the ordering of opportunity levels between the primary-subordinate and secondary sectors. Segmented-labor-market theorists (Piore 1975; Edwards 1979) suggest that career lines in the secondary sector offer the lowest opportunities for reward growth. Earlier we saw that a measure of sector based on the reasoning of Piore and Edwards weakly discriminated between the secondary and primary-subordinate compared with the large differences between these two sectors and the primary-independent.

Within sectors, we expect higher opportunity levels for men than for women, for status and complexity of jobs. For skill, we expect less sharp differences for the reasons outlined.

Resources. $(z = c_0 + \sum_i c_i x_i)$ We expect few consistent sex differences in resources at labor-force entry because the estimator taps measured and unmeasured resources. Further, our measures of resources are comprehensive, including some for which men have an advantage (that is, more formal schooling and higher occupational aspirations) and some for which women have a slight advantage (that is, the absence of military service and higher academic performance in high school). We expect overall personal resource differences by sector because of the social selection of higher-resource persons into primary-independent career lines compared with primary-subordinate and secondary career lines. We expect these patterns for all three work-role outcomes.

Equilibrium. [Predicted Maximum Reward Level: $y(m) = -z/b$] To be consistent with empirical evidence (Rosenfeld 1979; Sørensen 1979), men should have higher predicted levels of status, complexity, and skill reward levels than women. Further, men and women in the primary-independent sector should have a decided advantage in equilibrium reward levels compared with men and women in other sectors. We are uncertain as to gender differences within the primary-subordinate and secondary sectors.

Returns to Formal Schooling. [$c_i = (c_i^* b)/(e^{b\Delta t} - 1)$; $d_i = -c/b$] The fundamental parameter c_i measures the instantaneous effect of a resource on changes in reward level. The quantity d_i measures the expected effect of a resource when a person has achieved his or her maximum reward level, $y(m)$. The quantity depends on the instantaneous effect of the resource and the rate of opportunities. Thus a small instantaneous effect can be greatly magnified at equilibrium if the opportunity level is very high. This coefficient is comparable to parameters estimated in models that assume the career is in equilibrium

We expect men to receive larger returns to formal schooling than women receive for all three role outcomes (Featherman and Hauser 1976; Sewell, Hauser, and Wolf 1980; Sørensen 1979; Rosenfeld 1980). Particularly in the primary-independent sector, men's career lines offer more continuous employment at higher opportunity levels. If formal schooling measures knowledge acquisition and technical expertise, then these commodities require a stable, secure career line to yield their return, hence the advantage to the primary-independent sector and to males.

Returns to Degree Certification. Unlike the quantity of formal schooling, which is less observable to employers, degree certification is more visible and should be to the advantage of the job changer and more advantageous in discontinuous employment histories. When entering a job, changing jobs, or reentering the labor force, one can better rely on a degree to open employment doors than one can rely on years of formal schooling. Therefore, women should receive a higher return (instantaneous and at equilibrium) to degrees than men receive for all three role outcomes. For the same reason, men and women in the secondary sector and women in the primary-subordinate sector should receive a greater return to credentials than those in other sector-gender groups. Another reason to expect these differences is the relative scarcity of degrees across sectors. Nearly half of all the persons who begin their careers in the primary-independent sector have one or more B.A. level or higher-level degrees. Only 18 percent of those who begin careers in the primary-subordinate and secondary sectors hold bachelors or higher-level degrees. A degree is much more of a scarce resource that differentiates one from co-workers in the primary-subordinate and secondary sectors. On the surface, this reasoning may seem at variance with the human-capital and segmentation perspectives, but these traditions most often speak of schooling as a unitary concept and do not distinguish certification from formal schooling.

Variables and Estimation

We used equation 7.9 as the estimation equation to test the vacancy competition model. It requires information about jobs at two points in time, where the time interval is equally spaced for all respondents. For the Career Development Study sample, we sought a time interval that

1. maximized the change in job rewards
2. minimized sample attrition (an interval too early in people's lives would leave too many people still enrolled in school)
3. would place people at about the same point early in their work careers

For time 1 job we selected the first full-time job the respondent held after last leaving *regular, full-time* formal schooling. Part-time and nonregular (that is, noncollege or nonuniversity) schooling did not enter into the definition. This definition is closest to the model's assumption of fixed resources since it permitted all respondents to complete regular full-time schooling. Second, the definition minimizes heterogeneity in the career as all respondents' jobs are measured very early in their work histories.[7] Thus this job standardizes location in the career, and presumably career line, even though in real or calendar time, people began this job as early as 1965 for high school dropouts and as late as 1975. About 12 percent of respondents completed formal schooling after 1975 or were still enrolled in 1979 and were excluded from the analysis.[8] We assigned people in the sample to sectors based on this job.

For the temporal interval, we selected five years, that is, the job held five years after the date of starting first job.[9] The time interval provides 1,949 men and 1,527 women with the requisite data (67.9 percent of men and 51.3 percent of women who were interviewed in 1979). The bias and selection issues are much the same as those we addressed in the previous chapter and in chapter 2. With this five-year time interval, 60 percent of respondents are in different occupations at time 1 and time 2. A larger percentage (75.3 percent) changed jobs (that is, employer) one or more times between time 1 and time 2. The difference between the two estimates reflects people who change jobs but remain in the same occupation. Thus about one-quarter of the respondents held the same occupation with the same employer over the five-year interval.

Table 7-1 provides a description of the dependent variables and resource measures. We sought a comprehensive rather than limited measurement of resources, particularly for schooling. We conceptualize the first eighteen indicators as fixed resources at the time of entry into the labor force. Additionally, we measured three changing resource variables: (1) schooling undertaken between time 1 and time 2, (2) children born in the time interval, and (3) marital status at time 2. These measures permit a crude check on the validity of the fixed resources assumption in the vacancy competition model.

The dependent measures are scored in standard metrics for socioeconomic status (Duncan 1961) and substantive complexity (Spenner 1980). Skill level is more of an exploratory measure, based on data, people, and things and specific vocational preparation ratings from the *Dictionary of Occupational Titles* (U.S. Department of Labor 1965). Chapter 4 describes scale items and construction. Appendix C reports the zero-order correlations among all measures for men and women. Depending on the gender and the job, the correlation between status and complexity is in the range of $r = .8$ to .9, revealing fairly redundant measures. On the other hand, skill level measures a correlated but different dimension of roles, as the correlations between complexity or status with skill are in the range of $r = .35$ to .5.

Following the theory, we also scored all dependent variables, lag variables, and educational attainment in the Sørensen metric.[10] The transformation results in a ratio-type variable with a zero-point and an ex-

Table 7-1
Variable Labels, Sources, and Descriptions for the Dynamic Career Model

Symbol	Variable Name	Source	Description
MSERV	Military service	1979 survey	Scored 1 if R served in the regular military; scored 0 otherwise.
WKDIS	Work disability	1979 survey	Scored 1 if R reported any physical limitation or disability that limited the amount or kind of work he or she could do; scored 0 otherwise.
MOMEMX	Mother's employment	1979 survey	Scored 1 if R's mother was employed full-time during R's junior year of high school; scored 0 otherwise.
POPSEI	Father's occupational status	1979 survey	During R's junior year of high school, Duncan SEI value of detailed census occupation.
FTJBFE	Duration of full-time jobs before leaving formal education	1979 survey	Scored in months; elapsed time in all full-time jobs before month and year of last leaving full-time formal education.
GPA	Grade point average	High school transcript	Overall grade point average for high school years where A = 4.0, B = 3.0, C = 2.0, D = 1.0, and F = 0.0.
MA	Mental ability	Washington Pre-College Testing Program	Average of verbal and quantitative score; test typically taken during the fall of the senior year (see note b to table 6-1).
POPED	Father's education	1966 student questionnaire	1 = eighth grade or less; 2 = some high school but not a graduate; 3 = high school graduate; 4 = some college but not a graduate; 5 = college graduate; 6 = more than four years of college.
MOMED	Mother's education	1966 student questionnaire	Same as father's education.
OCCASP	Occupational aspiration	1966 student questionnaire	Duncan SEI value of occupation R realistically expected to have as his/her life's work.
SIBS	Number of siblings	1966 student questionnaire	Number of living brothers and sisters.
RURAL	Rural origin	1966 student questionnaire	Scored 1 if R lived in a place of fewer than 2,500 persons; scored 0 otherwise.
EDATT	Educational attainment	1979 survey	Years of regular (not vocational, technical, business or nursing) schooling completed.
LEDATT	Sørensen metric for educational attainment	(Sørensen 1979; see LSEIT1 below)	Exponential distribution score for years of regular schooling.
DEGREE	Degrees	1979 survey	Scored 1 if R obtained 1 or more B.A. or higher level (for example, M.A., Ph.D., M.D.) degrees; scored 0 otherwise.
VOCTECH	Vocational-technical training	1979 survey	Scored 1 if R attended full-time, one or more vocational, technical, business, or nursing schools; scored 0 otherwise.

Variable	Description	Source	Definition
OTHED	Other educational training	1979 survey	Other than formal full-time schooling measured in EDATT and vocational schooling measured in VOCTECH, scored 1 if R reported holding a journeyman's card or any additional schooling (includes government training programs, correspondence courses, adult-education courses, company training schools, and part-time schooling enrollments of two courses or fewer; excludes military training); scored 0 otherwise.
KIDST1	Number of children time 1	1979 survey	Number of R's children at the time the first job was begun.
MARSTT1	Marital status time 1	1979 survey	Scored 1 if R was married during the year in which time 1 job was begun.
SCHT2	Schooling between time 1 and time 2 jobs	1979 survey	Scored 1 if R obtained any schooling after entering time 1 job and before entering time 2 (five years after time 1) job; scored 0 otherwise (by definition of time 1 job this measure excludes full-time regular schooling).
KIDST2	Additional children between time 1 and time 2	1979 survey	Number of R's children born between entrance into time 1 job and time 2 job.
MARSTT2	Marital status time 2	1979 survey	Scored 1 if R was married during the year in which time 2 job was begun; scored 0 otherwise.
Job measures			
SEIT1 SEIT2	Socioeconomic status of time 1 and time 2 jobs	1979 survey	Duncan SEI value of detailed census occupation of time 1 and time 2 jobs (see text for definition).
CPLXT1 CPLXT2	Substantive complexity of time 1 and time 2 jobs	1979 survey, Spenner (1980)	Complexity of work value of detailed census occupation of time 1 and time 2 jobs (scores range from -3.23 [low] to 26.62 [high]; see Spenner [1980] for details).
SKLT1 SKLT2	Skill level and scope of time 1 and time 2 jobs	1979 survey, chapter 4	Linear combination of levels of involvement with data, people and things, and specific vocational preparation (see Spenner 1980). Components orthogonalized and weighted by principal components analysis (components = 4). Skill value of detailed census occupation of time 1 and time 2 jobs (scores range from .7 [high] to 9.26 [low]).
LSEIT1 LSEIT2 LCPLXT1 LCPLXT2 LSKLT1 LSKLT2	Sørensen metric for job measures	Sørensen (1979)	Exponential distribution for each job measure (see Sørensen 1979). For each job measure distribution, cumulative percentiles were obtained, cumulating from the top down (let these scores be $P[y]$). The desired score y is given by $y = -\log P(y)$. We generated the scores for census occupations from the April 1971 Current Population Survey, for all respondents using their current jobs ($n = 53{,}438$).

ponential or pyramidal distribution. Since the metric is new and is for comparison to the baseline models in the previous chapter, we report select results for transformed and untransformed metrics.

Finally, we use ordinary least squares (OLS) as an estimation technique.[11] In models of this type with a lagged dependent variable, OLS estimates are inefficient and inconsistent estimators of the true parameters to the extent that the model is misspecified (hence, our efforts at a more inclusive measurement of resource variables). A left-out variable will result in autocorrelation and dependence of error terms on regressors (see Hannan and Young 1977; Hanushek and Jackson 1977; Rosenfeld 1980; Rosenfeld and Nielsen 1981). The problem is important because unmeasured variables that are positively correlated with the lag variable will generate an upwardly biased estimate of b^*. The inefficiency is not such a severe problem here because of our relatively large sample size, particularly for the groups of total men and total women.

Rosenfeld (1980) partially solved the problems through use of modified generalized least squares (MGLS) (Hannan and Young 1977). She found the degree of error was very serious for nonwhites, which is of some consolation to us since the sample is largely white, and moderately serious for subgroups of whites. Yet this conclusion is difficult to evaluate. Rosenfeld used the untransformed metrics that may change the values of fundamental parameters, particularly b, and make a comparison between our models difficult. Second, the desirable properties of MGLS estimators are not invariant under nonmonotonic transformations, such as those performed in the calculation of fundamental parameters. The extent of slippage is unknown.

In summary, the estimation problem is complex, and our parameter estimates should be treated as approximations. We have tried to minimize the error through a detailed specification. It is of some consolation that our estimates of b^* are quite a bit lower than those reported by Sørensen (1979), who used only one resource variable. This is what one would expect since left-out variables will generally bias estimates of b^* upward.

Results

Table 7-2 reports means and standard deviations for all variables by gender. The baseline models in the previous chapter included many of the same independent variables for nearly the same sample. The means and standard deviations of these variables for both genders differ only trivially from those reported earlier, so we forgo discussion of them.

Several of the resource measures are new to this chapter. Nearly 40 percent of the men served in the military, while practically none of the women

Table 7-2
Means and Standard Deviations of Dynamic Model Variables by Gender

Variable	Men (N = 1,949) Mean	Men SD	Women (N = 1,527) Mean	Women SD
MSERV	.39	.49	.01	.11
WKDIS	.11	.31	.10	.30
MOMEMX	.62	.49	.64	.48
POPSEI	43.69	24.66	46.95	24.99
FTJBFE	10.75	18.73	5.82	13.79
GPA	2.44	.63	2.69	.60
MA	48.60	8.56	48.84	7.83
POPED	3.17	1.46	3.33	1.49
MOMED	3.19	1.14	3.23	1.15
OCCASP	59.34	25.59	54.71	18.22
SIBS	2.68	1.81	2.67	1.77
RURAL	.36	.48	.31	.46
EDATT	14.37	1.99	13.97	1.86
LEDATT	.85	.88	.70	.74
DEGREE	.35	.48	.28	.45
VOCTECH	.12	.32	.26	.44
OTHED	.34	.47	.22	.42
KIDST1	.15	.42	.14	.43
MARSTT1	.34	.47	.36	.48
SCHT2	.22	.42	.36	.48
KIDST2	.84	.97	.52	.75
MARSTT2	.56	.50	.58	.49
SEIT1	36.94	25.03	46.15	19.44
SEIT2	42.33	25.01	48.60	18.99
CPLXT1	9.08	7.34	12.61	5.11
CPLXT2	10.73	7.31	13.45	5.24
SKLT1[a]	5.67	1.88	6.50	2.08
SKLT2	5.41	1.85	6.28	2.14
LSEIT1	.78	.93	.88	.55
LSEIT2	.93	.94	.98	.59
LCPLXT1	.79	.89	1.02	.61
LCPLXT2	.95	.92	1.12	.68
LSKLT1	.87	.86	.68	.92
LSKLT2	.96	.88	.76	.98

Note: See table 7-1 for variable descriptions. The analysis sample definition excludes those who (1) never worked since high school; (2) last left formal full-time schooling after 1975; and (3) did not hold a full-time job five years after the year in which time 1 job was begun.
[a]Reverse scored.

served. As a classic human-capital concept, equal fractions of men and women (about 10 percent) report a physical limitation that limits the amount or kind of work that they can do. This is comparable to national data (President's Committee on Employment of the Handicapped 1977). Men average about eleven months of full-time labor force experience prior to last leaving full-time formal schooling, and women average somewhat less at 5.8 months. Further, the variability in early job experience is greater among men. Men are more likely than women to hold a degree (.35 versus .28), less likely to have taken vocational training (.12 versus .26), and more likely to have other educational experiences (.34 versus .22). For both genders, the number of children at time 1 is small but more likely to grow by time 2 for men (.84 versus .52 children). About one-third of men and women are married in the year that they left formal schooling; about 55 percent are married five years later. Finally, more women than men (36 percent versus 22 percent) obtain further schooling during the time 1-time 2 interval.

The dependent measures show the expected patterns by gender and reveal modest growth in all three work-role outcomes over the five-year time interval. The careers of men start about nine status points lower than women (36.94 versus 46.15), but men narrow the gap to about six status points after five years. A similar situation exists for substantive complexity of work in the early career. Women start higher than men and gain about .8 of one point in five years while men gain 1.75 points. For skill level, men enter their careers about one-half of one standard deviation higher than women, and each gender increases the skill levels of their jobs by nearly identical margins between time 1 and time 2 jobs.

For comparison purposes, we estimated equation 7.9 with the regular untransformed variables and with select variables scored in the exponential metric postulated by the theory. Table 7-3 provides select regression results. All equations include the fixed and changing resource variables. The outcomes are quite consistent with predictions from the theory and corroborate a similar analysis performed by Sørensen (1979). First, the Sørensen metric produces more meaningful outcomes for the opportunity level parameter (b) than the untransformed metric. The untransformed equations show women have greater career-line opportunities for growth in status and complexity than men; the Sørensen metric shows men have greater opportunities. Both metrics show women have greater opportunities for skill growth than men.

Second, the vacancy competition model interprets the constant (c_0^*, c_0) as reflecting unmeasured resources. A negative intercept makes no conceptual sense. Two of six constant terms are negative for each metric. The Sørensen metric for these two cases gives intercepts that are close to zero, although negative.[12] Third, the Sørensen metric equations better explain the total variation in the dependent variable (R^2) than untransformed metric equations, particularly for men. Overall, we take these results as strongly supporting use of the new metric. The new metric is theoretically derived, and it performs better than the old metric on conventional empirical criteria. All subsequent analyses use the new metric.

Table 7-3
Select Regression Results for the Dynamic Model by Gender, Job Measure, and Metric

| | Dependent Variable Metric | | | |
| | Untransformed Metric | | Sørensen Metric | |
Equation and Regression Result	Males	Females	Males	Females
Socioeconomic status				
b	−.829	−.816	−.541	−.771
constant	−21.886	3.607	−.139	.303
R^2	.515	.406	.616	.398
Complexity				
b	−.861	−.822	−.617	−.780
constant	−7.354	.958	−.063	.488
R^2	.491	.423	.558	.422
Skill level				
b	−.765	−.609	−.692	−.499
constant	5.131	3.603	.108	.435
R^2	.285	.396	.335	.433
N	1,949	1,527	1,949	1,527

Note: Each equation includes eighteen fixed resource variables, three changing resource variables, and the time 1 lag of the dependent variable. The Sørensen metric equations include educational attainment scored in the Sørensen metric (natural logarithm of the cumulative percentile); the untransformed metric equations use years of formal schooling. The results are unchanged if the changing resource variables are dropped.
[a]$b = \ln b^*$ where $b^* = $ lag regression coefficient.

Table 7-4 reports regression equations for men and women for each work-role outcome. We do not use these estimates (b^*, c_i^*) to test hypotheses that are more appropriately tested with the fundamental parameters (b, c_i). The regular regression coefficients offer, however, a general sense of how the overall equation performs. The coefficients in table 7-4 are in metric form, permitting gender comparisons for each role outcome, but they do not permit assessments of the relative importance of one variable compared with another within an equation.

The resource measures and lag coefficient explain much more of the variation in men's status and complexity growth than for women ($R^2 = .616$ and .558 versus .398 and .422). The opposite conclusion holds for skill growth ($R^2 = .335$ for men and .433 for women).

As we found for the equations in the previous chapter, there are broad similarities yet some marked differences in the resource variables that are

Table 7-4
Estimated Coefficients of the Dynamic Model by Job Outcome and Gender

Independent Variable[a]	Status		Dependent Variable Complexity		Skill	
	Male	Female	Male	Female	Male	Female
MSERV	−.015	−.009	−.041	−.025	.043	−.087
WKDIS	−.027	−.094*	−.041	−.156*	.003	−.199*
MOMEMX	.001	−.024	.060*	−.030	.007	.039
POPSEI	.001	.001*	.000	.001	−.000	.000
FTJBFE	.001	.002	.001	.002	−.001	.001
GPA	.027	.025	.019	.023	.090*	−.043
MA	.002	−.001	.000	−.002	−.001	−.002
POPED	.010	−.001	.027*	−.003	.021	−.006
MOMED	.012	−.018	.016	−.025	−.012	−.011
OCCASP	.002*	.003*	.002*	.002*	.000	−.000
SIBS	.005	−.004	.010	−.006	.006	−.009
RURAL	.002	.024	−.008	.013	.033	.027
LEDATT	.166*	.081*	.188*	.152*	.147*	.089*
DEGREE	.124*	.147*	.129*	.182*	.009	.277*
VOCTECH	−.037	−.056	.003	−.010	.036	.089
OTHED	.028	−.015	.027	.023	.077*	.048
KIDST1	−.064	−.066*	−.020	−.038	.040	.058
MARSTT1	−.015	−.014	−.006	−.016	−.033	.024
SCHT2	.033	.010	−.009	−.010	.039	.097
KIDST2	−.017	−.016	.004	−.004	.020	.013
MARSTT2	.123*	.088*	.056	.075*	.033	−.066
b*	.582*	.462*	.539*	.458*	.501*	.607*
constant	−.139	.303	−.063	.488	.108	.435
R^2	.616	.398	.558	.422	.335	.433
N	1,949	1,527	1,949	1,527	1,949	1,527

Note: All dependent variables are in the Sørensen metric. All coefficients are metric. See table 7-1 for variable descriptions. *Coefficient more than twice its standard error.

important for men compared to women. Most resource variables make very little difference for men or women, regardless of role outcome. The larger coefficients are confined to five or six specific resources. The most important resources for men and women, for all three career outcomes, are formal years of schooling and bachelors or higher degrees. For men, formal schooling appears the more formidable resource, and for women, degree-holding is more important. These patterns are accentuated when we consider the fundamental parameters.

For complexity and status growth, occupational aspirations are a significant resource for both genders. Occupational aspirations make little difference for growth in skill levels. Minimally, aspirations are indicative of different levels of goal orientations to overall aspects of work roles (status and complexity) but not a more specific aspect of work roles (skill level).

Aspirations may or may not reflect underlying motivational tendencies. All dynamic models of this type that we know leave aspirations unmeasured.

Several other resource variables have effects that exceed twice their standard error. Most of the effects are in the form of advantage to the careers of men and disadvantage to the careers of women. The presence of a work disability slows the growth of status, complexity, and skill levels in the early careers of women; it has no apparent effect for men. Men experience greater growth in job complexity as a function of maternal employment; women do not. High school grade point average is a significant resource for the skill growth in men's careers; it has no positive effect—indeed, its effect, if any, is negative—on the skill growth in women's careers. Men get a skill return to other forms of education; women do not. Children at the time of entry into the labor force slow status growth in women's careers. The coefficient is nearly as large for men and negative, but it is less than twice its standard error. Thus there is some support for Kanter's (1977) assertion that marriage and children benefit the careers of men but not women. For status, marriage has a more positive effect for men, but for complexity, marriage is of greater advantage to women. The presence of children has small effects, and, if anything, is more negative for women.

Finally, we note that the changing resource variables have little effect on growth in status, complexity, or skill, with the possible exception of marital status. Increments to schooling or the number of children have no effects that exceed twice the standard error for either gender for any role outcome. Being married five years after career entry provides a small boost to the status growth of men and women and a small return to the complexity growth of women. But the effects are small (in standardized regression coefficients, less than .07). Compared with equations with fixed resources, ignoring the changing resource variables would not alter any of our major conclusions based on fundamental parameters. Technically, we can say the fixed resource assumption of the theory involves some error. Practically, we can say that the error is probably very small—at least for resource changes as they involve schooling, children, and marital status.

Table 7-5 provides the estimates of fundamental parameters that we use to test hypotheses. The fundamental parameters are calculated with the algebraic manipulations reported in the hypotheses section. For example, consider the first two columns of estimates for males and females under socioeconomic status. The first row lists the estimate of the opportunity level parameter or the rate at which job opportunities that allow growth in status arrive in the career lines of men and women, respectively. This parameter is simply the natural logarithm of the lag regression coefficient. A smaller absolute value indicates a higher rate. A large negative number of -1 or more means the career reaches its status apex on entry into the labor force or even declines. In this case, men ($b = -.541$) have a much higher

Table 7-5
Parameter Estimates for the Vacancy Competition Model by Gender, Sector of Time 1 Job, and Job Outcome

| | | | Sector | | | | | |
| | | | Primary-Independent | | Primary-Subordinate | | Secondary | |
Job Outcome and Parameter	Male	Female	Male	Female	Male	Female	Male	Female
Socioeconomic status								
b	-.541	-.774	-.464	-.498	-.816	-1.070	-.650	-.877
c_0	-.138	.470	-.639	.258	.165	.691	.443	.577
c (LEDATT)	.221	.116	.206	.086	.396	.189	.044	.138
c (DEGREE)	.161	.211	.091	.118	.149	.297	.403	.347
z	.815	.795	1.213	1.126	.612	1.024	.602	.817
y (m)[a]	1.506	1.027	2.614	2.261	.758	.957	.927	.932
d (LEDATT)	.409	.150	.444	.173	.485	.177	.068	.157
d (DEGREE)	.298	.273	.196	.237	.183	.278	.620	.396
Complexity								
b	-.616	-.781	-.445	-.669	-.916	-.658	-.728	-1.981
c_0	-.047	.745	-.487	.766	.087	.678	.272	1.273
c (LEDATT)	.252	.213	.210	.218	.246	.180	.104	.313
c (DEGREE)	.169	.262	.031	.182	.318	.304	.552	.492
z	.778	.947	1.031	.939	.763	.748	.813	1.971
y (m)	1.263	1.213	2.317	1.404	.833	1.137	1.117	.995
d (LEDATT)	.409	.273	.472	.326	.269	.274	.143	.158
d (DEGREE)	.274	.335	.070	.272	.347	.462	.758	.248
Skill								
b	-.695	-.496	-.582	-.380	-1.317	-1.011	-.569	-.962
c_0	.218	.523	-.166	.632	.610	.370	.149	.022
c (LEDATT)	.205	.135	.210	.140	.022	.032	.076	.192
c (DEGREE)	.004	.340	.029	.271	.139	.239	.072	.584
z	.783	.498	.763	.338	1.149	.657	.642	.615
y (m)	1.127	1.004	1.311	.889	.872	.650	1.128	.639
d (LEDATT)	.295	.272	.361	.368	.017	.032	.134	.200
d (DEGREE)	.006	.685	.050	.713	.106	.236	.127	.607
N	1,949	1,527	977	705	537	402	435	420

Note: Table is based on fixed-resource variable equation. The dependent variable, lag 1 dependent variable, and educational attainment are scored in the Sørensen metric.

[a] If c_0 is negative then z is the sum of measured resources only.

rate of opportunities to move to higher-status jobs than women ($b =$ $-.774$). The second line (c_0) reports the unmeasured resources for status growth. It is based on an algebraic manipulation of the intercept in the regression equation. It is higher for women (.470 versus $-.138$), and we treat the negative coefficient for men as zero, meaning the equation probably includes all of the major personal resources relevant to status growth for this sample of men.

The third and fourth lines (c) report the instantaneous returns to formal schooling and degree certification. The coefficients are calculated from the raw regression coefficients and can be interpreted as the rate of return to schooling or certification at any given instant in the career. In this case, men get twice the return to schooling compared with women (.221 versus .116), and women get about one-quarter more of a return to degrees than men (.211 versus .161). The fifth row (z) is the total personal resources for status growth. It is calculated as a sum of the means for each variable for each group (that is, men and women), weighted by the fundamental parameter (c) or importance of each variable. For example, if military service has a negative effect on status growth for men and many men served in the military, then military service lowers the total personal resources that men have for status growth. Men and women have nearly equal measured personal resources for status growth (.815 and .795).

The sixth line gives the equilibrium value (apex of the career curve) or the maximum potential reward level based on the equation. The metric for the numbers is exponential. Appendix D assists the interpretation by giving the raw and exponential scores for all occupations for status, complexity, and skill. So for men, the equilibrium status level is 1.506, or about 65 on the Duncan scale. For women, the maximum potential status is lower at 1.027, or about 52 on the Duncan scale.

Finally, the last two lines in each panel report the effect of schooling and degrees at equilibrium. It is simply the instantaneous effect divided by the opportunity level. A high opportunity level (small absolute value for b) will accentuate the instantaneous effect. It is convenient to think of the d coefficients as the complete effect of schooling and degrees over the course of the career. In the case of status, the higher opportunity level in men's career lines gives them an even greater return to formal schooling compared with women (nearly three times as much) and allows men to catch up with women in the status returns to degrees over the career. For all of the parameters, the quality of the inferences assumes that the equation is correctly specified. Throughout, we do not emphasize statistical tests on the fundamental parameters because the application is not straightforward, and the statistical theory is not fully developed (Rosenfeld 1980). We review the outcomes by hypotheses for each parameter.

Opportunity Level (b)

The theory receives strong support and, by inference, so does the concept of career line. The worth of the career-line concept depends on the presence of differences in opportunity levels among hypothesized types of career lines. Such differences largely follow the hypothesized pattern. We expected men's career lines to contain an opportunity rate that was higher (*b* is smaller in absolute value) than the career lines of women. Further, we expected higher opportunity levels for career lines in the primary-independent sector compared with primary-subordinate and secondary sectors. Within sectors, we expected an advantage for men, and we reasoned that the patterns would be more clear for status and complexity and less clear for skill.

For status and complexity outcomes, men have more opportunity for growth in their careers and, by inference, in the career lines that they occupy than do women. The opportunity parameters in men's career lines are $-.541$ and $-.616$ for status and complexity, compared with $-.774$ and $-.781$, or 25 to 40 percent lower for the career lines followed by women. The gender differences are less in the primary-independent sector and greater in the primary-subordinate and secondary sectors.

Recall, the measure of sector is for the sector of first job, and it says nothing about the sectoral location of subsequent jobs. This measurement strategy flows logically from the notion of port of entry to career lines. Presumably, more people are in port-of-entry jobs in the first job after the completion of formal schooling than for any other job in the work course. The gender difference in opportunity level also holds within each sector for complexity and status, with the exception of complexity in the primary-subordinate sector. Men are exposed to vacancy regimes in their career lines that range from 7 percent to 170 percent higher in vacancy opportunity rates depending on sector and role outcome. If we ignore gender and focus on sector for status and complexity, the hypothesized pattern is also found. Career lines in the primary-independent sector offer much more opportunity for growth in status and complexity compared with other sectors (from nearly one-half again as much opportunity to more than twice as much).

We expected the opportunity differences between secondary and primary-subordinate sectors to be complicated, and they are. Women in the primary-subordinate sector have the very lowest opportunities for growth in status ($b = -1.070$), while women in the secondary sector face the lowest opportunities for complexity growth ($b = -1.981$).

The skill growth in career lines exhibits a pattern in opportunity levels different from status and complexity but a pattern that is still meaningful in context of the vacancy competition model. Recall, the skill measure taps mental, interpersonal, and manipulative levels of task performance along with total job-specific training. In general, women have higher opportunity levels for expanding the skill level and scope of jobs in their career lines compared with men. This holds in both primary sectors but not in the secondary sector, where the opportunity levels for men are higher ($b = -.569$ versus $-.962$). Given the nature of the skill measure, the pattern of opportunity levels by gender is not surprising. More important for the theory, the primary-independent sector provides opportunity levels for growth in skill that are better than career lines in the other two sectors.

Resources (z)

Women have more resources for growth in complexity; men have more resources for growth in job skill; the genders are about equal in personal resources for status growth. In general, men have more resources for growth in role outcomes if their career lines are in the primary-independent sector, while women have equal or greater resources of growth in role outcomes if career-line locations are in other sectors.

We did expect one sector difference of greater personal resources in career lines in the primary-independent sector, and the difference occurs. Those in the primary-independent sector—particularly men—have more resources for growth in reward levels than persons in other sectors. Thus there is some evidence that those with more resources relevant to growth in status, complexity, and skill are more likely to be socially selected or allocated to career lines in the primary-independent sector (see Beck, Horan, and Tolbert 1980, for complementary evidence).[13]

The resource level for women in the secondary sector for complexity growth and for men in the primary-subordinate for skill growth are anomalously high. We are unsure why. Further, we note that the negative unmeasured resource levels (c_0) that occur in five out of twenty-four equations are also unexpected. One explanation says that negative intercepts occur because not all variables in the equation are scored in the exponential metric. Alternately, the equations may have fully or overparameterized personal resources in these cases, leaving effectively no unmeasured personal resources.

Equilibrium [Predicted Maximum Reward Level, y(m)]

We expected and find that men have higher predicted levels of maximum achievement than women for all three work-role outcomes. The predicted gender difference at the apex of the career is about twelve points on the untransformed status scale and about one-half of a scale point in the complexity and the skill scales. For status and complexity, this occurs because men have higher opportunities for growth, even though their resource levels are nearly equal or lower compared to women. For skill, women have higher opportunity levels but much lower resources for using the opportunities. As a result, men have slightly higher equilibrium levels of skill than women [$y(m)$= 1.127 versus 1.004]. It is important to note that typical attainment models do not permit this type of fine-grained interpretation of how structure and personal resources shape careers.

The sector differences in equilibrium values are much as expected:

1. Higher levels are found in the primary-independent compared to primary-subordinate and secondary sectors.
2. Men have the advantage in the primary-independent and secondary sectors.
3. Unexpectedly, women in the primary-subordinate sector have higher equilibrium levels than men for status and complexity role outcomes. Perhaps this reflects women's location in higher-status and more complex clerical career lines, while men in primary-subordinate career lines tend to do lower-status and less complex machine-related work.
4. Also unexpected and not consistent with the speculation of sector theorists, the equilibrium levels in the secondary sector generally exceed the primary-subordinate equilibrium levels.

Returns to Formal Schooling and Credentials (c_i, d_i)

We expected men to receive higher returns to formal schooling than women and higher returns in career lines in the primary-independent sector compared with other sectors. In contrast, we expected the higher return from degrees to accrue to women and in primary-subordinate and secondary sectors. In general, this is what we find, although with several significant exceptions. First we consider growth in status.

Men receive about twice the returns that women receive to years of formal schooling (c_i = .221 versus .116). When the opportunity level of the career line is taken into account, and the effect of formal schooling is assessed over the career, the return of men has grown to nearly three times that of women (d_i = .409 versus .150). The greater opportunities that men have by virtue of exposure to higher rates of vacancies that permit status growth yield men a bonus in returns to formal schooling when the effects are cumulated over time. This conclusion cannot be obtained from a static model. Further, these estimates suggest that typical regression models underestimate the true gender difference in returns to formal schooling.

An equally subtle return to certification occurs for men and women for socioeconomic status. As hypothesized, the instantaneous return to degrees is 25 percent higher for women than men. But when we factor in the higher opportunities for status growth that men experience, the difference disappears, and male-female returns to degrees are about equal at the status apex of the career. Again, this subtle type of career effect could not be ferreted out in typical models. Such dynamic model outcomes offer powerful testimony to the necessity of considering the opportunity levels in career lines and the explicit consideration of change over time when studying work-role outcomes.

Considered by sector, the status growth returns to schooling and degrees form a complex pattern. In both primary sectors, men receive greater returns to formal schooling, and women receive greater returns to degree certification. The gender differences are slightly greater when considered over the career compared with the instantaneous effect because men have higher opportunity levels. In the secondary sector, the pattern is reversed. Women receive a higher return to formal schooling and men a slightly higher return to degrees. Again, opportunity level differences increase the gender difference at equilibrium.

The highest overall returns to degrees, as hypothesized, occur in the secondary sector. The highest return to formal schooling is not in the primary-independent, as we expected, but in the primary-subordinate sector for males. Considered over the career, women's returns to formal schooling differ very little by sector.

On balance, the hypotheses receive support. The anomalies center on two questions. First, in the secondary sector, why do women receive the greater return to formal schooling ($c = .138$ versus $.044$) and men the greater return to degrees ($c = .403$ versus $.347$)? Second, why do men in the primary-subordinate sector receive the highest return to formal schooling compared with any other sector-gender subgroup ($c = .396$, $d = .485$)?

The pattern of returns to schooling and degree resources are much the same for complexity and skill level. Recall that we expected men to receive greater returns to formal schooling and women greater returns to degrees. Further, we hypothesized that degrees would yield their greatest return in secondary-sector career lines. Several generalizations summarize the results.

1. Men generally receive a greater return to formal schooling then women. For complexity growth, men's higher opportunity levels accentuate the difference at equilibrium; for skill growth, women's greater opportunities narrow the gender difference at equilibrium.
2. The marked exception is the secondary sector. Women receive the greater return to formal schooling, but because men have higher opportunity levels in this sector, the gender differences are minimal at equilibrium for both skill and complexity growth.
3. Women receive much higher returns to degree certification for skill and complexity growth. The only exception is the secondary sector for com-

plexity growth, where the instantaneous effect is slightly greater for men (.552 versus .492), and the equilibrium effect is much greater for men (.758 versus .248).

4. On balance, the greatest returns to formal schooling are in the primary-independent sector, and the greatest returns to certification are in the secondary sector. Beck, Horan, and Tolbert (1980) found that women received higher earnings returns to schooling in periphery industries. Our findings for occupational role rewards over the career are consistent with this and suggest the pattern may even be stronger for the returns to degrees compared with formal schooling. The marked exception is the extremely high skill return that women in primary-independent career lines receive for degree certification over the career ($d = .713$).

Career Curves for Role Outcomes

The career curves for status, complexity, and skill level by gender conveniently summarize the predicted outcomes under the vacancy competition model. Figure 7-1 displays the curves calculated over the interval from labor force entry to thirty-five years of work experience. We use the reward level of first job as the initial time point.[14] For no role outcome have men or women fully reached the equilibrium value, which represents an infinity of labor-force experience. However, from 92 percent to 99 percent of equilibrium values are obtained by thirty-five years.

The curves show initial levels of job rewards, the rate of growth in rewards over the work course, and differences in rewards on approaching retirement. The calculation of the curves includes both the rates of vacancy occurrence for better jobs in career lines and returns to fixed resources.

The status curves are the most interesting. Men enter the labor force in jobs of lower status than women by about nine points on the Duncan scale. The model predicts that status growth in men's careers will overtake women's levels of status within five years of labor-force participation. Our data show that men's status remains about six points below women's status level after five years of work experience. At the time of interview in 1979, where men and women average about six and one-half years of work experience since last leaving school, the difference has narrowed to three points on the Duncan scale.

Thus there is some error in the curves (overpredicting actual status), but the changes in the real profiles follow the pattern predicted by the model. The growth in status is much more pronounced for men than for women. After fifteen years of work experience, men have reached 91 percent of their equilibrium value, and women have reached 97 percent. As others have

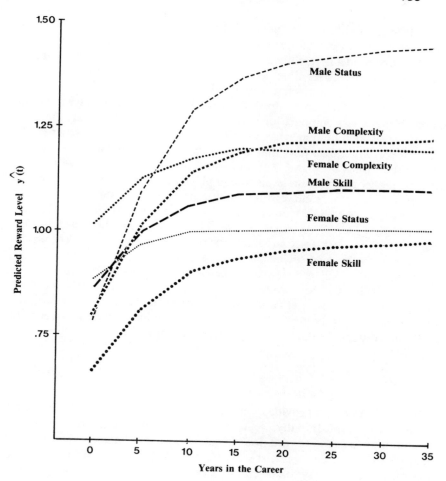

Figure 7-1. Predicted Career Curves for Status, Complexity, and Skill by Gender

suggested, the larger portion of status differentiation occurs within fifteen years of labor-force entry, when most working men and women are in their middle or late thirties (Otto and Haller 1979; Rosenfeld 1980).

The dynamic model offers a more refined view of status growth in the career than the baseline model in the previous chapter. Although women have resources for status growth that are nearly equal to men, and they enter the labor force in higher-status jobs, the status of men grows more rapidly and approaches a higher equilibrium; over their careers, men receive a larger return on personal resources. Compared with the dynamic model, the baseline model offers no explicit link to career lines, leaves obscure the change in rewards over time, and underestimates the return to select personal resources by as much as one-third.

The career curves for complexity of work show that men enter the labor force in much less complex jobs than women do but will surpass the complexity level of jobs that women hold after fifteen or twenty years in the labor force. The career lines that men occupy provide more opportunities to take other jobs of higher substantive complexity. The model predicts slightly higher equilibrium levels of complexity for men than for women. In contrast to the status curves that show a decided advantage for men, the complexity curves show women will enjoy more complex work on average over the first half of the work course. This strengthens the counsel to examine multiple work-role outcomes, for over the career the patterns do not always match those of socioeconomic status.

Finally, the skill profiles show men entering the work force in much higher skilled jobs than women. The gap is sufficiently large that even though women have better career-line opportunities for growth in skill, the difference will still be over 60 percent of the original gender difference in skill after thirty-five years of labor-force participation.

Summary

The models and data provide independent assessment of the validity of the career-line concept. Initially, we used a synthetic cohort that involves strong assumptions to examine variations in career lines. On balance, the evidence suggested the concept was a reasonable one. Yet the possibility remained that the noise of the synthetic cohort was greater than the signal of career lines in the data.

In this chapter the analysis was unencumbered by the assumptions of the synthetic cohort and drew on the strength of data from event histories of jobs for a large sample of men and women. Our reasoning involved several premises. If career lines are operative in the economy, then we should be able to detect some evidence of their effect in people's job histories after adjusting for differences in personal resources. If men follow different career lines than women—and there are many reasons to believe that they do—then the effect of career lines should be detectable in separate analyses by gender. Further, if sectors of the economy contain ports of entry to different types of career lines, then classifying job histories on the basis of port of entry of jobs in the history should reveal signals of a career-line effect. We selected role continuity (that is, status, complexity, and skill level) as the conceptual property of career lines for study. Role continuity is the logical choice because of the large base of theory and analytical methods to study job rewards compared with other career-line properties. We selected the first full-time job after formal schooling to capture the effects of ports of entry in sectors that grant access to types of career lines.

We estimated a status-attainment model in chapter 6 to establish a baseline for a dynamic career-line model and to establish the quality of the (new) data base. We used Sørensen's (1977) vacancy competition model as a theoretical framework that predicted an effect for career lines and personal resources on growth in job rewards over time. We interpreted vacancy chains as embedded in career lines any time the career line involves a job change. Sørensen's theory implies a particular differential equation that explains changes in job rewards over time.

The model estimates for men and women and for sector-gender groups provide fairly strong and consistent support for Sørensen's theory. The test represents an independent replication of Sørensen's model. More important, the test results confirm what would be expected if different career lines operate within economic sectors and for men compared with women. The critical parameter b, reflecting the opportunity level for reward growth in career lines, was ordered consistent with predictions for most gender and sector comparisons. Further, the vacancy competition model provides a plausible interpretation of how career lines combine with personal resources to shape individual careers.

Compared with the baseline model, the dynamic model offers a more refined view of careers. First, dynamic models depict change over time rather than the level of an outcome at one point in time. Second, the dynamic model incorporates a parameter for the effect of career lines in shaping career profiles. Third, the dynamic model gives explicit attention to the way the career approaches equilibrium. We found, for example, that the baseline model underestimates the return to personal resources that men receive compared with women.

The test has limitations. The OLS estimates are subject to sizable error to the extent that important variables are left out of the model.[15] The measures of sector are weak and reflect the state of the art. A more complete test of the theory would use all of the information in the job histories, in an event history type of analysis (Tuma, Hannan, and Groeneveld 1979). The importance of changing resources is an unresolved empirical issue. Finally, we examined a limited part of the conceptual domain of career lines—differences in continuities of role rewards as they might flow from ports of entry. An expanded dynamic model would include other role rewards and other conceptual features of career lines. This would require an expanded version of the theory, one that further partitions the rate of vacancy occurrence into different sources of structural heterogeneity.

Yet, weighing the evidence, we find that the concept of career line is reasonable and promising. Our evidence strongly suggests that theories seeking to explain careers must take career lines into account.

The application of the vacancy competition model in this chapter speaks in several ways to any eventual theory of careers. First, the model estimates clearly showed an effect of structure on career outcomes. In our application, the structure effects were consistently organized by gender and sector and were consistent with predictions and interpretations derived from a career-line perspective. Second, the estimates demonstrated the advantage of explicitly considering time and change in a dynamic framework. A number of more refined, more accurate conclusions were possible with the dynamic model compared with baseline models that leave the dynamic features of careers unattended. Finally, a career-line perspective applied in the vacancy competition model offers a plausible theoretical interpretation of how social structure and personal resources combine to shape careers.

There may be other ways to combine person and structure, but the important point for a theory of careers is the necessity to consider both person and structure (and their interplay) to the exclusion of neither. The career-line perspective offers a beginning.

Notes

1. The major statement of the theory is in Sørensen (1977). Evidence on predictions from the theory can be found in Sørensen (1978, 1979, 1980), Rosenfeld (1980), and Sørensen and Tuma (1978). For discussion and background to the ideas and methods, consult Sørensen (1974, 1975a, 1975b), Coleman (1968), Goldberg (1958), Kalleberg and Hudis (1979), Nielsen and Rosenfeld (1981), Rosenfeld and Nielsen (1981), and Halaby (1980).

2. We restrict our application of the theory to occupational role characteristics.

3. The discrete variable analog is the geometric distribution.

4. Our subsequent estimation equation attempts to capture some of the effect of changing resources, if indeed they change. We find some truth in both assumptions: Resources change (at least during the late twenties and early thirties) after entry into the labor force but not enough to make a big difference.

5. Coleman (1964, 1968) provided much of the original motivation for the use of differential equation models in sociology.

6. Following Sørensen (1977, 1979), we interpret b as a measure of the rate of occurrence of vacancies that offer a reward level gain. By use of the term opportunity we mean this rate and no more or less. We label a high rate, high opportunity and a low rate, low opportunity. Recall that a high

rate is a small absolute value of b, assuming b is less than zero. There is some disagreement over the interpretation of b (see Rosenfeld and Nielsen 1981). We view the disagreement as flowing from the two forms of this kind of differential equation model (which can be shown to be mathematically similar, yet may involve very different theoretical mechanisms and interpretations). We use the so-called negative feedback form of the model and believe that our interpretation of b is consistent with it.

7. Additionally, we constructed a variable that measured months of full-time job experience before last leaving formal education to control for any remaining heterogeneity in work histories. The variable made no difference, which lends confidence to the selection of time intervals and jobs (see Sørensen 1980, for a related result).

8. Many of those enrolled in school after 1975 are people who started school late or interrupted their schooling careers rather than persons enrolled in post-secondary education for eight, nine, or more consecutive years. About 13 percent of all sample members obtained from seventeen to twenty years of formal schooling by the date of interview in 1979. Truncated to 1975, 11 percent of this subsample has obtained from seventeen to twenty years of formal schooling. Thus, the schooling distributions are censored only slightly by the selection of first job after schooling after 1975.

9. We experimented with a thirty-six-month interval and rejected it because it provided much less change. We rejected a seventy-two-month interval because it moved the first job truncation year to 1974, excluding another 5 percent of sample members who were enrolled in school. All measures are in month and year; however, if a person did not hold a job in the sixtieth month after starting the first job, we searched for a job in the calendar year (that closest to the sixtieth month) and included the case on that basis. In the case of multiple jobs at the same time, we randomly selected one.

10. The procedure first obtains the cumulative percentile of scores $[P(y)]$ in the untransformed distribution, cumulating from the top down (highest reward level equals the lowest percentile). The transformed score is $y = -\log P(y)$. The scores range from 0 to about 6.9 (high). We experimented with the transformation for several resource variables, which the theory would also specify in an exponential metric. Among the variables we checked, only transformed educational attainment makes a consistent difference in the equation. Transformed educational attainment affects the size and sign of the intercept but leaves other fundamental parameters relatively unaltered compared with the equation that uses untransformed educational attainment. We did not check dichotomous variables. To give the reader an example, the following select years of schooling receive exponential scores (in parentheses): 12 (.12), 14 (.62), 16 (1.09), 18 (3.04) and 20 (4.51); and select Duncan SEI scores: 6 (.01), 26 (.40), 46 (.88), 66 (1.55),

86 (3.86). Appendix D provides the exponential scores for all occupation categories.

11. We hope to perform the modified generalized least-squares estimation in the future. Even MGLS estimates are not invariant under non-monotonic transformations, as are performed in the calculation of fundamental parameters. We are unaware of any statistical software that performs maximum likelihood estimation (the estimators being invariant under transformation) for continuous time, continuous dependent variable models.

12. Using Sørensen's equation with education as the only resource measure, we obtain all positive intercepts in the Sørensen metric equations and negative intercepts in untransformed metric equations.

13. Sector boundaries are far from rigid. About 64 percent of men and 62 percent of women remain in the same sector over the five year time-interval. Between time 1 and time 2, larger percentages are upwardly mobile across sectors (24 percent of men and 22 percent of women) than are downwardly mobile (12 percent of men and 15 percent of women).

14. We obtained the predicted values with the equation (see Rosenfeld 1980, p. 606).

$$\widehat{Y}(t) = (\widehat{e^{bt}})\ \overline{Y}_0 + (1 - \widehat{e^{bt}})\ Y(m)$$

15. Our estimates of the model using only voluntary job shifts are closely comparable to the estimates reported here.

8

Retrospect and Prospect

Retrospect

We began with the concepts of career line and career. Careers are individual employment biographies. We attached no evaluative connotations or restrictions to the concept. It encompasses upward and downward mobility, job histories of all types, continuous as well as discontinuous employment histories. As a concept, career is not explanatory but merely descriptive of the sequence of jobs a person holds over his or her working lifetime. Careers are the grist for explanation—the material that we seek to understand.

Our study uses career line as a concept to explain some of the variation in people's careers. Career lines reference the patterns of job changes that people regularly make over the course of their work histories. Career line is a structural concept because it defines normative patterns of work-role entry, exit, rates of progression, job change, and work-role outcomes. The concept of career line offers a conceptual bridge between the larger structures in the economy—industries, occupations, labor markets and firms—and the expectations and behaviors of people in jobs. Career lines have their origins in larger structural arenas, yet they are the stage on which individual employment biographies are acted out.

Career lines do not unequivocally determine where people go in the labor market. Rather, they shape workers' expectations and behaviors. As workers, we are all more or less accurate observers of the career-line structure in the economy. We have some expectation that our present jobs will lead somewhere or that they will not. Some types of job moves are more likely, and others are less likely. As labor-force participants, we know career paths exist "out there."

It is not that we cannot deviate from the path. Indeed, we all know of at least one mail-room clerk who became vice-president. But we also know that type of move is unusual. Most of us are subject to a more restricted regime that determines where one can go from this job or that job. The collective perception of career lines is an interesting topic in its own right.

The most important goal of this book is to establish and investigate the concept of career line. The agenda for doing so came from Spilerman (1977), who earlier provided the most developed statement of the concept.

We approached the agenda items with two data sets and corresponding modes of analysis. The census data, in conjunction with the assumptions of the synthetic cohort, accommodated the estimation of the large number of detailed career lines for the economy. This strategy's costs were the strong assumptions of the synthetic cohort. The Career Development Study data complemented the census approach to career lines—that is, not allowing the great detail in job categories but containing a wealth of information from personal life histories—to permit study of how people's careers mesh with the career-line structure.

The analytical design for studying career lines involved a dual strategy. The census and Career Development data permitted independent yet complementary strategies for the validation of the career-line concept. Each design relied on a particular type of reasoning to validate the notion of career line. For the census data, we sought the identification of normative patterns of job progressions for detailed job categories but without the benefit of considering the differences among people that might explain aggregate job patterns. The Career Development data provided consideration for individual differences that generate job patterns but required aggregation by gender and sector to detect career-line differences. That we could detect empirical signal of career lines with two independent methods and data bases is stronger and more compelling support for a new concept than evidence based on a single method or data base. That there are threats to the validity of each method or alternate explanations for findings from each data set is undeniable. Yet an alternate explanation must go further, and the threat to validity is lessened if two separate sources offer support for a concept.

We began by defining several properties of career lines. The properties are features of career lines, distinct from causes and consequences of career lines or features of individual work histories. The elementary properties provide a basis for defining higher-order or derived concepts such as the order-disorder in career lines or careers. We defined five properties: size, differentiation, holding power, ports of entry and exit, and role continuity.

Size references variations in the volume of workers that moves through the career line. Size varies over developmental and historical time. *Differentiation* indexes the number and work course location of job transitions in a career line or set of career lines. *Holding power* refers to the probability of continuing in a career line. *Ports of entry and exit* refer to the age-specific labor force and non-labor force positions through which workers enter and exit career lines. As with other career-line properties, ports index statistically normative patterns of entry and exit. Ports of entry and exit vary in their age-width and work course location. *Work-role continuity* refers to the levels of role requirements, routines, and rewards associated with jobs in a career line. A review of literature found several research traditions and theoretical perspectives that contained hypotheses consistent with a career-line perspective. We illustrated several of the properties with a measure of career lines taken from the census data.

We next sought a more systematic empirical description of the variation in properties of career lines. We reasoned that a valid concept and measure would exhibit meaningful variation in several ways. We examined variations and properties over the work course, by both the major occupation group in which a career line had its origin or destination and the gender composition of the career line. The operational measures of elementary properties in the census data were fallible approximations to the concepts. For one property—size—the data were not well suited to examine variations. For another property—differentiation—the measure was weak, and for other properties, the measures held greater face validity.

We found some well-documented empirical patterns. Career lines contained a sharp increase in holding power over the work course, across socioeconomic levels, and by gender composition of the career line. Career lines followed by males and composed of higher-status jobs had somewhat higher holding power than female and lower-status career lines. Consistent with conventional wisdom, career lines contained a slight increase in differentiation during ages in the late twenties and thirties and then progressively less differentiation over the work course, perhaps corresponding to settling into the career. But the work-course variation in differentiation was not so large that it supported popular themes of midlife crises or career changes of any sizable fraction of the population at the same age. If such perspectives are valid, our data suggest they must be reconciled with the socioeconomic level of career lines because the age of maximum differentiation varied substantially for career lines in different occupation groups.

The measures for ports of entry and exit index the relative concentration versus diffuseness of origins to and destinations from career-line categories. We did not find a strong trend in the diffuseness of ports other than a decline in ports of entry and an increase in ports of exit during the last decade of the work course. Late in the work course, the recruitment sources for career lines were less dispersed across the labor force, in part, because the large ports of entry involving military, college, and non-labor force origins are much less traveled transitions. At the same time, ports of exit were more diffuse late in the work course, signaling a more varied pattern of job changing for older workers. We found that entry to career lines from out of the labor force increased slightly then declined steadily over the work course.

The patterns of entry and exit varied markedly by the major occupation group and gender composition of the career line. For example, higher-status and male career lines had more diffuse ports of entry early in the work course. Female career lines with clerical destinations contained a precipitous increase in the diffuseness of entry ports for workers in their forties. We interpreted these patterns as a more orderly and a more certain regime of job transitions for male and higher-status career lines in the years of high role responsibility during the middle of the work course. In contrast, female and some lower-status career lines contained an inverted U-shaped pattern of exits over the work course: more concentrated exit destinations early and late in the work course and more diffuse exit ports during the middle years of the work course. The major refuges for those entering career lines from out of the labor force are female, androgynous, clerical, and service career lines. The differences were strongest when many careers, in the popular sense of the term, are established during ages in the late twenties and thirties.

For the role continuity in career lines, we found well-documented patterns for earnings. Median earnings grow over the work course, more so for men than women, and more for high-status than low-status career-line locations. Additionally—patterns of growth aside—starting and average earnings are ordered by the status and sex composition of the career-line category: They are highest for predominantly male career lines, lowest for predominantly female career lines, and intermediate for androgynous career lines. In contrast, the skill distance of career-line transitions revealed only one major pattern: progressive decline over the work course. This held for all major occupation groups and for career lines of varying gender composition.

The portrait of career lines in the American economy is no more certain than the design and assumptions that generated it. Our data referred to the 1965-to-1970 quinquennium. We used a synthetic cohort to take the job transitions of successive five-year age cohorts and translate them into a synthetic work course. We doubt that the conclusions are far off the mark, but they probably do contain a modest level of distortion. Further, we have not adjusted inferences for the way the occupational structure has changed in size and job composition for successive age cohorts whose careers began as early as the 1920s and as late as 1970. The conclusions reflect both the intragenerational mobility regime and the age, job, and age-job compositional changes in the labor force over recent history. Both types of effects are meaningful sources of variation in the career-line structure. The data design simply precluded sorting out the effects of one from the other.

In short, the empirical description of career lines is probably more tentative than is usually the case for samples of this size and is bounded by the job-transition experiences of a set of age cohorts at a single point in history, 1965 to 1970. The conclusions are better viewed as hypotheses to be confirmed than as confirmed hypotheses. Applied to other age cohorts at historical points other than 1965 to 1970, the inferences are suggestive, not definitive. Yet, based on the empirical patterns in career lines, we were optimistic about the theoretical utility of the concept and proceeded with the research agenda.

In chapter 5, we examined several initial hypotheses about the origins of the career-line structure. From neoclassical literatures, we reasoned that career lines were among the devices that met the technical skill levels required by organizations and the economy. Career lines should provide a supply of labor at optimal skill levels for the efficient production of goods and services. From a neoclassical perspective, we expected variation in the properties of career lines to be structured around the skill level of jobs in the career line. Segmentation perspectives suggested that career lines are located in sectors of the economy. Sectors form from larger control imperatives in the economy. Hence, we expected variation in the properties of career lines by the sector location of jobs in the career line.

We found evidence for the two perspectives. The neoclassical predictions received some support for career-line holding power, ports of entry including entrance from out of the labor force, and role continuity as indexed by earnings. Sector predictions were supported for career-line holding power, ports of exit, entry from out of the labor force, and for indicators of role continuity. So to some extent, the data were consistent with the hypothesis that career lines are formed in response to the skill levels inherent in jobs. Further, the data were also consistent with the hypothesis that career lines are formed and maintained in sectors of the economy. The sector location of the career line shaped some of its features, particularly if the career line was located in the primary-independent versus secondary sector.

We hesitate to describe the support for predictions from either perspective as overwhelming. Perhaps more refined tests will produce such support. We also hesitate to say that one perspective was more successful than the other in explaining career-line variation. The conventional R^2 criterion for variance explained suggests both perspectives taken together leave substantial room for other hypotheses about the sources of career-line variation.

In the final part of the book, we shifted the focus to careers and career lines. Instead of directly making inferences about career lines, we used the career histories of Career Development Study respondents to inform the study of career lines. The goal of this part of the study was to describe how workers' careers are a joint product of personal resources and career lines.

Chapter 6 contained estimates of a baseline model for the early careers of men and women. The equations embodied the well-known status-attainment model (Sewell, Hauser, and Wolf 1980). The validation of status-attainment findings served several purposes. It provided a theoretical and empirical baseline for an expanded treatment of careers, one that explicitly takes career lines into account. Typical applications of this status-attainment model leave career and career line concepts unspecified. Most models ignore the underlying dynamic model when first job and current job are included in the same equation. The validation provided a comparison point to evaluate the properties of a new data set. Finally, the validation offered an independent replication of an important research model but on a more recent sample from a different part of the nation.

In general, we found more similarity than difference between our estimates and those in other studies. We confirmed many of the gender differences found in other studies for the way men and women attain years of schooling and occupational status. On balance, we considered the validation of the data set successful. If there was a difference between our estimates of the status-attainment model and earlier studies, it was less pronounced differences between men and women, particularly for educational outcomes. Career Development Study women aspired to, received encouragement for, and actually obtained higher education at rates higher than earlier cohorts of high school students and more closely approximated the rates of men than did earlier cohorts. Further, some of the structural parameters of the educational-attainment process contained less of a gender difference than did past studies. We interpreted the smaller gender differences in terms of changes in American society in the last ten to fifteen years, particularly in the educational arena.

Yet some gender differences persist as large as those estimated in other studies, particularly in the occupational arena. Of substantive importance to the study of careers are the occupational status returns to years of formal schooling. Men received a larger status return to formal schooling than women in their first job and current job at about age 30. Men received twice the status return in their first job, which replicates previous studies (Sewell, Hauser, and Wolf 1980), and nearly twice the status return to schooling in their current jobs, which is at variance with some previous estimates. Schooling is the most important personal resource for attainment in the work career. How would the conclusions about schooling change in a more refined model, one that took into account career lines and the dynamic nature of careers?

Chapter 7 pursued a more refined model of careers. The model was more comprehensive in four ways. First, the formulation and estimation were explicitly dynamic. A dynamic differential equation model permitted the study of *change* in work-role outcomes over time. Second, we sought a formulation that plausibly explained how social structure embodied in career lines and personal resources combined to shape careers. We used Sørensen's (1977) vacancy competition model as a framework. Third, the formulation considered both the resources of workers before and after entry into the labor force. Finally, we expanded consideration of work-role outcomes from the traditional measure of socioeconomic status to also include two other features of role continuity: the complexity and skill level of work.

Sørensen's (1977) model is a theory of the structure of inequality and the process of attainment. In brief, it says that the valued job rewards that contribute to work-role continuity are distributed like a pyramid (exponentially) in society. Job vacancies that carry opportunities for growth in rewards move in the social structure (vacancy chains). Workers are exposed to the structure of inequality and the opportunity regime by virtue of the level or position in social structure that they occupy and the rate at which opportunities arrive at that level. We reasoned that career lines that involve job changes with gains in rewards are vacancy chains. In extreme form, each career line or career-line set in the economy contains a potentially unique opportunity level or rate at which vacancies that allow reward growth occur. Finally, the theory postulates that the extent to which people take advantage of opportunities for gains in job rewards depends on personal resources such as schooling, ability, and background. Thus the eventual achievement levels in people's careers depend not only on personal resources but on the structural opportunity levels embodied in career lines.

Our design generated separate estimates for men and women and for each gender within sectors for port of entry jobs. We assumed that the first full-time job after the completion of formal schooling captured port of entry jobs to generic classes of career lines. That is, each set of estimates reflects a group of career lines or a different vacancy competition regime. Based on the model and results from earlier chapters, we made hypotheses about several key parameters: the opportunity level or rate of vacancy occurrence, personal resources, maximum predicted achievement levels, and the instantaneous and career returns to formal schooling and degree certification.

We found support for the vacancy competition model and for a career-line perspective. For example, men have higher opportunity levels than women have for status and complexity reward growth. Port of entry jobs to career lines in the primary-independent sector carried higher opportunity levels than port of entry jobs in the primary-subordinate and secondary sectors. More often than not, men experience vacancy occurrence rates for reward growth within sectors that were higher than the rates experienced by women. These outcomes were largely consistent with expectation. They were fully consistent with a perspective that says career lines shape individual careers.

The dynamic model permitted additional and more fine-grained interpretations than could be obtained from the baseline model. For status and complexity outcomes, women have personal resources for achievement that are greater than or nearly equal to those of men. Yet because men have more opportunities for status and complexity growth—by virtue of the career lines they occupy—their eventual levels of status and complexity over the career will surpass those of women. For skill growth, men enter the labor force in much more skilled jobs than women and have higher resource levels for skill growth. Women only modestly narrow the gap over the work course even though they have higher opportunity levels for skill growth.

The advantage of an explicit dynamic formulation can be seen in the results for returns to formal schooling and degrees. In the baseline model we found that men received about twice the status return to a year of formal schooling compared with women. In the dynamic model, the instantaneous effect of schooling on status growth was about twice as much for men as for women. When considered over the career—that is, taking into account the higher opportunity levels of men, which act as a multiplier on the instantaneous effect—men received nearly three times the total return to formal schooling as women. The baseline model, by virtue of ignoring the opportunity level differences in career lines, may underestimate the real gender difference in returns to formal schooling by one-third to one-half of the real difference. Many similar accentuations or levelings of differences over the career occurred for the role returns to degree credentials. Finally, we note that the outcomes for status, complexity, and skill, when compared, are related but hardly synonymous. It would be erroneous to conclude that the outcomes for socioeconomic status reflect the career profiles well, the career-lines effects, or the importance of specific personal resources for other role outcomes.

The dynamic model outcomes provided an independent line of support for a career-line perspective. The model offered a plausible logic for the way that personal resources and career lines combine to shape careers. The analyses considered multiple work-role outcomes and provided for the study of change in role outcomes over time. Considered in conjunction with evidence from the earlier chapters, the dynamic model outcomes suggest that the career-line concept and perspective warrant further attention and investigation.

In the next section we outline the importance of a career-line perspective for the conventional views of careers and speculate on some areas for further investigation and policy implication.

Prospect

The value of a concept is no greater than what it can offer to contemporary thinking about a topic. If whole areas of inquiry are rejected in the press to advance a new concept, then the advocates are asking too much and offering too little. No less important, the initial proposal for conceptual or methodological reform is most often found wanting or many of the crucial details lacking. But in the process of finding that ideas are wanting or the details lacking, other new and better ideas are found, and there is incremental progress in the scientific process by the scholarly community that joins in the dialogue. Our work is no different. If at the beginning, there existed a new concept, some ideas, and some fuzziness, there now exists a used concept, more ideas, and still some fuzziness. But along the way, some things were learned that speak to conventional approaches to careers.

Career as Personal Preference and Life Stage

Among the premises that underlie many psychological and vocational-development approaches to careers are the trait-factor assumption and the notion of life stage (Super 1957; Holland 1973). The trait-factor assumption suggests people (personality) and work environments fall into types. The quality of the match between personality and environment motivates individual behavior and accounts for the variation in career experiences. The life stage notion suggests that people pass through stages of career development during specific ages, exhibiting the characteristic behaviors while in each stage (such as stabilization or consolidation). In each assumption, personal choice and the free actor are paramount considerations.

The social-science community has not taken these ideas very seriously as accurate descriptions of how careers work. Yet these ideas more than any others from social science form the cornerstones of conventional guidance counseling. The advocates and their ideas are well known and vocal in the American public and policymaking domains.

The career-line concept and our evidence are based on neither the trait-factor or life stage assumptions as found in vocational development. Career lines are "out there" as normative patterns of jobs staying and changing. They are not merely the aggregate result of many personal choices, although our culture and ideology may convince us so. Rather, there is evidence that career lines exist, that large numbers of workers follow these normative paths among jobs, and that they form partly in response to the organization of work, the logic of production in firms, and the economic sectors and labor markets in the economy as these are shaped by larger structural forces. Rather than personal choice being the paramount consideration in the course of the career, the prior network or the career-line structure is paramount. Personal choice occurs within the framework of the career-line structure. The fruitful research questions, we submit, pertain to how the career-line structure originates, changes, and is maintained, and how personal choices occur within it.

Our data were no more consistent with monolithic notions of life stage or notions of critical ages for "career change" that characterize any sizable fraction of workers. There are meaningful age variations in career-line properties such as the work course increases in holding power or the decrease in skill distance, but they are continuous over the age range rather than discrete to a particular age. If the variations in career-line phenomena occur around discrete life stages, then our data suggest that such explanations must take into account why the variations are specific to career lines of one gender composition and not another and to career lines of one socioeconomic level and not others. Examples include the precipitous increase in the diffuseness of entry portals during the forties for clerical career lines but not others; the peak in career-line differentiation during the middle thirties for managers and skilled career lines but different age-specific peaks for other career lines; or the great difference in career-line differentiation early in the work course for female but not male or androgynous career lines. The life stage notion may eventually prove fruitful, but many present versions of the thesis are simply not accurate descriptions of career-line phenomena.

Career as Orderly Progression and Individual Achievement

The notion that one has a career only if the progression of jobs is orderly has its origins in the case studies of a decade or more ago and is still common in occupational sociology (Hall 1975). A career-line perspective suggests another approach to orderly progression in the career. Rather than restricting careers to a subgroup of the population, those who have ever been employed have a career merely because of their employment biography. The career more or less approximates patterns in the career-line structure. Order might be more profitably defined in terms of the nature of this approximation.

Alternately, career lines can be studied in terms of their elementary properties. "Order" and other global designations such as dead end or career blockage might be more rigorously conceptualized as derived features of career lines, constituted by different mixtures of elementary property variations. Interesting research questions include the extent to which workers' perceptions of the career-line structure are accurate and the consequences of such, or the antecedents and consequences of the career closely or not closely approximating career-line patterns.

We gave detailed attention at several points to individual achievement approaches as found in the human-capital and status-attainment paradigms. Career and career line are undeveloped concepts in these traditions. The unit of explanation and analysis is the individual. Social structure plays a distant role. A career-line perspective provides a way for the study of individual achievement to bring social structure into sharper focus. People may attain first jobs as suggested in the status-attainment tradition, but once entered, first jobs and jobs early in the work course act as ports of entry to career lines. The exposure times to different opportunity regimes and to the career-line structure are underway.

Sørensen's model offers a starting point to inform the study of individual achievement with the structural perspective implied by career lines. There are several logical next steps in advancing the theory and application of the model. Our application of the model links only one feature of career lines to careers: the rate of occurrence of job opportunities that offer growth in rewards. How can the vacancy competition model accommodate other properties of career lines such as differentiation or ports of entry and exit? Our ordinary least squares estimates involve statistical problems. More complicated estimation strategies can solve some of the problems, such as the possible inconsistency and inefficiency of estimates. Other problems, such as tests of significance and the invariance of parameters under certain transformations, will require developments in statistical theory. Finally, we made eight sets of estimates for the model for three role outcomes. A logical extension would expand the estimates to other population subgroups, additional role outcomes, and more disaggregated groups of career lines.

Careers as Labor Markets

We also gave detailed attention to several ideas from segmentation perspectives. Most segmentation writers hypothesize qualitatively different work histories for one type of labor market or sector compared with another, but actual tests of the hypothesis and accumulation of evidence on its operation are infrequent. Perhaps one of the reasons is the continuing debate over the definition and measurement of markets and sectors. Althauser and Kalleberg (1981a) offer one of the more careful reviews and attempts at resolution. They note that some definitions of markets and sectors equate sector with career lines of a particular type. Other definitions treat career lines as consequences of the organization of labor markets or economic sectors. Our study of career lines does not directly speak to this issue. Whether cause or consequence, we think the career-line perspective can inform segmentation perspectives. Career-line concepts offer segmentation perspectives a more explicit linkage between social structure and individual behavior without, in Granovetter's (1981, p. 20) terms, an immediate causal reductionism to the level of individual attitudes and work behaviors.

Althauser and Kalleberg (1981a) go on to offer their redefinition of an internal labor market, one we submit could readily be investigated in the framework of career-line concepts and measures. In the redefinition, internal labor markets refer to clusters of jobs. Three structural features define a cluster of jobs as an internal labor market: a job ladder that permits entry only at the bottom and contains a progressive development of knowledge or skill with movement up the ladder. We submit that identification of "clusters of jobs" should be in terms of career-line criteria, that is, statistically normative patterns of job transition. The criterion of "entrance at the bottom" is one of age-specific concentration of ports of entry and is directly measurable as such.

Finally, skill progression in career lines is an issue of role continuity, and the examples in chapters 4, 5, and 7 offer precedent. In short, a career-line perspective is consistent with current studies of segmentation, and career-line concepts and measures have the potential to inform segmentation hypotheses.

Final Notes

Our work used young concepts and relatively new data sets and analyses. Thus it would be presumptuous to attribute finality or a high degree of certainty to specific conclusions. Future work may refine these. We encourage and invite this. Our most certain conclusion suggests that the concept of career line is very reasonable and promising. It can help explain aspects of work life that heretofore unduly stretched the credibility of individual or structural explanations, taken alone.

It would be presumptuous to make specific policy recommendations on the basis of this type of work; yet we feel there are two lines of policy that stand to benefit from a career-line perspective. First, the contemporary guidance counseling enterprise is at variance with a career-line perspective. The logic of such counseling, when it occurs, stresses personal choice, assumes a single job or occupation for a lifetime, and pretends that one gets where one is going in the career, directly and fairly quickly in age terms.

The research on career lines suggests revisions in each of these assumptions. Choice is not paramount and may play a relatively minor role once the "decision" is made to enter a career line. If one "chooses" to leave— and it is amazing how some career lines foster so many more "choices" to leave—then where one goes is far from an open contest, statistically. The notion of a single job with the same employer over the work course is fiction, for it characterizes a very small fraction of workers. Finally, we find sizable variations in the rates of progression, patterns of entry and exit, opportunity levels for reward growth, and returns to personal resources, around the social and institutional axes of gender, age, sector, and the socioeconomic and skill levels in career lines. Some change in the counseling enterprise would seem appropriate in order to recognize these other aspects of "choice."

Second, a career-line perspective carries implications for the tractableness of inequalities in work life. To the extent that career lines schedule and shape career outcomes, then societal manipulations of personal resource distributions such as schooling are limited in their efficacy and occur in the context of the career-line structure. As Sørensen (1977) has noted in discussing policy implications of his model, the returns to personal resources over the career are highly conditioned by the opportunity regime in which workers enact their employment biographies.

Policy modifications of the career-line structure are likely to be difficult. At several points in the discussion we identified but did not analytically separate two sources of variation in mobility regimes: changes in the distributions of people to jobs (such as growth or decline in the economy) and net of this, the underlying transition regime that probabilistically links one job to another. Featherman and Hauser (1978) found that a large portion of the changes in upward intergenerational and intragenerational mobility experienced by recent cohorts of American men could be traced to variations in the distributions of people to jobs rather than to changes in the underlying regime. Career-line patterns may involve many of the same sources of change and are likely no more tractable to conscious policy manipulation. Instead, for career lines as for other patterns of inequality—whatever the prospects for programmed social change—understanding the phenomena is the first course of action.

Bibliography

Alexander, Karl L., and Eckland, Bruce K. "Sex Differences in the Educational Attainment Process." *American Sociological Review* 39(1974): 668-682.

Alexander, Karl L.; Eckland, Bruce K.; and Griffin, Larry J. "The Wisconsin Model of Socioeconomic Achievement: A Replication." *American Journal of Sociology* 81(1975):324-342.

Althauser, Robert P., and Kalleberg, Arne L. "Firms, Occupations and the Structure of Labor Markets: A Conceptual Analysis and Research Agenda." In *Sociological Perspectives on Labor Markets*, edited by Ivar Berg. New York: Academic Press, 1981*a*.

————. "Studying Labor Markets and Careers within Firms: Strategies, Issues, and Implications." Paper presented at the Annual Meetings of the American Sociological Association, 1981*b*, Toronto.

Alwin, Duane F., and Hauser, Robert M. "The Decomposition of Effects in Path Analysis." *American Sociological Review* 40(1975):37-47.

Angrist, Shirley S., and Almquist, Elizabeth M. *Careers and Contingencies: How College Women Juggle with Gender*. New York: Dunellen, 1975.

Averitt, Robert T. *The Dual Economy*. New York: Norton, 1968.

Baron, James N., and Bielby, William T. "Bringing the Firms Back In: Stratification, Segmentation, and the Organization of Work." *American Sociological Review* 45(1980):737-765.

————. "Workers and Machines: Dimensions and Determinants of Technical Relations in the Workplace." *American Sociological Review* 47 (1982): in press.

Beck, E.M.; Horan, Patrick M.; and Tolbert, Charles M. II. "Stratification in a Dual Economy: A Sectoral Model of Earnings Determination." *American Sociological Review* 43(1978):704-720.

————. "Industrial Segmentation and Labor Market Discrimination." *Social Problems* 28(1980):113-130.

Becker, Gary S. *Human Capital: A Theoretical and Empirical Analysis, with Special Reference to Education*. 2d ed. New York: Columbia University Press, 1975.

Berg, Ivar, ed. *Sociological Perspectives on Labor Markets*. New York: Academic Press, 1981.

Bibb, Robert, and Form, William H. "The Effects of Industrial, Occupational, and Sex Stratification on Wages in Blue-Collar Markets." *Social Forces* 55(1977):974-996.

Bielby, William T., and Baron, James N. "Economic 'Dualism' and Work Organization: Case Studies From the Core." Paper presented at the

Annual Meetings of the American Sociological Association, 1980, New York.

Bielby, William T.; Hauser, Robert M.; and Featherman, David L. "Response Errors of Black and Nonblack Males in Models of the Intergenerational Transmission of Socioeconomic Status." *American Journal of Sociology* 82(1977):1242-1288.

Blau, Peter M., and Duncan, Otis D. *The American Occupational Structure*. New York: Wiley, 1967.

Blau, Peter M., and Schoenherr, Richard. *The Structure of Organizations*. New York: Basic Books, 1971.

Bowles, Samuel, and Gintis, Herbert. *Schooling in Capitalist America: Educational Reform and the Contradictions of Economic Life*. New York: Basic Books, 1976.

Cain, Glen G. "The Challenge of Segmented Labor Market Theories to Orthodox Theory." *Journal of Economic Literature* 14(1976): 1215-1257.

Cain, Pamela S., and Treiman, Donald J. "The *Dictionary of Occupational Titles* as a Source of Occupational Data." *American Sociological Review* 46(1981):253-278.

Call, Vaughn R.A.; Otto, Luther B.; and Spenner, Kenneth I. *Tracking Respondents: A Multi-Method Approach*. Lexington, Mass.: Lexington Books, D.C. Heath, 1982.

Chinoy, Ely. *Automobile Workers and the American Dream*. New York: Doubleday, 1955.

Coleman, James S. *Introduction to Mathematical Sociology*. New York: Free Press of Glencoe, 1964.

_____ . "The Mathematical Study of Change." In *Methodology in Social Research*, edited by Hubert M. Blalock, Jr., and Ann B. Blalock, pp. 428-478. New York: McGraw-Hill, 1968.

Collins, Randall. *The Credential Society: An Historical Sociology of Education and Stratification*. New York: Academic Press, 1979.

Coser, Rose Laub. "The Complexity of Roles as a Seedbed of Individual Autonomy." In *The Idea of Social Structure: Papers in Honor of Robert K. Merton*, edited by Lewis A. Coser, pp. 236-263. New York: Harcourt, 1975.

Davis, Kingsley, and Moore, Wilbert, E. "Some Principles of Stratification." *American Sociological Review* 2(1945):242-249.

Doeringer, Peter B., and Piore, Michael J. *Internal Labor Markets and Manpower Analysis*. Lexington, Mass.: Lexington Books, D.C. Heath, 1971.

Duncan, Otis Dudley. "A Socioeconomic Index for All Occupations." In *Occupations and Social Status*, edited by Albert J. Reiss, Jr., pp. 109-138. New York: Free Press, 1961.

――――. "Methodological Issues in the Analysis of Social Mobility." In *Social Structure and Mobility in Economic Development*, edited by Neil J. Smelser and Seymour Martin Lipset, pp. 51-97. Chicago: Aldine, 1966.

――――. "Social Stratification and Mobility." In *Indicators of Social Change*, edited by Eleanor B. Sheldon and Wilbert E. Moore, pp. 675-719. New York: Russell Sage Foundation, 1968.

Duncan, Otis D.; Featherman, David L.; and Duncan, Beverly. *Socioeconomic Background and Achievement*. New York: Seminar Press, 1972.

Eckaus, Richard S. *Estimating the Returns to Education: A Disaggregated Approach*. Berkeley, Calif.: The Carnegie Commission on Higher Education, 1973.

Edwards, Richard C. *Contested Terrain: The Transformation of the Workplace in the Twentieth Century*. New York: Basic Books, 1979.

Featherman, David L. "A Research Note: A Social Structural Model for the Socioeconomic Career." *American Journal of Sociology* 77(1971): 293-304.

――――. "Comments on Models for the Socioeconomic Career." *American Sociological Review* 38(1973):785-791.

Featherman, David L., and Hauser, Robert M. "Sexual Inequalities and Socioeconomic Achievement in the U.S., 1962-1973." *American Sociological Review* 41(1976):462-483.

――――. "The Measurement of Occupation in Social Surveys." In *The Process of Stratification: Trends and Analyses*, edited by R.M. Hauser and D.L. Featherman, pp. 51-80. New York: Academic Press, 1977.

――――. *Opportunity and Change*. New York: Academic Press, 1978.

Field, Alexander James. "Industrialization and Skill Intensity: The Case of Massachusetts." *The Journal of Human Resources* 15(1980):149-175.

Fligstein, Neil; Hicks, Alexander; and Morgan, Phil. "Towards a Theory of Income Determination." Mimeographed. National Opinion Research Center, 1982.

Fligstein, Neil, and Wolf, Wendy. "Sex Similarities in Occupational Attainment: Are the Results Due to the Restriction of the Sample to Employed Women?" *Social Science Research* 7(1978):197-212.

Form, William H., and Miller, Delbert C. "Occupational Career Patterns as a Sociological Instrument." *American Journal of Sociology* 54(1949): 317-329.

Freedman, Marcia K. *Labor Markets: Segments and Shelters*. Montclair, N.J.: Allanheld, Osmun & Company, 1976.

Freeman, Richard B., and Medoff, James L. "New Estimates of Private Sector Unionism in the United States." *Industrial and Labor Relations Review* 32(1979):143-174.

Gaertner, Karen N. "The Structure of Organizational Careers." *Sociology of Education* 53(1980):7-20.

Goldberg, Samuel. *Introduction to Difference Equations.* New York: Wiley, 1958.

Goldner, Fred. "Demotion in Industrial Management." *American Sociological Review* 30(1965):714-724.

Grandjean, Burke D. "History and Career in a Bureaucratic Labor Market." *American Journal of Sociology* 86(1981):1057-1092.

Granovetter, Mark. "Toward a Sociological Theory of Income Differences." In *Sociological Perspectives on Labor Markets,* edited by Ivar Berg, pp. 11-48. New York: Academic Press, 1981.

Gross, Edward. "Plus Ca Change . . .? The Sexual Structure of Occupations Over Time." *Social Problems* 16(1968):198-208.

Halaby, Charles N. "Dynamic Models and Attainment in the Workplace." *Social Science Research* 9(1980):1-36.

Hall, Oswald. "The Stages of a Medical Career." *American Journal of Sociology* 55(1948):243-253.

Hall, Richard H. *Occupations and the Social Structure.* (1959). 2d ed. Englewood Cliffs, N.J.: Prentice-Hall, 1975.

Haller, Archibald O., and Portes, Alejandro. "Status Attainment Processes." *Sociology of Education* 46(1973):51-91.

Haller, Archibald O., and Spenner, Kenneth I. "Occupational Income Differentiation in Status Attainment." *Rural Sociology* 42(1977): 517-535.

Hannan, Michael, T., and Tuma, Nancy Brandon. "Methods for Temporal Analysis." In *Annual Review of Sociology,* vol. 5, edited by Alex Inkeles, James Coleman, and Ralph H. Turner, pp. 303-328. Palo Alto, Calif.: Annual Reviews, Inc., 1979.

Hannan, Michael T., and Young, Alice A. "Estimation in Panel Models: Results on Pooling Cross-Sections and Time Series." In *Sociological Methodology 1977,* edited by David R. Heise, pp. 52-83. San Francisco: Jossey-Bass, 1977.

Hanushek, Eric A., and Jackson, John E. *Statistical Methods for Social Scientists.* New York: Academic Press, 1977.

Heckman, James J. "Sample Selection Bias as a Specification Error." *Econometrica* 47(1979):153-161.

Henderson, James M., and Quandt, Richard E. *Microeconomic Theory: A Mathematical Approach.* 2d ed. 1958. Reprint. New York: McGraw-Hill, 1971.

Hodson, Randy. "Labor in the Monopoly, Competitive, and State Sectors of Production." *Politics and Society* 9(1978):429-480.

Hogan, Dennis P. *Transitions and Social Change.* New York: Academic Press, 1981.

Holland, John L. *Making Vocational Choices: A Theory of Careers.* Englewood Cliffs, N.J.: Prentice-Hall, 1973.

Horan, Patrick M. "Is Status Attainment Research Atheoretical?" *American Sociological Review* 43(1978):534-541.

Hout, Michael, and Morgan, William R. "Race and Sex Variations in the Causes of the Expected Attainments of High School Seniors." *American Journal of Sociology* 81(1975):364-394.

Janowitz, Morris. *The Professional Soldier: A Social and Political Portrait*. New York: Free Press, 1960.

Jencks, Christopher. *Inequality: A Reassessment of the Effect of Family and Schooling in America*. New York: Basic Books, 1972.

_____ . *Who Gets Ahead? The Determinants of Economic Success in America*. New York: Basic Books, 1979.

Kalleberg, Arne L., and Hudis, Paula M. "Wage Change in the Late Career: A Model for the Outcomes of Job Sequences." *Social Science Research* 8(1979):16-40.

Kalleberg, Arne L., and Sørensen, Aage B. "The Sociology of Labor Markets." In *Annual Review of Sociology*, vol. 5, edited by Alex Inkeles, James Coleman, and Ralph H. Turner, pp. 351-379. Palo Alto, Calif.: Annual Reviews, Inc., 1979.

Kalleberg, Arne L.; Wallace, Michael; and Althauser, Robert P. "Economic Segmentation, Worker Power and Income Inequality." *American Journal of Sociology* 87(1981):651-683.

Kanter, Rosabeth Moss. *Men and Women of the Corporation*. New York: Basic Books, 1977.

Kaufman, Robert L.; Hodson, Randy; and Fligstein, Neil. "Defrocking Dualism: A New Approach to Defining Industrial Sectors." *Social Science Research* 10(1981):1-31.

Kaufman, Robert L., and Spilerman, Seymour. "The Age Structures of Occupations and Jobs." *American Journal of Sociology* 87(1982):827-851.

Kelley, Jonathan. "Causal Chain Models for the Socioeconomic Career." *American Sociological Review* 38(1973a):481-493.

_____ . "History, Causal Chains and Careers: A Reply." *American Sociological Review* 38(1973b):791-796.

Kerckhoff, Alan C. "The Status Attainment Process: Socialization or Allocation?" *Social Forces* 55(1976):368-381.

Kerr, Clark. "The Balkanization of Labor Markets." In *Labor Mobility and Economic Opportunity*, edited by E.W. Bakke, et al., pp. 92-110. New York: Wiley, 1954.

Kerr, Clark; Dunlop, John T.; Harbison, Frederick H.; and Meyers, Charles A. *Industrialism and Industrial Man*. New York: Oxford University Press, 1964.

Kimberly, John R. "Organizational Size and the Structuralist Perspective: A Review, Critique, and Proposal." *Administrative Science Quarterly* 21(1976):571-597.

Kluegel, James R. "The Causes and Cost of Racial Exclusion from Job Authority." *American Sociological Review* 43(1978):285-301.

Kohn, Melvin L. *Class and Conformity*. 2d ed. Chicago and London: University of Chicago Press, 1977.

Kohn, Melvin L., and Schooler, Carmi. "Occupational Experience and Psychological Functioning: An Assessment of Reciprocal Effects." *American Sociological Review* 38(1973):97-118.

_____ . "The Reciprocal Effects of Substantive Complexity of Work and Intellectual Flexibility: A Longitudinal Assessment." *American Journal of Sociology* 84(1978):24-52.

Leigh, Duane E. *An Analysis of the Determinants of Occupational Upgrading*. New York: Academic Press, 1978.

Levinson, Daniel J. *The Seasons of a Man's Life*. New York: Knopf, 1978.

Lipset, Seymour M., and Bendix, Reinhard. "Social Mobility and Occupational Career Patterns. I. Stability of Jobholding." *American Journal of Sociology* 57(1952a):366-374.

_____ . "Social Mobility and Occupational Career Patterns. II. Social Mobility." *American Journal of Sociology* 57(1952b):494-504.

Lipset, Seymour Martin, and Malm, F. Theodore. "First Jobs and Career Patterns." *American Journal of Economics and Sociology* 14(1954): 247-261.

March, James C., and March, James G. "Almost Random Careers: The Wisconsin School Superintendency, 1940-1972." *Administrative Science Quarterly* 22(1977):377-409.

Marini, Margaret Mooney. "Sex Differences in the Process of Occupational Attainment: A Closer Look." *Social Science Research* 9(1980):307-361.

Martin, N.H., and Strauss, Anselm L. "Patterns of Mobility within Industrial Organizations." In *Industrial Man*, edited by W. Lloyd Warner and N.H. Martin, pp. 85-101. New York: Harper & Row, 1959.

Mayer, Thomas. "Models in Intragenerational Mobility." In *Sociological Theories in Progress*, vol. 2, edited by Joseph Berger, Morris Zelditch, Jr., and Bo Anderson, pp. 308-357. Boston: Houghton Mifflin, 1972.

McClendon, McKee J. "The Occupational Status Attainment Processes of Males and Females." *American Sociological Review* 41(1976):52-64.

McLaughlin, Steven D. "Occupational Sex Identification and the Assessment of Male and Female Earnings Inequality." *American Sociological Review* 43(1978):909-921.

Miller, Ann R.; Treiman, Donald J.; Cain, Pamela S.; and Roos, Patricia A.,eds. *Work, Jobs, and Occupations: A Critical Review of the Dictionary of Occupational Titles*. Washington, D.C.: National Academy Press, 1980.

Miller, Joanne; Schooler, Carmi; Kohn, Melvin L.; and Miller, Karen A. "Women and Work: The Psychological Effects of Occupational Conditions." *American Journal of Sociology* 85(1979):66-94.

Mincer, Jacob. *Schooling, Experience, and Earnings*. New York: Columbia University Press, 1974.

Neugarten, Bernice L., and Datan, Nancy. "Sociological Perspectives on the Life Cycle." In *Life-Span Developmental Psychology: Personality and Socialization*, edited by Paul B. Baltes and K. Warner Schaie, pp. 53-69. New York: Academic Press, 1973.

Nielsen, Francois, and Rosenfeld, Rachel A. "Substantive Interpretations of Differential Equation Models." *American Sociological Review* 46(1981):159-174.

Norwood, Janet L. "The Job Outlook for College Graduates through 1990." *Occupational Outlook Quarterly* 23(1979):2-7.

Otto, Luther B.; Call, Vaughn R.A.; and Spenner, Kenneth I. *Design for a Study of Entry into Careers*. Lexington, Mass.: Lexington Books, D.C. Heath, 1981.

Otto, Luther B., and Haller, Archibald, O. "Evidence for a Social Psychological View of the Status Attainment Process: Four Studies Compared." *Social Forces* 57(1979):887-914.

Otto, Luther B.; Spenner, Kenneth I.; and Call, Vaughn R.A. *Career Line Prototypes*. Boys Town, Nebr.: Boys Town Center, 1980.

Palmer, Gladys L. *Labor Mobility in Six Cities*. New York: Social Science Research Council, 1954.

Parsons, Talcott. *Essays in Sociological Theory*. 1949. Revised edition. New York: Free Press of Glencoe, 1954.

Peng, Samuel S.; Fetters, William B.; and Kolstad, Andrew I. *High School and Beyond: A National Longitudinal Study for the 1980's*. Washington, D.C.: National Center for Education Statistics, 1981.

Piore, Michael J. "Notes for a Theory of Labor Market Stratification." In *Labor Market Segmentation*, edited by Richard C. Edwards et al., pp. 125-150. Lexington, Mass.: D.C. Heath, 1975.

President's Committee on Employment of the Handicapped. *One in Eleven: Handicapped Adults in America*. Washington, D.C.: U.S. Government Printing Office, 1977.

Reich, Michael; Gordon, David M.; and Edwards, Richard C. "Dual Labor Markets: A Theory of Labor Market Segmentation." *American Economic Review* 63(1973):359-365.

Roe, Anne, *The Psychology of Occupations*. New York: Wiley, 1957.

Roos, Patricia A. "Gender Differences in Intergenerational Occupational Mobility: A Cross-National Study." Paper presented at the Annual Meetings of the American Sociological Association, 1981, Toronto.

Rosenbaum, James E. "Tournament Mobility: Career Patterns in a Corporation." *Administrative Science Quarterly* 24(1979a):220-241.

_____ . "Organizational Career Mobility: Promotion Chances in a Corporation during Periods of Growth and Contraction." *American Journal of Sociology* 85(1979b):21-48.

Rosenberg, S. "The Dual Labor Market: Its Existence and Consequences." Ph.D. dissertation, University of California, Berkeley, 1975.

Rosenfeld, Rachel A. "Women's Occupational Careers: Individual and Structural Explanations." *Sociology of Work and Occupations* 6 (1979): 283-311.

———. "Race and Sex Differences in Career Dynamics." *American Sociological Review* 45(1980):583-609.

Rosenfeld, Rachel A., and Nielsen, Francois. "Inequality and Careers: A Dynamic Model of Socioeconomic Achievement." Mimeographed. National Opinion Research Center, 1981.

Rumberger, Russell W., and Carnoy, Martin. "Segmentation in the U.S. Labour Market: Its Effects on the Mobility and Earnings of Whites and Blacks." *Cambridge Journal of Economics* 4 (1980):117-132.

Rush, James C.; Peacock, Andrew C.; and Milkovich, George T. "Career Stages: A Partial Test of Levinson's Model of Life/Career Stages." *Journal of Vocational Behavior* 16(1980):347-359.

Sewell, William H.; Haller, Archibald O.; and Portes, Alejandro. "The Educational and Early Occupational Attainment Process." *American Sociological Review* 34(1969):82-92.

Sewell, William H., and Hauser, Robert M. "Causes and Consequences of Higher Education: Models of the Status Attainment Process." *American Journal of Agricultural Economics* 54(1972):851-861.

———. *Education, Occupation, and Earnings: Achievement in the Early Career.* New York: Academic Press, 1975.

Sewell, William H.; Hauser, Robert M.; and Wolf, Wendy C. "Sex, Schooling, and Occupational Status." *American Journal of Sociology* 86(1980):551-583.

Sofer, Cyril. *Men in Mid-Career: A Study of British Managers and Technical Specialists.* Cambridge: Cambridge University Press, 1970.

Sørensen, Aage B. "A Model for Occupational Careers." *American Journal of Sociology* 80(1974):44-57.

———. "The Structure of Intragenerational Mobility." *American Sociological Review* 40(1975a):456-471.

———. "Growth in Occupational Achievement: Social Mobility or Investment in Human Capital." In *Social Indicators Model*, edited by Kenneth C. Land and Seymour Spilerman, pp. 335-360. New York: Russell Sage Foundation, 1975b.

———. "The Structure of Inequality and the Process of Attainment." *American Sociological Review* 42(1977):965-978.

———. "Mathematical Models in Sociology." In *Annual Review of Sociology*, edited by Ralph H. Turner, James Coleman, and Renee C. Fox, pp. 345-371. Palo Alto, Calif.: Annual Reviews, Inc., 1978.

_____ . "A Model and a Metric for the Analysis of the Intragenerational Status Attainment Process." *American Journal of Sociology* 85(1979): 361-384.

_____ . "Career Patterns and Job Mobility: Toward a Theory of Attainment and Opportunity." Paper presented at the Japan-U.S. Conference on Social Stratification and Mobility, 1980, Hawaii.

Sørensen, Aage B., and Tuma, Nancy Brandon. "Labor Market Structures and Job Mobility." Paper presented at the Ninth World Congress of Sociology, 1978, Uppsala, Sweden.

Spaeth, Joe L. "Vertical Differentiation among Occupations." *American Sociological Review* 44(1979):746-762.

Spenner, Kenneth I. "From Generation to Generation: The Transmission of Occupation." Ph.D. dissertation, University of Wisconsin, 1977.

_____ . "Temporal Changes in Work Content." *American Sociological Review* 44(1979):968-975.

_____ . "Occupational Characteristics and Classification Systems: New Uses of the *Dictionary of Occupational Titles* in Social Research." *Sociological Methods & Research* 9(1980):239-264.

_____ . "Occupations, Role Characteristics, and Intergenerational Transmission." *Sociology of Work and Occupations* 8(1981):89-112.

Spenner, Kenneth I., and Featherman, David L. "Achievement Ambitions." In *Annual Review of Sociology*, vol. 4, edited by Ralph H. Turner, James Coleman, and Renee C. Fox, pp. 373-420. Palo Alto, Calif.: Annual Reviews, Inc., 1978.

Spilerman, Seymour. "Careers, Labor Market Structure, and Socioeconomic Achievement." *American Journal of Sociology* 83(1977):551-593.

Stewman, Shelby. "Two Markov Models of Open System Occupational Mobility: Underlying Conceptualizations and Empirical Tests." *American Sociological Review* 40(1975):298-321.

Super, Donald E. *The Psychology of Careers*. New York: Harper & Row, 1957.

_____ . "Vocational Development in Adolescence and Early Adulthood: Tasks and Behaviors." In *Career Development: Self-Concept Theory*, edited by D.E. Super, R. Starishevsky, N. Matlin, and J.P. Jordaan. New York: College Entrance Examination Board, 1963.

Sweet, James A. *Women in the Labor Force*. New York: Seminar Press, 1973.

Telesky, Carol W. "Synthetic Cohort Analysis of Careers in Retail Sales: An Evaluation of the Utility of Spilerman's Approach." Paper presented at the Annual Meetings of the American Sociological Association, 1979, Boston.

Thurow, Lester C. *Generating Inequality*. New York: Basic Books, 1975.

Tolbert, Charles; Horan, Patrick M.; and Beck, E.M. "The Structure of Economic Segmentation: A Dual Economy Approach." *American Journal of Sociology* 85(1980):1095-1116.

Treiman, Donald J. "Industrialization and Social Stratification." In *Social Stratification: Research and Theory for the 1970s*, edited by Edward O. Laumann, pp. 207-234. Indianapolis, Ind.: Bobbs-Merrill Company, 1970.

_____ . *Occupational Prestige in Comparative Perspective*. New York: Academic Press, 1977.

Treiman, Donald J., and Terrell, Kermit. "Sex and the Process of Status Attainment: A Comparison of Working Women and Men." *American Sociological Review* 40(1975):174-200.

Tuma, Nancy Brandon. "Rewards, Resources, and the Rate of Mobility: A Nonstationary Multivariate Stochastic Model." *American Sociological Review* 41(1976):338-360.

Tuma, Nancy Brandon; Hannan, Michael T.; and Groeneveld, Lyle P. "Dynamic Analysis of Event Histories." *American Journal of Sociology* 84(1979):820-854.

Tyree, Andrea, and Treas, Judith. "The Occupational and Marital Mobility of Women." *American Sociological Review* 39(1974):293-302.

U.S. Bureau of the Census. *Alphabetical Index of Industries and Occupations, 1970 Census of Population*. Washington, D.C.: U.S. Government Printing Office, 1971.

_____ . *Public Use Samples of Basic Records from the 1970 Census: Description and Technical Documentation*. Washington, D.C.: U.S. Government Printing Office, 1972.

U.S. Department of Labor. *Dictionary of Occupational Titles*. 3d ed. 2 vols. Washington, D.C.: U.S. Government Printing Office, 1965.

Wallace, Michael, and Kalleberg, Arne L. "Economic Organization of Firms and Labor Market Consequences: Toward a Specification of Dual Economy Theory." In *Sociological Perspectives on Labor Markets*, edited by Ivar Berg, pp. 77-117. New York: Academic Press, 1981.

Wells, Robert V. "On the Dangers of Constructing Artificial Cohorts in Times of Rapid Social Change." *Journal of Interdisciplinary History* 9(1978):103-110.

White, Harrison C. *Chains of Opportunity*. Cambridge, Mass.: Harvard University Press, 1970.

Wilensky, Harold L. "Work, Careers, and Social Integration." *International Social Science Journal* 12(1960):543-560.

_____ . "Orderly Careers and Social Participation: The Impact of Work History on Social Integration in the Middle Mass." *American Sociological Review* 26(1961):521-539.

Wilson, Kenneth L., and Portes, Alejandro. "The Educational Attainment Process: Results from a National Sample." *American Journal of Sociology* 81(1975):343-363.

Wolf, Wendy C., and Fligstein, Neil D. "Sex and Authority in the Workplace: The Causes of Sexual Inequality." *American Sociological Review* 44(1979):235-252.

Wright, Erik Olin, and Perrone, Luca. "Marxist Class Categories and Income Inequality." *American Sociological Review* 42(1977):32-55.

**Appendix A:
Career-Line Categories in
Terms of Their 1970 U.S.
Census Occupation-Industry
Elements**

CAREER-LINE CATEGORY	SECTOR[a]	GENDER COMPOSITION[b]	INCLUDED 1970 CENSUS OCCUPATIONS	INCLUDED 1970 CENSUS INDUSTRIES
PROFESSIONAL, TECHNICAL, AND KINDRED WORKERS				
Accountants—accounting firms	P-I	M	001	889
Accountants—public administration	P-I	A	001	907-937
Accountants—finance and professional services	P-I	A	001	707-718,828-888,890-897
Accountants—manufacturing industries	P-I	M	001	107-398
Accountants—other industries	P-I	A	001	017-106,407-699,727-809,938-999
Architects	P-I	M	002	all
Computer programmers	P-I	A	003	all
Other computer specialists (except programmers)	P-I	M	004,005	all
Aeronautical and astronautical engineers	P-I	M	006	all
Chemical engineers	P-I	M	010	all
Civil engineers	P-I	M	011	all
Electrical and electronic engineers	P-I	M	012	all
Industrial engineers	P-I	M	013	all
Mechanical engineers	P-I	M	014	all
Sales engineers	P-I	M	022	all
Other engineers	P-I	M	015,020,021,023	all
Foresters and conservationists	P-I	M	025	all
Lawyers	P-I	M	031	all
Librarians, archivists and curators	P-I	F	032,033	all
Mathematical specialists	P-I	A	034,035,036	all
Chemists	P-I	M	045	all
Other life and physical scientists	P-I	M	042-044,051-054	all
Operations and systems researchers and analysts	P-I	M	055	all
Personnel and labor relations workers	P-I	A	056	all
Dentists	P-I	M	062	all
Pharmacists	P-I	M	064	all

Occupation				
Physicians, medical and osteopathic	P-I	M	065	all
Other medical practitioners	P-I	M	061,063,071,072,073	all
Dieticians	P-I	F	074	all
Registered nurses—hospitals	P-I	F	075	838
Registered nurses—settings other than hospitals	P-I	F	075	017-837,839-999
Therapists	P-I	A	076	all
Clinical laboratory technologists and technicians	P-I	F	080	all
Other health technologists and technicians	P-I	A	081-085	all
Clergymen	P-I	M	086	all
Social scientists	P-I	A	091-096	all
Social workers	P-I	A	100	all
Recreation workers	P-I	M	101	all
College teachers—natural sciences	P-I	A	102-112	all
College teachers—other than natural sciences	P-I	F	113-140	all
Elementary school teachers	P-I	F	142	all
Prekindergarten and kindergarten teachers	P-I	A	143	all
Secondary school teachers	P-I	A	144	all
Other teachers—except college and university	P-I	M	141,145	all
Chemical technicians	P-I	M	151	all
Draftsmen	P-I	M	152	all
Electrical and electronic engineering technicians	P-I	M	153	all
Surveyors	P-I	M	161	all
Other engineering and science technicians	P-I	M	150,154,155,156,162	all
Air pilots, controllers, and flight engineers	P-I	M	163,164,170	all
Other technicians (except health, engineering, and science)	P-I	M	165,171,172,173	all
Vocational and educational counselors	P-I	A	174	all
Athletes and kindred workers	P-I	A	180	all
Designers	P-I	A	183	all
Editors and reporters	P-I	A	184	all
Musicians and composers	P-I	A	185	all
Painters and sculptors	P-I	A	190	all
Photographers	P-I	M	191	all

CAREER-LINE CATEGORY	SECTOR[a]	GENDER COMPOSITION[b]	INCLUDED 1970 CENSUS OCCUPATIONS	INCLUDED 1970 CENSUS INDUSTRIES
Public relations men and publicity writers	P-I	A	192	all
Other writers, artists, and entertainers	P-I	A	175,181,182,193,194	all
Research workers, not specified	P-I	A	195	all
Other professionals	P-I	A	024,026,030,090	all
MANAGERS AND ADMINISTRATORS, EXCEPT FARM				
Assessors, controllers and inspectors—public administration	P-I	M	201,213,215	all
Bank officers and financial managers	P-I	M	202	all
Buyers and shippers	P-I	A	203,205	all
Credit men	P-I	A	210	all
Funeral directors	P-I	M	211	all
Health administrators	P-I	A	212	all
Building managers and superintendents	P-I	A	216	all
Office managers, n.e.c.	P-I	A	220	all
Ship officers, pilots and pursers	P-I	M	221	all
Officials and administrators—public administration, n.e.c.	P-I	M	222	all
Officials of lodges, societies, and unions	P-I	M	223	all
Postmasters and mail superintendents	P-I	A	224	all
Purchasing agents and buyers, n.e.c.	P-I	M	225	all
Railroad conductors	P-I	M	226	all
Restaurant, cafeteria, and bar managers	P-I	A	230	all
Sales managers and department heads, retail trade	P-I	A	231	all
Sales managers, except retail trade	P-I	M	233	all
School administrators	P-I	A	235,240	all
Managers, n.e.c.—general building contractors, construction	P-I	M	245	067
Managers, n.e.c.—other construction industries	P-I	M	245	068-077
Managers, n.e.c.—manufacturing, machinery	P-I	M	245	177-209

Occupation				
Managers, n.e.c.—manufacturing, other durable goods	P-I	M	245	107-176,210-259
Managers, n.e.c.—manufacturing, printing and publishing	P-I	M	245	338-339
Managers, n.e.c.—manufacturing, chemicals, petro, rubber	P-I	M	245	347-387
Managers, n.e.c.—manufacturing, other nondurable goods	P-I	M	245	268-337,388-398
Managers, n.e.c.—transportation	P-I	M	245	407-429
Managers, n.e.c.—communications and utilities	P-I	M	245	447-479
Managers, n.e.c.—wholesale trade	P-I	M	245	507-588
Managers, n.e.c.—food, retail	P-I	M	245	628-638
Managers, n.e.c.—general merchandise, retail	P-I	M	245	607-627
Managers, n.e.c.—motor vehicles, retail	P-I	M	245	639-647,649
Managers, n.e.c.—gas stations, retail	P-I	M	245	648
Managers, n.e.c.—apparel and shoe stores	P-I	A	245	657,658
Managers, n.e.c.—other retail	P-I	M	245	659-698
Managers, n.e.c.—finance, insurance, and real estate	P-I	M	245	707-718
Managers, n.e.c.—business and repair services	P-I	M	245	727-759
Managers, n.e.c.—personal services	P-I	A	245	769-798
Managers, n.e.c.—other industries	P-I	M	245	017-066,799-999
SALES WORKERS				
Advertising agents and salesmen	P-I	M	260	all
Demonstrators, auctioneers, hucksters, and peddlers	S	F	261,262,264	all
Insurance agents, brokers, and underwriters	P-I	M	265	all
Newsboys	S	A	266	all
Real estate agents and brokers	P-I	A	270	all
Stock and bond salesmen	P-I	M	271	all
Sales representative—manufacturing, durables	P-I	M	280-285	107-259
Sales representative—manufacturing, nondurables	P-I	M	280-285	268-398

CAREER-LINE CATEGORY	SECTOR[a]	GENDER COMPOSITION[b]	INCLUDED 1970 CENSUS OCCUPATIONS	INCLUDED 1970 CENSUS INDUSTRIES
Sales representative—wholesale: food products	S	M	280-285	527
Sales representative—wholesale: machinery equipment	P-I	M	280-285	539
Sales representative—wholesale: other industries	S	M	280-285	017-058,507-509, 528-538,557-599
Sales clerks—retail: lumber and hardware	S	M	280-285	607-608
Sales clerks—retail: department and mail order stores	S	F	280-285	609
Sales clerks—retail: grocery stores	P-S	A	280-285	628
Salesmen—retail: motor vehicles	P-I	M	280-285	639
Salesmen—retail: furniture and appliances	S	A	280-285	667,668
Sales clerks—retail: apparel, excluding shoe	S	F	280-285	657
Sales clerks—retail: drug stores	P-S	F	280-285	677
Salesmen and sales clerks—other retail trade	S	A	280-285	617-627,629-638,647-649,658,669,678-699
Salesmen of services and construction	P-I	M	280-285	067-078,407-499,707-747
Salesmen and sales clerks in other industries	S	A	280-285	748-999
CLERICAL AND KINDRED WORKERS				
Bank tellers	P-S	F	301	all
Billing clerks	P-S	F	303	all
Bookkeepers—finance, insurance, real estate	S	F	305	707-718
Bookkeepers—manufacturing, durable goods	S	F	305	107-259
Bookkeepers—manufacturing, nondurables	P-I	F	305	268-398
Bookkeepers—wholesale trade	P-I	F	305	507-588
Bookkeepers—motor vehicles—retail	P-I	F	305	639-649
Bookkeepers—other retail	P-I	F	305	607-638,657-698
Bookkeepers—professional services	S	F	305	828-897
Bookkeepers—public administration	P-S	A	305	907-937
Other bookkeepers	S	F	305	017-078,407-499, 727-827,947-999

Occupation				
Cashiers	P-S	F	310	all
Clerical supervisors, n.e.c.	P-I	A	312	all
Collectors, bill and account	S	A	313	all
Counter clerks, except food	S	F	314	all
Dispatchers and starters, vehicle	S	M	315	all
Estimators, investigators, enumerators	P-I	A	320,321	all
Expediters and production controllers	P-I	M	323	all
File clerks	P-S	F	325	all
Insurance adjusters, examiners, and investigators	P-I	A	326	all
Library attendants and assistants	S	F	330	all
Mail carriers, post office	P-S	M	331	all
Mail handlers, except post office	P-S	A	332	all
Bookkeeping and billing machine operators	P-S	F	341	all
Computer and peripheral equipment operators	P-I	A	343	all
Key punch operators	P-S	F	345	all
Other office machine operators	P-S	F	342,344,350,355	all
Payroll and timekeeping clerks	P-S	A	360	all
Postal clerks	S	A	361	all
Receptionists	P-S	F	364	all
Secretaries, legal	P-I	F	370	all
Secretaries, medical	P-I	F	371	all
Secretaries, n.e.c.—elementary and secondary schools	P-I	F	372	857
Secretaries, n.e.c.—colleges and universities	P-I	F	372	858
Secretaries, n.e.c.—health industries	P-I	F	372	828-848
Secretaries, n.e.c.—religious and nonprofit organizations	P-I	F	372	877,887
Secretaries, n.e.c.—other professional service organizations	P-I	F	372	849,859-869,878, 879,888-897
Secretaries, n.e.c.—manufacturing industries, durables	P-I	F	372	107-267
Secretaries, n.e.c.—manufacturing industries, nondurables	P-I	F	372	268-399
Secretaries, n.e.c.—wholesale and retail trade	P-I	F	372	507-699

CAREER-LINE CATEGORY	SECTOR[a]	GENDER COMPOSITION[b]	INCLUDED 1970 CENSUS OCCUPATIONS	INCLUDED 1970 CENSUS INDUSTRIES
Secretaries, n.e.c.—insurance firms	P-I	F	372	717
Secretaries, n.e.c.—financial and real estate firms	P-I	F	372	707-709,718
Secretaries, n.e.c.—public administration	P-I	F	372	907-937
Secretaries, n.e.c.—other industries	P-I	F	372	017-078,407-499, 727-817,947-999
Shipping and receiving clerks—manufacturing	S	M	374	107-398
Shipping and receiving clerks—except manufacturing industries	S	M	374	017-106,407-999
Statistical clerks	P-S	A	375	all
Stenographers	P-S	F	376	all
Stock clerks and storekeepers—manufacturing	P-S	M	381	107-398
Stock clerks and storekeepers—except manufacturing industries	P-S	A	381	017-106,407-999
Telephone and telegraph operators	P-S	F	384,385	all
Ticket, station, and express agents	S	A	390	all
Typists—banking, insurance, real estate	S	F	391	707-718
Typists—professional and related organizations	S	F	391	828-897
Typists—local, state, and federal government	S	F	391	907-937
Typists—other industries	S	F	391	017-706,719-827,938-999
Other clerical workers—manufacturing, durables	S	A	311,333,334, 362,363,382, 383,392-395	259
Other clerical workers—manufacturing, nondurables	P-S	A	311,333,334,362,363,382, 383,392-395	268-398
Other clerical workers—transportation	S	A	311,333,334,362,363,382 383,392-395	407-479
Other clerical workers—wholesale and retail trade	P-S	F	311,333,334,362,363,382, 383,392-395	507-698

Occupation				
Other clerical workers—finance industries	S	S	311,333,334,362,363,382, 383,392-395	707-718
Other clerical workers—professional services	S	F	311,333,334,362,363,382, 383,392-395	828-897
Other clerical workers—local, state, and federal government	S	A	311,333,334,362,363,382, 383,392-395	907-937
Other clerical workers—other industries	S	A	311,333,334,362,363,382, 383,392-395	017-078,727-827 938-999
CRAFTSMEN AND KINDRED WORKERS				
Bakers	P-I	A	402	all
Blacksmiths, forgemen, heat treaters	P-I	M	403,442,446	all
Brickmasons and stonemasons	P-I	M	410,411	all
Bulldozer operators	P-S	M	412	all
Cabinetmakers and furniture finishers	P-I	M	413,443	all
Carpenters—general building contractors	P-I	M	415,416	067
Carpenters—special trade contractors	P-I	M	415,416	069
Carpenters—other construction industries	P-I	M	415,416	068,077
Carpenters—other nonconstruction industries	P-I	M	415,416	017-066,078-999
Carpet and floor installers	P-I	M	420,440	all
Cement and concrete finishers	P-I	M	421	all
Compositors and typesetters	P-I	M	422,423	all
Cranemen, derrickmen, and hoistmen	P-S	M	424	all
Decorators and window dressers	P-I	A	425	all
Electricians—special trade contractors	P-I	M	430,431	069
Electricians—except special trade contractors	P-I	M	430,431	017-068,070-999
Electric power linemen and cablemen	P-I	M	433	all
Excavating, grading and road machine operators; except bulldozer	S	M	436	all
Foremen, n.e.c.—construction	P-I	M	441	067-077
Foremen, n.e.c.—manufacturing, metals	P-I	M	441	139-169
Foremen, n.e.c.—manufacturing, machinery	P-I	M	441	177-209
Foremen, n.e.c.—manufacturing, transportation equipment	P-I	M	441	219-238

CAREER-LINE CATEGORY	SECTOR[a]	GENDER COMPOSITION[b]	INCLUDED 1970 CENSUS OCCUPATIONS	INCLUDED 1970 CENSUS INDUSTRIES
Foremen, n.e.c.—manufacturing, textiles and apparel	P-I	A	441	307-327
Foremen, n.e.c.—chemicals, petro and rubber	P-I	M	441	347-387
Foremen, n.e.c.—other manufacturing	P-I	M	441	107-138,239-299, 328-339,388-398
Foremen, n.e.c.—transportation, communications, and utilities	P-I	M	441	407-479
Foremen, n.e.c.—wholesale and retail trade	P-I	M	441	507-698
Foremen, n.e.c.—other industries	P-I	M	441	017-057,707-999
Inspectors, scalers and graders; log and lumber and n.e.c. other	P-I	M	450,452	all
Jewelers and watchmakers	P-I	M	453	all
Job and die setters, metal	P-I	M	454	all
Locomotive firemen and engineers	P-I	M	455,456	all
Machinists—manufacturing, machinery	P-I	M	461,462	177-209
Machinists—manufacturing, durables (except machinery)	P-I	M	461,462	107-169,210-259
Machinists—other industries	P-I	M	461,462	017-106,260-999
Air conditioning, heating, and refrigeration repairmen	P-I	M	470	all
Aircraft mechanics and repairmen	P-I	M	471	all
Automobile body repairmen	P-I	M	472	all
Automobile mechanics—motor vehicle dealers	P-I	M	473,474	639
Automobile mechanics—gas stations	P-I	M	473,474	648
Automobile mechanics—auto repair services	P-I	M	473,474	757
Automobile mechanics—other industries	P-I	M	473,474	017-638,640-647, 649-756,758-999
Other mechanics and repairmen	P-I	M	475,480,483,484,491-495	all
Heavy equipment mechanics, including diesel—manufacturing	P-I	M	481	107-399
Heavy equipment mechanics—other industries (except manufacturing)	P-I	M	481	017-106,400-999

Occupation				
Household appliance and accessory installers and mechanics	P-I	M	482	all
Radio and television mechanics	P-I	M	485	all
Railroad and car shop mechanics	P-I	M	486	all
Millwrights	P-I	M	502	all
Molders, metal	P-I	M	503,504,514	all
Painters—special trade contractors	P-I	M	510,511	069
Painters—except special trade contractors	P-I	M	510,511	017-068,070-999
Plasterers and paperhangers	P-I	M	512,520,521	all
Pattern and model makers, excluding paper	P-I	M	514	all
Plumbers—special trade contractors	P-I	M	522,523	069
Plumbers—except special trade contractors	P-I	M	522,523	017-068,070-999
Pressmen and plate printers	P-I	M	530,531	all
Roofers and slaters	P-I	M	534	all
Sheetmetal workers and tinsmiths	P-I	M	535,536	all
Stationary engineers	P-I	M	545	all
Structural metal craftsmen	P-I	M	550	all
Tailors	P-I	A	551	all
Telephone installers and repairmen	P-I	M	552	all
Telephone linemen and splicers	P-I	M	554	all
Tool and die makers	S	M	561,562	all
Upholsterers	P-I	M	563	all
Other craft workers—manufacturing industries	P-I	M	401,404,405,426,434,435,444,445,501,505,506,515,516,525,533,540-543,546,560,571-575	107-399
Other craft workers—other industries	P-I	M	401,404,405,426,434,435,444,445,501,505,506,515,516,525,533,540-543,546,560,571-575	017-106,400-999

OPERATIVES, EXCEPT TRANSPORT

Occupation				
Assemblers—manufacturing, metals and non-electric machinery	P-S	A	602	139-198
Assemblers—electrical machinery and equipment	P-S	F	602	199-209

CAREER-LINE CATEGORY	SECTOR[a]	GENDER COMPOSITION[b]	INCLUDED 1970 CENSUS OCCUPATIONS	INCLUDED 1970 CENSUS INDUSTRIES
Assemblers—transportation equipment	P-S	A	602	219-238
Assemblers—other industries	P-S	A	602	017-138,239-999
Bottling and canning operatives	P-S	A	604	all
Checkers and inspectors—electrical and transportation equipment	P-S	A	610	199-238
Checkers and inspectors—manufacturing, other durables	S	A	610	107-198,239-267
Checkers and inspectors—manufacturing, nondurables	P-S	F	610	268-398
Clothing ironers and pressers	P-S	F	611	all
Cutting operatives, n.e.c.	P-S	A	612	all
Dressmakers and seamstresses, except factory	P-I	F	613	all
Drillers, earth	P-S	M	614	all
Dry wall installers and lathers	P-S	M	615	all
Filers, polishers, sanders and buffers	P-S	A	621	all
Furnacemen, smeltermen, and pourers	P-S	M	622	all
Garage workers and gas station attendants	S	M	623	all
Graders and sorters	P-S	F	624,625	all
Laundry and dry cleaning operatives, n.e.c.	P-S	A	630	all
Meat cutters and butchers—manufacturing	S	A	633	all
Meat cutters and butchers—except manufacturing	P-S	M	631	all
Mine operatives, n.e.c.	P-S	M	640	all
Mixing operatives	P-S	M	641	all
Packers and wrappers, except meat and produce—nondurable goods	P-S	F	643	268-397
Packers and wrappers, except meat and produce—other industries	P-S	A	643	017-267,398-999
Painters, manufactured articles	S	M	644	all
Photographic process workers	P-I	A	645	all
Drill press operatives	P-S	A	650	all
Grinding machine operatives	S	M	651	all

Lathe and milling machine operatives	P-S	M	652	all
Precision machine operatives, n.e.c.	S	M	653	all
Punch and stamping press operatives	P-S	A	656	all
Sawyers	S	M	662	all
Sewers and stitchers—apparel and accessories	P-S	F	663	319
Sewers and stitchers—except apparel and accessories	P-S	F	663	017-318,320-999
Shoemaking operatives	P-S	A	664	all
Stationary firemen	P-I	M	666	all
Knitters, loopers and toppers	P-S	A	671	all
Spinners, twisters and winders	P-S	A	672	all
Weavers	P-S	A	673	all
Textile operatives other	P-S	A	670,674	all
Welders and flame-cutters—manufacturing	P-I	M	680	107-399
Welders and flame-cutters—except manufacturing industries	P-I	M	680	017-106,400-999
Winding operatives, n.e.c.	P-S	A	681	all
Other operatives—construction	P-S	M	601,603,605,620,626, 634-636,642,660,661, 665,690,692,694,695	067-077
Other operatives—lumber and wood products	P-S	A	601,603,605,620,626, 634-636,642,660,661, 665,690,692,694,695	107-118
Other operatives—stone, clay, and glass products	P-S	M	601,603,605,620,626, 634-636,642,660,661, 665,690,692,694,695	119-138
Other operatives—primary iron and steel industries	P-S	M	601,603,605,620,626, 634-636,642,660,661, 665,690,692,694,695	139-147

CAREER-LINE CATEGORY	SECTOR[a]	GENDER COMPOSITION[b]	INCLUDED 1970 CENSUS OCCUPATIONS	INCLUDED 1970 CENSUS INDUSTRIES
Other operatives—other metal industries	P-S	M	601,603,605,620,626, 634-636,642,660,661, 665,690,692,694,695	148-169
Other operatives—electrical machinery	P-S	A	601,603,605,620,626, 634-636,642,660,661, 665,690,692,694,695	199-209
Other operatives—nonelectrical machinery	P-S	A	601,603,605,620,626, 634-636,642,660,661, 665,690,692,694,695	177-198
Other operatives—transportation equipment	P-S	M	601,603,605,620,626, 634-636,642,660,661, 665,690,692,694,695	219-238
Other operatives—other durable goods	P-S	A	601,603,605,620,626, 634-636,642,660,661, 665,690,692,694,695	239-259
Other operatives—food industries	P-S	A	601,603,605,620,626, 634-636,642,660,661, 665,690,692,694,695	268-298
Other operatives—apparel	P-S	F	601,603,605,620,626, 634-636,642,660,661, 665,690,692,694,695	319-327
Other operatives—paper products	P-S	A	601,603,605,620,626, 634-636,642,660,661, 665,690,692,694,695	328-337
Other operatives—printing and publishing	P-S	A	601,603,605,620,626, 634-636,642,660,661, 665,690,692,694,695	338-339
Other operatives—chemicals	S	M	601,603,605,620,626, 634-636,642,660,661, 665,690,692,694,695	347-369
Other operatives—petroleum products	P-S	A	601,603,605,620,626, 634-636,642,660,661, 665,690,692,694,695	377-387

Other operatives—other nondurable goods	P-S	A	601,603,605,620,626, 634-636,642,660,661, 665,690,692,694,695	299,307-318,388-399
Other operatives—wholesale and retail trade	P-S	A	601,603,605,620,626, 634-636,642,660,661, 665,690,692,694,695	507-699
Other operatives—other industries	S	M	601,603,605,620,626, 634-636,642,660,661, 665,690,692,694,695	017-058,407-499,707-999
TRANSPORT EQUIPMENT OPERATIVES				
Bus drivers, urban rail transit conductors and motormen	S	A	703,704	all
Deliverymen and routemen—wholesale and retail trade	P-S	M	705	507-699
Deliverymen and routemen—except wholesale and retail trade industries	P-S	M	705	017-506,700-999
Forklift and tow motor operatives	P-S	M	706	all
Railroad brake and switchmen	S	M	712,713	all
Taxicab drivers and chauffeurs	S	M	714	all
Truck drivers—construction	P-S	M	715	067-078
Truck drivers—manufacturing industries	P-S	M	715	107-399
Truck drivers—other transportation, communications, and utilities	P-S	M	715	407-416,418-499
Truck drivers—wholesale trade	P-S	M	715	507-599
Truck drivers—retail trade	P-S	M	715	607-699
Truck drivers—trucking services	P-S	M	715	417
Truck drivers—other industries	P-S	M	715	017-066,079-106,707-999
Transport equipment operatives	P-S	M	701,710,711	all
LABORERS, EXCEPT FARM				
Construction laborers—general building and special trade contractors	P-S	M	750,751	067,069
Construction laborers—general contractors excluding building	P-S	M	750,751	068

CAREER-LINE CATEGORY	SECTOR[a]	GENDER COMPOSITION[b]	INCLUDED 1970 CENSUS OCCUPATIONS	INCLUDED 1970 CENSUS INDUSTRIES
Construction laborers—other industries	S	M	750,751	017-066,070-999
Freight and material handlers	P-S	M	753	all
Garbage collectors	P-S	M	754	all
Gardeners and groundskeepers, excluding farm	S	M	755	all
Longshoremen, stevedores, and teamsters	P-S	M	760,763	all
Lumbermen, raftsmen, and woodchoppers	S	M	761	all
Stock handlers—grocery stores	P-S	A	762	628
Stock handlers—except grocery stores	P-S	A	762	017-627,629-999
Vehicle washers and equipment cleaners	P-S	M	764	all
Warehousemen, n.e.c.	P-S	M	770	all
Other laborers—manufacturing durables	P-S	M	740,752,780,785	107-259
Other laborers—manufacturing nondurables	P-S	A	740,752,780,785	268-399
Other laborers—transportation	S	M	740,752,780,785	407-429
Other laborers—other industries	S	M	740,752,780,785	017-106,447-999
FARMERS, FARM MANAGERS, FARM LABORERS, AND FARM FOREMEN				
Farmers (owners and tenants)	P-I	M	801	all
Farm managers and foremen	P-I	M	802,821	all
Farm laborers, wage workers	S	A	822	all
Self-employed farm service laborers and unpaid farm workers	S	A	823,824	all
SERVICE WORKERS, EXCEPT PRIVATE HOUSEHOLD				
Chambermaids and maids, except private household	S	F	901	all
Cleaners and charwomen	P-S	A	902	all
Janitors—elementary and secondary schools	S	M	903	857
Janitors—manufacturing firms	S	M	903	107-399
Janitors—public administration	S	M	903	907-937
Janitors—other industries	S	M	903	017-106,400-856, 858-906,938-999

Bartenders	S	A	910	all
Busboys	P-S	A	911	all
Cooks—eating and drinking places	P-I	A	912	669
Cooks—elementary and secondary schools	P-I	F	912	857
Cooks—other industries	P-I	A	912	017-668,670-856,858-999
Dishwashers	S	A	913	all
Food counter and fountain workers	P-S	F	914	all
Waiters—eating and drinking places	P-S	F	915	669
Waiters—other industries	P-S	F	915	017-668,670-999
Food service workers, n.e.c., excluding private household	S	F	916	all
Dental assistants	P-I	F	921	all
Nursing aides, orderlies, and attendants—except hospitals	S	F	925	017-837,839-999
Nursing adies, orderlies, and attendants—hospitals	S	F	925	838
Practical nurses	P-I	F	926	all
Other health service workers	S	F	922,923,924	all
Airline stewardesses	S	F	931	all
Attendants and ushers, recreation and amusement	S	A	932,953	all
Attendants, personal service other	S	A	933,934,945	all
Barbers	P-I	M	935	all
Child care workers, excluding private household	S	F	942	all
Hairdressers and cosmetologists	P-I	F	944	all
Housekeepers, excluding private household	P-I	F	950	all
Other personal service workers	S	A	940,941,943,952,954	all
Firemen, fire protection	P-I	M	961	all
Guards and watchmen	P-S	M	962	all
Policemen and detectives	S	M	964	all
Other protective service workers	S	A	960,963,965	all

CAREER-LINE CATEGORY	SECTOR[a]	GENDER COMPOSITION[b]	INCLUDED 1970 CENSUS OCCUPATIONS	INCLUDED 1970 CENSUS INDUSTRIES
PRIVATE HOUSEHOLD WORKERS				
Child care workers, private household	S	F	980	all
Cooks, housekeepers, and laundresses—private household	S	F	981,982,983	all
Maids and servants, private household	S	F	984	all

[a]P-I = Primary-Independent

P-S = Primary-Secondary

S   = Secondary

[b]F = Female

M = Male

A = Androgynous

Appendix B: Summary of Job Characteristics Based on the *Dictionary of Occupational Titles*

Several measures depend on job characteristics available for jobs listed in the third edition, *Dictionary of Occupational Titles* (U.S. Department of Labor 1965). Here, we summarize several measures: levels of involvement with data, people, and things, specific vocational preparation, repetitiveness, variety, and control in work. Volume 2 of the *Dictionary* (U.S. Department of Labor 1965, pp. 649-656) contains a full description of the variables. Spenner (1980) described the procedures used to map measures for *Dictionary of Occupational Title* jobs into census titles. Miller and colleagues (1980) discussed measurement issues involved in the use of variables from the *Dictionary*.

Levels of Involvement with Data, People, and Things

Data include the "information, knowledge and conceptions related to data, people or things, obtained by observation, investigation, interpretation, visualization, mental creation; incapable of being touched; written data take the form of numbers, words, symbols; other data are ideas, concepts, oral verbalization" (U.S. Department of Labor 1965, p. 649). People include "human beings; also animals dealt with on an individual basis as if they were human" (U.S. Department of Labor 1965, p. 649). Things include "inanimate objects as distinguished from human beings; substances or materials; machines, tools, equipment; products" (U.S. Department of Labor 1965, p. 650). The scales of measurement for each variable were as follows:

Data	*People*	*Things*
0 Synthesizing	0 Mentoring	0 Setting up
1 Coordinating	1 Negotiating	1 Precision working
2 Analyzing	2 Instructing	2 Operating-controlling
3 Compiling	3 Supervising	3 Driving-operating
4 Computing	4 Diverting	4 Manipulating
5 Copying	5 Persuading	5 Tending
6 Comparing	6 Speaking-signaling	6 Feeding-offbearing
7 ⎰ No significant	7 Serving	7 Handling
8 ⎱ relationship	8 No significant relationship	8 No significant relationship

Specific Vocational Preparation

Specific vocational preparation references the "amount of time required to learn the techniques, acquire information, and develop the facility needed for average performance in a specific job-worker situation" (U.S. Department of Labor 1965, p. 652). School, work, military, institutional, or avocational environment can provide such training. The measure does not include the orientation time required of all workers to become accustomed to a job. If relevant, the measure would include vocational education, apprenticeship training, in-plant and on-the-job training, and essential experience in other jobs. The scale values were as follows:

1 = short demonstration only
2 = anything beyond short demonstration up to and including thirty days
3 = over thirty days up to and including three months
4 = over three months up to and including six months
5 = over six months up to and including one year
6 = over one year up to and including two years
7 = over two years up to and including four years
8 = over four years up to and including ten years
9 = over ten years.

Variety, Repetitiveness, Specific Instruction and Control

The *Dictionary* includes measures for several "different types of situations to which workers must adjust" (U.S. Department of Labor 1965, p. 654). The items are coded only if they are characteristic of a job, with a present-absent scoring system. The items were as follows:

1. Situations involving a variety of duties often characterized by frequent change (variety).
2. Situations involving repetitive or short-cycle operations carried out according to set procedures or sequences (repetitive).
3. Situations involving doing things only under specific instruction, allowing little or no room for independent action or judgment in working out job problems (specific instruction).
4. Situations involving the direction, control, and planning of an entire activity or the activities of others (control).

**Appendix C:
Correlations among Variables
in the Dynamic Model
(Chapter 7)**

Variables and Correlation (men below diagonal, N = 1,949; women above diagonal, N = 1,527)

	MSERV	WKDIS	MOMEMX	POPSEI	FTJBFE	GPA	MA	POPED	MOMED	OCCASP	SIBS	RURAL	EDATT	LEDATT	DEGREE	VOCTECH	OTHED
MSERV		-.015	-.039	-.013	.013	-.055	-.033	-.012	-.044	-.038	.011	.009	-.014	-.024	-.001	.005	.015
WKDIS	-.053		.072	-.022	.009	-.049	.020	-.044	-.038	.046	-.124	.012	-.075	-.054	-.093	.061	.097
MOMEMX	.086	.029		-.123	-.006	-.078	-.053	-.115	-.048	.010	-.017	.046	-.029	-.022	-.027	.049	.041
POPSEI	-.114	.001	-.009		.014	.196	.210	.576	.328	.118	-.102	-.211	.333	.285	.283	-.117	.032
FTJBFE	-.065	-.010	-.004	.082		.055	.074	.071	.094	.092	-.032	-.041	.271	.240	.161	-.142	.054
GPA	-.305	-.013	-.075	.220	.057		.590	.220	.222	.340	-.071	.022	.492	.437	.438	-.201	.010
MA	-.211	.019	-.010	.235	.024	.663		.208	.179	.264	-.051	-.110	.358	.315	.331	-.178	.053
POPED	-.171	-.014	-.038	.572	.054	.275	.248		.477	.168	-.116	-.215	.355	.300	.277	-.110	.052
MOMED	-.147	-.007	.065	.393	.052	.271	.252	.508		.160	-.145	-.115	.338	.273	.273	.065	.006
OCCASP	-.218	-.018	.032	.324	.098	.466	.397	.338	.290		-.071	-.048	.366	.292	.282	-.155	.004
SIBS	.088	-.017	-.046	-.094	-.004	-.106	-.041	-.072	-.089	-.151		.086	-.172	-.128	-.132	-.037	.001
RURAL	.034	.025	.022	-.245	-.067	-.032	-.099	-.244	-.147	-.209	.130		-.138	-.113	-.116	.050	.022
EDATT	-.331	-.060	-.020	.308	.198	.636	.453	.351	.312	.554	-.155	-.125		.924	.841	-.330	.052
LEDATT	-.287	-.047	-.026	.261	.132	.573	.423	.292	.275	.460	-.133	-.093	.914		.751	-.278	.060
DEGREE	-.327	-.050	-.023	.256	.117	.615	.427	.297	.264	.465	-.097	-.119	.820	.690		-.275	.038
VOCTECH	.075	.033	-.011	-.104	-.025	-.154	-.118	-.055	-.068	-.148	.038	.021	-.190	-.058	-.200		-.116
OTHED	-.024	.001	.028	.045	.036	-.072	-.024	.024	.006	-.028	-.005	.003	-.078	-.058	-.092	.034	
KIDST1	.024	.008	-.006	-.036	.135	-.033	-.031	-.042	-.031	-.020	.051	.023	.015	.001	.003	-.003	.028
MARSTT1	-.045	-.029	-.012	.037	.119	.132	.056	.022	.027	.104	-.013	-.057	.203	.177	.155	-.042	-.007
SCHT2	.011	.026	-.025	-.022	.038	-.058	-.022	-.005	-.003	.008	-.024	-.018	.002	.016	-.050	.542	.028
KIDST2	-.045	.008	-.009	-.122	.049	-.093	-.127	-.140	-.128	-.137	.099	.054	-.147	-.125	-.135	-.008	.020
MARSTT2	-.039	-.029	.028	.024	.123	.036	.009	-.017	-.000	-.010	-.029	-.012	.079	.078	.047	-.028	.044
SEIT1	-.185	-.042	-.035	.220	.106	.415	.301	.228	.157	.372	-.114	-.106	.562	.529	.501	-.113	-.084
SEIT2	-.214	-.051	-.013	.268	.137	.436	.330	.274	.210	.416	-.113	-.116	.599	.546	.539	-.127	-.046
CPLXT1	-.210	-.033	-.045	.222	.141	.402	.293	.233	.180	.350	-.088	-.084	.560	.595	.491	-.102	-.071
CPLXT2	-.231	-.054	-.001	.255	.163	.417	.300	.266	.221	.385	-.089	-.098	.589	.539	.522	-.111	-.029
SKLT1	.106	.018	.014	-.072	-.055	-.205	-.147	-.099	-.110	-.168	.036	.035	-.283	-.308	-.215	.043	-.006
SKLT2	.070	.025	.008	-.078	-.024	-.210	-.135	-.116	-.096	-.136	.026	.008	-.258	-.278	-.200	.034	-.051
LSEIT1	-.178	-.050	-.057	.201	.048	.451	.344	.230	.175	.361	-.112	-.080	.571	.595	.486	-.122	-.082
LSEIT2	-.206	-.051	-.040	.245	.089	.459	.356	.265	.221	.395	-.103	-.095	.603	.609	.515	-.131	-.047
LCPLXT1	-.196	-.030	-.054	.198	.108	.412	.304	.226	.186	.320	-.083	-.076	.569	.595	.469	-.104	-.080
LCPLXT2	-.222	-.043	-.007	.225	.119	.418	.313	.268	.230	.358	-.072	-.093	.587	.595	.494	-.114	-.043
LSKLT1	-.117	-.031	-.022	.081	.045	.242	-.183	.128	.131	.191	-.045	-.038	.339	.383	.253	-.046	.023
LSKLT2	-.094	-.022	-.016	.078	.023	.246	.175	.127	.105	.172	-.030	-.013	.318	.351	.243	-.028	.023

Appendix C

	KIDST1	MARSTT1	SCHT2	KIDST2	MARSTT2	SEIT1	SEIT2	CPLXT1	CPLXT2	SKLT1	SKLT2	LSEIT1	LSEIT2	LCPLXT1	LCPLXT2	LSKLT1	LSKLT2
MSERV	.006	.006	.018	.034	.007	-.044	-.029	-.011	-.022	.048	.033	-.052	-.028	-.020	-.015	-.041	-.030
WKDIS	-.013	-.003	.045	.018	-.043	-.021	-.065	-.063	-.116	-.047	.040	-.004	-.068	-.038	-.105	.042	-.040
MOMEMX	.024	.056	.026	.009	.031	-.035	-.040	-.026	-.039	-.030	-.031	-.027	-.046	-.024	-.045	.032	.038
POPSEI	-.028	-.024	-.031	-.133	-.029	.169	.189	.178	.209	-.085	-.097	.169	.194	.174	.193	.057	.065
FTJBFE	-.006	-.024	-.128	-.050	.021	.079	.128	.135	.160	-.052	-.068	.095	.133	.150	.159	.050	.062
GPA	-.065	.091	-.044	-.107	.048	.291	.303	.313	.301	-.129	-.131	.294	.293	.313	.289	.112	.098
MA	-.014	.111	-.029	-.014	.030	.201	.204	.195	.179	-.094	-.098	.210	.202	.216	.188	.079	.063
POPED	-.052	.036	.011	-.155	.017	.175	.183	.195	.196	-.080	-.078	.172	.179	.184	.178	.051	.056
MOMED	-.018	.029	.012	-.133	.047	.195	.154	.199	.152	-.104	-.091	.188	.153	.187	.145	.095	.080
OCCASP	-.059	.056	-.036	-.045	.017	.312	.309	.234	.232	-.056	-.053	.298	.291	.229	.225	.027	.036
SIBS	.089	-.013	-.025	.123	-.007	-.147	-.122	-.144	-.127	.080	.079	-.127	-.107	-.135	-.112	-.080	-.079
RURAL	.085	.070	.010	.092	.044	-.103	-.065	-.113	-.090	.062	.020	-.091	-.063	-.111	-.078	-.042	-.026
EDATT	-.095	.053	-.037	-.204	-.000	.400	.442	.510	.514	-.325	-.331	.446	.457	.548	.514	.305	.299
LEDATT	-.081	.036	.008	-.172	-.017	.373	.412	.502	.503	-.362	-.358	.445	.442	.573	.526	.353	.335
DEGREE	-.093	.025	-.065	-.184	-.014	.330	.385	.426	.459	-.336	-.357	.373	.412	.465	.470	.315	.325
VOCTECH	.013	-.038	.609	.013	-.038	-.200	-.215	-.149	-.175	.051	.024	-.201	-.212	-.166	-.180	-.009	.016
OTHED	.014	-.013	-.060	-.033	-.069	-.009	.003	.022	.028	-.029	-.040	-.004	-.004	.016	.027	.031	.037
KIDST1	.395	.347	.006	-.043	.177	-.105	-.117	-.068	-.079	-.023	-.022	-.097	-.106	-.068	-.076	.024	.024
MARSTT1	-.031	-.006	-.024	.190	.534	-.001	.012	.023	.014	-.025	-.029	.007	.022	.026	-.046	.034	.023
SCHT2	.009	.201	-.020	-.043	.243	-.088	-.077	-.019	-.038	.053	-.083	-.078	-.074	-.032	-.046	.079	.107
KIDST2	.240	.576	-.011	.374	-.064	-.140	-.120	-.146	-.126	.068	.065	-.143	-.113	-.142	-.108	-.056	-.061
MARSTT2	.054	.199	-.030	-.111	.243	-.026	.041	-.019	.036	.024	.030	-.029	.042	-.018	.032	-.015	-.036
SEIT1	.014	.176	.001	-.102	.061	.646	.887	.577	.454	-.282	-.127	.954	.522	.724	.408	.191	.087
SEIT2	.058	.211	-.032	-.108	.103	.578	.874	.578	.773	-.138	-.243	.576	.936	.445	.712	.091	.167
CPLXT1	.015	.170	-.008	-.104	.081	.766	.577	.629	.584	-.359	-.208	.776	.444	.949	.541	.330	.206
CPLXT2	-.030	-.152	.033	.017	.096	.454	.773	.584	.584	.214	-.356	.476	.755	.573	.930	.201	.331
SKLT1	-.015	-.102	.010	.000	-.066	-.282	-.138	-.359	-.314	.510	-.478	-.333	-.167	-.451	-.259	-.949	-.585
SKLT2	.036	.186	-.057	-.096	.078	-.127	-.243	-.208	-.356	-.478	.596	-.386	-.310	-.282	-.457	-.599	-.947
LSEIT1	.004	.173	-.028	-.094	.112	.954	.576	.776	.476	-.333	-.386	.748	.614	.783	.463	.262	.150
LSEIT2	.050	.202	-.052	-.083	.098	.522	.936	.444	.755	-.167	-.310	.804	.614	.460	.779	.131	.257
LCPLXT1	.023	.172	-.034	-.074	.101	.724	.445	.949	.573	-.451	-.282	.594	.768	.704	.589	.434	.282
LCPLXT2	.026	.159	-.031	-.032	.075	.408	.712	.541	.930	-.259	-.457	.536	.398	.615	.548	.256	.453
LSKLT1	.026	.112	.009	-.015	.068	.191	.091	.330	.201	-.478	-.507	.356	.443	.427	.427	.552	.634
LSKLT2										-.490	-.927	.356	.443	.395	.548	.552	.634

Note: Consult chapter 7, table 7-1 for variable definitions.

**Appendix D:
Select Raw and Exponential
Metric Scores for 1970
Census Occupations**

Code and Occupation Category	1	2	3	4	5	6	7
001 Accountants	1	76.8	1.90	17.49	1.45	8.97	0.01
002 Architects	1	85.2	3.77	15.33	1.22	3.13	2.10
003 Computer programmers	1	65.0	1.44	17.73	1.51	8.57	0.04
004 Computer systems analysts	1	65.0	1.44	18.99	1.77	7.52	0.18
005 Computer specialists, n.e.c.	1	65.0	1.44	22.19	2.27	5.07	0.82
006 Aeronautical and astronautical engineers	1	87.0	4.14	15.21	1.19	3.34	1.73
010 Chemical engineers	1	89.9	4.42	15.19	1.18	3.49	1.61
011 Civil engineers	1	84.0	2.50	13.53	1.01	3.00	2.23
012 Electrical and electronic engineers	1	84.0	2.50	15.06	1.16	3.53	1.57
013 Industrial engineers	1	85.5	3.86	17.62	1.48	7.66	0.16
014 Mechanical engineers	1	80.2	2.15	15.07	1.16	2.84	2.36
015 Metallurgical and materials engineers	1	83.1	2.44	16.07	1.34	3.82	1.24
020 Mining engineers	1	85.0	3.65	14.22	1.09	2.76	2.50
021 Petroleum engineers	1	81.0	2.16	15.80	1.28	4.05	1.12
022 Sales engineers	1	87.0	4.14	17.56	1.47	3.63	1.52
023 Engineers, n.e.c.	1	86.9	3.96	15.45	1.24	3.93	1.17
024 Farm management advisers	1	83.0	2.40	22.66	2.40	2.43	2.92
025 Foresters and conservationists	1	48.0	0.90	09.62	0.71	5.52	0.73
026 Home management advisers	1	83.0	2.40	20.27	1.94	3.46	1.65
030 Judges	1	93.0	5.30	26.62	6.21	1.24	4.27
031 Lawyers	1	92.3	4.96	25.97	4.96	1.78	3.35
032 Librarians	1	60.0	1.18	18.62	1.68	6.71	0.36
033 Archivists and curators	1	74.6	1.82	17.42	1.44	4.92	0.87
034 Actuaries	1	81.0	2.16	17.96	1.57	9.09	0.01
035 Mathematicians	1	80.0	2.03	20.58	2.02	9.00	0.01
036 Statisticians	1	81.0	2.16	18.16	1.60	8.84	0.02
042 Agricultural scientists	1	80.0	2.03	14.38	1.10	3.63	1.51
043 Atmospheric and space scientists	1	62.0	1.29	18.18	1.61	8.60	0.04
044 Biological scientists	1	80.0	2.03	14.53	1.11	2.74	2.66
045 Chemists	1	79.4	2.00	14.98	1.15	2.96	2.29
051 Geologists	1	80.0	2.03	15.67	1.26	2.76	2.50

Code	Occupation							
052	Marine scientists	1	80.0	2.03	15.67	1.26	2.76	2.50
053	Physicists and astronomers	1	80.0	2.03	16.74	1.37	3.32	1.77
054	Life and physical scientists, n.e.c.	1	77.2	1.91	20.94	2.09	8.47	0.06
055	Operations and systems researchers and analysts	1	65.7	1.52	18.13	1.59	7.23	0.24
056	Personnel and labor relations workers	1	83.6	2.48	20.40	2.00	4.64	0.95
061	Chiropractors	1	75.0	1.85	24.07	2.92	0.70	4.71
062	Dentists	1	96.0	6.21	25.80	4.71	1.31	3.86
063	Optometrists	1	79.0	1.96	24.07	2.92	0.70	4.71
064	Pharmacists	1	81.3	2.32	12.95	0.96	3.14	2.02
065	Physicians, medical and osteopathic	1	92.1	4.71	24.99	4.42	0.83	4.42
071	Podiatrists	1	58.0	1.11	23.25	2.53	1.45	3.65
072	Veterinarians	1	78.0	1.94	20.65	2.05	2.11	3.22
073	Health practitioners, n.e.c.	1	58.0	1.11	18.82	1.71	4.31	1.04
074	Dietitians	1	39.0	0.61	17.00	1.40	6.66	0.38
075	Registered nurses	1	44.3	0.81	15.95	1.31	8.19	0.08
076	Therapists	1	59.9	1.17	17.90	1.56	5.68	0.67
080	Clinical laboratory technologists and technicians	1	48.0	0.90	09.95	0.74	3.11	2.15
081	Dental hygienists	1	48.0	0.90	14.84	1.14	7.14	0.26
082	Health record technologists and technicians							
083	Radiologic technologists and technicians	1	60.0	1.18	15.92	1.29	8.58	0.04
084	Therapy assistants	1	48.0	0.90	13.99	1.08	6.14	0.54
085	Health technologists and technicians, n.e.c.	1	48.0	0.90	18.82	1.71	4.31	1.04
086	Clergymen	1	52.2	1.05	13.81	1.05	6.34	0.46
090	Religious workers, n.e.c.	1	52.0	1.03	26.41	5.30	1.28	4.14
091	Economists	1	56.7	1.09	23.48	2.69	2.69	2.69
092	Political scientists	1	74.4	1.80	19.23	1.81	6.78	0.35
093	Psychologists	1	81.0	2.16	20.64	2.03	4.93	0.87
094	Sociologists	1	81.0	2.16	24.65	4.14	2.96	2.27
095	Urban and regional planners	1	81.0	2.16	24.34	3.22	3.79	1.25
096	Social scientists, n.e.c.	1	65.0	1.44	18.55	1.66	6.98	0.28
		1	81.0	2.16	20.37	1.98	7.87	0.13
100	Social workers	1	64.0	1.41	23.45	2.62	1.48	3.58

Code and Occupation Category	1	2	3	4	5	6	7
101 Recreation workers	1	67.0	1.57	22.46	2.34	3.78	1.35
102 Agriculture teachers	1	84.0	2.50	24.34	3.22	3.78	1.25
103 Atmospheric, earth, marine, and space teachers	1	84.0	2.50	21.47	2.16	3.45	1.66
104 Biology teachers	1	84.0	2.50	24.34	3.22	3.79	1.25
105 Chemistry teachers	1	84.0	2.50	23.66	2.80	3.70	1.44
110 Physics teachers	1	84.0	2.50	24.34	3.22	3.79	1.25
111 Engineering teachers	1	84.0	2.50	23.65	2.76	3.91	1.17
112 Mathematics teachers	1	84.0	2.50	24.21	3.12	3.76	1.35
113 Health specialties teachers	1	84.0	2.50	23.10	2.50	4.07	1.11
114 Psychology teachers	1	84.0	2.50	24.34	3.22	3.78	1.25
115 Business and commerce teachers	1	84.0	2.50	24.34	3.22	3.78	1.25
116 Economics teachers	1	84.0	2.50	24.34	3.22	3.78	1.25
120 History teachers	1	84.0	2.50	23.78	2.88	3.96	1.14
121 Sociology teachers	1	84.0	2.50	24.34	3.22	3.78	1.25
122 Social science teachers, n.e.c.	1	84.0	2.50	24.14	3.06	4.12	1.09
123 Art, drama, and music teachers	1	53.2	1.08	23.61	2.72	3.64	1.51
124 Coaches and physical education teachers	1	64.0	1.41	23.32	2.56	3.71	1.43
125 Education teachers	1	84.0	2.50	24.11	3.02	3.73	1.37
126 English teachers	1	84.0	2.50	23.03	2.48	3.67	1.48
130 Foreign language teachers	1	84.0	2.50	23.42	2.59	3.59	1.54
131 Home economics teachers	1	72.0	1.71	23.71	2.83	3.42	1.69
132 Law teachers	1	84.0	2.50	24.34	3.22	3.78	1.25
133 Theology teachers	1	84.0	2.50	24.34	3.22	3.78	1.25
134 Trade, industrial, and technical teachers	1	84.0	2.50	20.65	2.05	3.36	1.71
135 Miscellaneous teachers, college and university	1	84.0	2.50	24.22	3.17	3.76	1.35
140 Teachers, college and university, subject not specified	1	84.0	2.50	22.91	2.44	3.73	1.40

Code	Occupation							
141	Adult education teachers	1	61.3	1.26	21.37	2.13	3.33	1.74
142	Elementary school teachers	1	71.2	1.69	21.43	2.15	2.80	2.44
143	Prekindergarten and kindergarten teachers	1	72.0	1.71	17.84	1.55	4.87	0.89
144	Secondary school teachers	1	70.2	1.65	21.81	2.21	3.19	1.94
145	Teachers, except college and university, n.e.c.	1	62.3	1.38	22.37	2.32	3.00	2.23
150	Agriculture and biological technicians, except health	1	62.0	1.29	07.87	0.43	3.68	1.45
151	Chemical technicians	1	62.0	1.29	09.08	0.61	3.67	1.47
152	Draftsmen	1	67.0	1.57	11.47	0.84	3.24	1.85
153	Electrical and electronic engineering technicians	1	62.0	1.29	11.23	0.81	3.07	2.19
154	Industrial engineering technicians	1	64.1	1.43	10.41	0.76	6.65	0.39
155	Mechanical engineering technicians	1	62.0	1.29	09.88	0.74	2.45	2.88
156	Mathematical technicians	1	53.0	1.07	18.02	1.58	8.94	0.01
161	Surveyors	1	48.4	0.95	16.80	1.38	8.48	0.06
162	Engineering and science technicians, n.e.c.	1	62.0	1.29	10.22	0.75	3.72	1.42
163	Airplane pilots	1	79.0	1.96	11.56	0.86	4.69	0.93
164	Air traffic controllers	1	69.0	1.62	17.17	1.43	7.21	0.24
165	Embalmers	1	60.8	1.20	16.10	1.35	5.87	0.61
170	Flight engineers	1	48.0	0.90	09.43	0.66	3.18	1.96
171	Radio operators	1	69.0	1.62	12.10	0.92	6.05	0.57
172	Tool programmers, numerical control	1	62.0	1.29	11.90	0.89	7.35	0.20
173	Technicians, n.e.c.	1	62.0	1.29	11.81	0.88	4.04	1.13
174	Vocational and educational counselors	1	65.0	1.44	23.47	2.66	1.76	3.41
175	Actors	1	60.0	1.18	19.04	1.78	4.51	0.99
180	Athletes and kindred workers	1	59.4	1.15	16.99	1.40	3.68	1.46
181	Authors	1	76.0	1.88	20.07	1.93	8.92	0.02
182	Dancers	1	45.0	0.83	18.33	1.64	4.48	1.00
183	Designers	1	70.5	1.66	13.09	0.98	2.82	2.40
184	Editors and reporters	1	82.0	2.34	21.09	2.10	6.22	0.52
185	Musicians and composers	1	52.0	1.03	21.91	2.25	4.85	0.90
190	Painters and sculptors	1	67.0	1.57	13.02	0.97	2.25	3.06
191	Photographers	1	50.0	0.99	11.67	0.87	1.69	3.51

Code and Occupation Category	1	2	3	4	5	6	7
192 Public relations men and publicity writers	1	82.0	2.34	20.05	1.91	6.24	0.51
193 Radio and television announcers	1	65.0	1.44	20.27	1.94	4.36	1.02
194 Writers, artists, and entertainers, n.e.c.	1	40.2	0.66	17.76	1.51	5.60	0.70
195 Research workers, not specified	1	65.0	1.44	17.77	1.52	4.72	0.92
201 Assessors, controllers, and treasurers; local public administration	1	61.2	1.25	19.58	1.84	6.53	0.41
202 Bank officers and financial managers	1	79.5	2.02	21.73	2.19	4.70	0.92
203 Buyers and shippers, farm products	1	50.5	1.01	19.65	1.88	6.00	0.58
205 Buyers, wholesale and retail trade	1	72.1	1.74	18.62	1.68	5.77	0.64
210 Credit men	1	74.0	1.77	19.59	1.85	7.33	0.20
211 Funeral directors	1	59.0	1.14	18.92	1.75	6.97	0.29
212 Health administrators	1	74.1	1.78	21.89	2.23	3.43	1.68
213 Construction inspectors, public administration	1	57.6	1.10	16.77	1.37	6.56	0.31
215 Inspectors, except construction, public administration	1	66.7	1.56	11.39	0.84	6.71	0.36
216 Managers and superintendents, building	1	32.0	0.49	15.84	1.29	5.74	0.64
220 Office managers, n.e.c.	1	75.1	1.86	19.62	1.86	7.13	0.26
221 Officers, pilots, and pursers; ship	1	49.9	0.99	13.61	1.03	1.28	3.96
222 Officials and administrators; public administration, n.e.c.	1	67.3	1.60	19.05	1.80	5.74	0.65
223 Officials of lodges, societies, and unions	1	59.8	1.16	22.54	2.36	3.65	1.49
224 Postmasters and mail superintendents	1	61.3	1.26	17.67	1.49	6.53	0.40
225 Purchasing agents and buyers, n.e.c.	1	74.7	1.82	18.30	1.62	5.42	0.76
226 Railroad conductors	1	58.2	1.13	15.93	1.30	6.90	0.31
230 Restaurant, cafeteria, and bar managers	1	37.6	0.59	16.39	1.35	6.27	0.50
231 Sales managers and department heads, retail trade	1	70.6	1.68	19.39	1.82	4.50	0.99
233 Sales managers, except retail trade	1	74.7	1.82	22.75	2.42	3.13	2.05
235 School administrators, college	1	77.9	1.93	22.21	2.29	4.57	0.96

Code	Occupation							
240	School administrators, elementary and secondary	1	71.7	1.70	24.70	4.27	2.66	2.76
245	Managers and administrators, n.e.c.	1	62.0	1.29	18.54	1.65	5.28	0.79
260	Advertising agents and salesmen	1	66.1	1.55	17.50	1.45	6.19	0.54
261	Auctioneers	3	40.0	0.64	14.81	1.13	5.80	0.62
262	Demonstrators	3	35.0	0.56	12.90	0.94	4.96	0.85
264	Hucksters and peddlers	3	08.8	0.06	13.25	0.99	4.98	0.84
265	Insurance agents, brokers, and underwriters	1	66.0	1.54	17.09	1.42	6.50	0.42
266	Newsboys	3	27.0	0.42	08.54	0.52	6.91	0.31
270	Real estate agents and brokers	1	62.0	1.29	16.00	1.32	6.20	0.53
271	Stock and bond salesmen	1	72.3	1.75	19.89	1.90	6.55	0.40
281	Sales representatives, manufacturing industries	1	65.0	1.44	15.56	1.25	5.62	0.70
282	Sales representatives, wholesale trade	1	60.9	1.21	15.29	1.21	5.76	0.64
283	Sales clerks, retail trade	3	39.0	0.61	11.55	0.85	6.21	0.52
284	Salesmen, retail trade	3	39.0	0.61	14.37	1.09	5.77	0.63
285	Salesmen of services and construction	1	52.7	1.06	13.92	1.06	5.74	0.65
301	Bank tellers	2	52.0	1.03	15.06	1.16	6.77	0.34
303	Billing clerks	2	44.0	0.73	11.02	0.78	8.22	0.08
305	Bookkeepers	3	50.8	1.01	13.43	1.00	8.77	0.03
310	Cashiers	2	44.0	0.73	11.30	0.83	5.87	0.60
311	Clerical assistants, social welfare	2	44.0	0.73	11.95	0.89	7.26	0.23
312	Clerical supervisors, n.e.c.	1	43.6	0.72	17.81	1.54	6.67	0.38
313	Collectors, bill and account	3	43.3	0.71	12.15	0.92	6.68	0.37
314	Counter clerks, except food	3	44.0	0.73	09.66	0.72	7.22	0.24
315	Dispatchers and starters, vehicle	3	39.9	0.64	14.59	1.11	5.87	0.61
320	Enumerators and interviewers	1	44.0	0.73	13.86	1.05	6.28	0.49
321	Estimators and investigators, n.e.c.	1	59.2	1.14	15.37	1.23	7.11	0.27
323	Expediters and production controllers	1	43.7	0.72	13.46	1.01	7.02	0.28
325	File clerks	2	44.0	0.73	11.29	0.82	7.80	0.14
326	Insurance adjusters, examiners, and investigators	1	62.1	1.37	18.72	1.70	7.42	0.19

Code and Occupation Category	1	2	3	4	5	6	7
330 Library attendants and assistants	3	44.0	0.73	13.57	1.02	6.62	0.39
331 Mail carriers, post office	2	53.0	1.07	10.48	0.77	7.66	0.16
332 Mail handlers, except post office	2	43.0	0.70	08.73	0.56	7.72	0.16
333 Messengers and office boys	3	28.2	0.44	05.52	0.30	7.88	0.12
334 Meter readers, utilities	3	44.0	0.73	09.45	0.69	9.26	0.00
341 Bookkeeping and billing machine operators	2	44.9	0.82	11.21	0.81	8.29	0.07
342 Calculating machine operators	2	45.0	0.83	09.69	0.72	7.79	0.15
343 Computer and peripheral equipment operators	1	45.0	0.83	09.47	0.69	4.47	1.01
344 Duplicating machine operators	2	45.0	0.83	02.70	0.17	6.49	0.43
345 Keypunch operators	2	45.0	0.83	06.65	0.37	4.22	1.07
350 Tabulating machine operators	2	45.0	0.83	05.35	0.29	7.18	0.25
355 Office machine operators, n.e.c.	2	45.0	0.83	05.27	0.29	5.73	0.66
360 Payroll and timekeeping clerks	2	44.0	0.73	12.43	0.93	8.68	0.03
361 Postal clerks	3	44.7	0.81	13.04	0.98	6.80	0.34
362 Proofreaders	3	44.0	0.73	09.38	0.65	9.67	0.00
363 Real estate appraisers	3	67.8	1.61	11.59	0.86	8.54	0.05
364 Receptionists	2	44.0	0.73	12.93	0.95	6.75	0.35
370 Secretaries, legal	1	61.0	1.22	15.22	1.20	7.28	0.22
371 Secretaries, medical	1	61.0	1.22	15.21	1.19	7.27	0.22
372 Secretaries, n.e.c.	1	61.9	1.28	15.41	1.24	7.30	0.22
374 Shipping and receiving clerks	3	24.2	0.37	05.23	0.28	7.42	0.19
375 Statistical clerks	2	43.7	0.72	11.63	0.87	7.91	0.12
376 Stenographers	2	61.0	1.22	11.51	0.85	8.78	0.03
381 Stock clerks and storekeepers	2	44.0	0.73	06.44	0.36	7.72	0.16
382 Teacher aides, except school monitors	3	63.2	1.40	12.99	0.96	5.66	0.68
383 Telegraph messengers	3	22.0	0.32	11.95	0.89	7.26	0.23
384 Telegraph operators	2	47.0	0.89	09.85	0.73	7.00	0.28
385 Telephone operators	2	45.0	0.83	04.97	0.26	2.66	2.72
390 Ticket, station, and express agents	3	59.8	1.16	14.81	1.13	6.33	0.47
391 Typists	3	61.0	1.22	10.39	0.75	8.29	0.07

Code	Occupation						
392	Weighers	3	41.9	0.68	01.04	0.08	7.41	0.20
394	Miscellaneous clerical workers	3	43.7	0.72	11.14	0.79	7.84	0.13
395	Not specified clerical workers	3	44.0	0.73	11.14	0.79	7.84	0.13
401	Automobile accessories installers	1	21.6	0.30	10.49	0.77	3.93	1.16
402	Bakers	1	21.9	0.31	04.41	0.25	5.50	0.74
403	Blacksmiths	1	16.0	0.13	08.03	1.45	3.54	1.55
404	Boilermakers	1	32.6	0.51	08.80	0.58	3.08	2.16
405	Bookbinders	1	39.0	0.61	02.36	0.15	7.15	0.25
410	Brickmasons and stonemasons	1	27.0	0.42	06.80	0.38	4.53	0.98
411	Brickmasons and stonemasons, apprentices	1	32.0	0.49	06.89	0.38	4.21	1.07
412	Bulldozer operators	2	19.7	0.27	02.46	0.15	6.22	0.52
413	Cabinetmakers	1	22.3	0.34	08.18	0.47	2.75	2.62
415	Carpenters	1	18.9	0.22	08.59	0.52	4.20	1.08
416	Carpenter apprentices	1	31.0	0.47	08.49	0.51	4.27	1.06
420	Carpet installers	1	12.0	0.09	06.16	0.34	4.12	1.09
421	Cement and concrete finishers	1	19.0	0.23	03.02	0.20	7.41	0.19
422	Compositors and typesetters	1	52.0	1.03	07.30	0.40	5.05	0.83
423	Printing trades apprentices, except pressmen	1	40.0	0.64	05.41	0.30	5.63	0.69
424	Cranemen, derrickmen, and hoistmen	2	21.0	0.28	02.21	0.14	5.94	0.59
425	Decorators and window dressers	1	40.0	0.64	12.80	0.94	1.40	3.77
426	Dental laboratory technicians	1	48.0	0.90	10.71	0.78	5.05	0.83
430	Electricians	1	44.0	0.73	09.49	0.70	3.20	1.91
431	Electrician apprentices	1	37.0	0.58	09.41	0.65	3.22	1.90
433	Electric power linemen and cablemen	1	49.0	0.96	08.59	0.52	3.51	1.59
434	Electrotypers and stereotypers	1	55.0	1.09	08.24	0.48	7.05	0.27
435	Engravers, except photoengravers	1	47.0	0.89	04.94	0.26	5.14	0.81
436	Excavating, grading, and road machine operators; except bulldozer	3	22.8	0.34	02.68	0.17	6.17	0.54
440	Floor layers, except tile setters	1	17.3	0.18	03.03	0.20	6.13	0.55
441	Foremen, n.e.c.	1	49.7	0.98	16.06	1.33	2.17	3.17
442	Forgemen and hammermen	1	23.0	0.35	04.08	0.24	5.66	0.67
443	Furniture and wood finishers	1	17.8	0.19	06.34	0.36	4.67	0.93

Code and Occupation Category	1	2	3	4	5	6	7
444 Furriers	1	39.5	0.65	11.35	0.83	2.76	2.50
445 Glaziers	1	25.2	0.39	04.45	0.25	5.53	0.73
446 Heat treaters, annealers, and temperers	1	21.7	0.31	02.70	0.17	5.44	0.75
450 Inspectors, scalers, and graders; log and lumber	1	22.4	0.34	03.62	0.22	8.13	0.10
452 Inspectors, n.e.c.	1	41.2	0.68	08.46	0.50	6.86	0.33
453 Jewelers and watchmakers	1	36.4	0.58	09.64	0.72	3.48	1.62
454 Job and die setters, metal	1	33.5	0.53	07.83	0.43	2.80	2.48
455 Locomotive engineers	1	57.8	1.11	08.67	0.55	5.31	0.78
456 Locomotive firemen	1	45.0	0.83	08.70	0.56	5.29	0.79
461 Machinists	1	32.9	0.51	09.17	0.61	2.54	2.83
462 Machinist apprentices	1	41.0	0.67	08.32	0.49	2.93	2.32
470 Air conditioning, heating, and refrigeration	1	27.0	0.42	08.95	0.60	3.79	1.24
471 Aircraft	1	48.0	0.90	09.55	0.70	3.29	1.80
472 Automobile body repairmen	1	19.0	0.23	07.08	0.39	3.94	1.15
473 Automobile mechanics	1	19.0	0.23	08.82	0.59	3.39	1.70
474 Automobile mechanic apprentices	1	25.0	0.38	09.43	0.66	3.18	1.93
475 Data processing machine repairmen	1	27.0	0.42	11.28	0.81	3.19	1.93
480 Farm implement	1	27.0	0.42	09.34	0.64	3.12	2.13
481 Heavy equipment mechanics, including diesel	1	26.6	0.41	08.82	0.59	3.27	1.81
482 Household appliance and accessory installers and mechanics	1	27.0	0.42	07.09	0.40	4.61	0.96
483 Loom fixers	1	10.0	0.06	09.43	0.66	2.29	2.96
484 Office machine	1	35.9	0.56	11.19	0.80	3.47	1.64
485 Radio and television	1	36.0	0.57	09.56	0.71	3.24	1.84
486 Railroad and car shop	1	20.5	0.28	08.10	0.47	4.27	1.05
491 Mechanic, except auto, apprentices	1	34.0	0.54	06.96	0.39	4.09	1.10
492 Miscellaneous mechanics and repairmen	1	26.5	0.41	07.60	0.42	3.73	1.39
495 Not specified mechanics and repairmen	1	27.0	0.42	08.06	0.46	3.49	1.60

501	Millers; grain, flour, and feed	1	19.0	0.23	05.27	0.29	6.07	0.56
502	Millwrights	1	31.0	0.47	09.31	0.63	3.22	1.88
503	Molders, metal	1	12.0	0.09	06.04	0.34	4.32	1.03
504	Molder apprentices	1	33.0	0.52	08.65	0.53	3.85	1.18
505	Motion picture projectionists	1	43.0	0.70	08.07	0.46	4.08	1.11
506	Opticians, and lens grinders and polishers	1	39.0	0.61	05.92	0.33	3.51	1.58
510	Painters, construction and maintenance	1	16.4	0.15	03.88	0.23	5.53	0.72
511	Painter apprentices	1	29.0	0.45	08.65	0.53	3.85	1.18
512	Paperhangers	1	13.7	0.11	03.90	0.23	5.49	0.74
514	Pattern and model makers, except paper	1	43.0	0.70	07.86	0.43	3.32	1.75
515	Photoengravers and lithographers	1	63.0	1.39	07.78	0.43	4.95	0.86
516	Piano and organ tuners and repairmen	1	38.0	0.60	08.27	0.48	3.13	2.07
520	Plasterers	1	25.0	0.38	04.23	0.25	5.65	0.68
521	Plasterer apprentices	1	29.0	0.45	08.65	0.53	3.85	1.18
522	Plumbers and pipe fitters	1	34.0	0.54	08.84	0.59	3.85	1.23
523	Plumber and pipe fitter apprentices	1	33.0	0.52	08.79	0.58	3.85	1.23
525	Power station operators	1	50.0	0.99	07.75	0.42	6.94	0.30
530	Pressmen and plate printers, printing	1	46.3	0.89	05.38	0.29	6.04	0.58
531	Pressman apprentices	1	40.0	0.64	03.45	0.22	6.19	0.53
533	Rollers and finishers, metal	1	22.0	0.32	00.88	0.06	6.88	0.31
534	Roofers and slaters	1	15.1	0.13	06.78	1.37	3.73	1.38
535	Sheetmetal workers and tinsmiths	1	33.0	0.52	09.08	0.61	3.24	1.86
536	Sheetmetal apprentices	1	33.0	0.52	09.43	0.66	3.18	1.96
540	Shipfitters	1	34.0	0.54	08.74	0.56	4.55	0.97
542	Shoe repairmen	1	12.0	0.09	07.45	0.41	3.96	1.14
543	Sign painters and letterers	1	16.9	0.16	08.74	0.56	3.52	1.56
545	Stationary engineers	1	45.2	0.87	05.98	0.33	5.59	0.71
546	Stone cutters and stone carvers	1	24.0	0.36	03.31	0.21	5.91	0.60
550	Structural metal craftsmen	1	33.7	0.54	04.98	0.27	4.90	0.88
551	Tailors	1	22.0	0.32	05.90	0.33	4.65	0.94
552	Telephone installers and repairmen	1	48.8	0.96	07.58	0.41	3.31	1.78
554	Telephone linemen and splicers	1	49.0	0.96	08.74	0.56	3.00	2.21
560	Tile setters	1	28.2	0.44	04.69	0.26	4.95	0.86

Code and Occupation Category	1	2	3	4	5	6	7
561 Tool and die makers	1	49.2	0.98	09.32	0.64	2.55	2.80
562 Tool and die maker apprentices	1	41.0	0.67	09.43	0.66	2.29	2.96
563 Upholsterers	3	21.1	0.29	03.39	0.22	5.22	0.80
571 Specified craft apprentices, n.e.c.	1	34.5	0.56	08.65	0.53	3.85	1.18
572 Not specified apprentices	1	39.0	0.61	08.65	0.53	3.85	1.18
575 Craftsmen and kindred workers, n.e.c.	1	25.7	0.40	04.18	0.24	5.15	0.81
601 Asbestos and insulation workers	2	32.0	0.49	03.35	0.21	6.81	0.34
602 Assemblers	2	17.2	0.18	00.97	0.07	6.61	0.39
603 Blasters and powdermen	2	11.0	0.08	09.33	0.64	3.13	2.03
604 Bottling and canning operatives	2	18.4	0.22	−0.84	0.01	6.67	0.37
605 Chainmen, rodmen, and axmen; surveying	2	25.0	0.38	03.14	0.20	8.47	0.06
610 Checkers, examiners, and inspectors; manufacturing	2	19.2	0.25	03.94	0.23	6.27	0.49
611 Clothing ironers and pressers	2	17.8	0.19	01.34	0.09	5.45	0.75
612 Cutting operatives, n.e.c.	2	18.8	0.22	01.54	0.10	6.29	0.48
613 Dressmakers and seamstresses, except factory	1	23.0	0.35	05.53	0.31	3.78	1.34
614 Drillers, earth	2	21.6	0.30	02.36	0.15	6.27	0.50
615 Dry wall installers and lathers	2	24.5	0.37	04.08	0.24	6.51	0.42
620 Dyers	2	12.0	0.09	01.77	0.11	6.09	0.56
621 Filers, polishers, sanders, and buffers	2	18.7	0.22	00.96	0.07	6.45	0.43
622 Furnacemen, smeltermen, and pourers	2	18.1	0.20	01.44	0.09	5.93	0.59
623 Garage workers and gas station attendants	3	17.9	0.19	03.41	0.22	6.68	0.37
624 Graders and sorters, manufacturing	2	17.0	0.16	00.21	0.04	7.80	0.14
625 Produce graders and packers, except factory and farm	2	12.2	0.10	−0.27	0.02	8.12	0.11
626 Heaters, metal	2	29.0	0.45	05.64	0.31	4.55	0.98
630 Laundry and dry cleaning operatives, n.e.c.	2	15.0	0.12	−0.07	0.02	7.04	0.27
631 Meat cutters and butchers, except manufacturing	2	28.8	0.45	04.68	0.25	7.33	0.21

633	Meat cutters and butchers, manufacturing	3	16.4	0.14	02.60	0.16	5.84	0.62
634	Meat wrappers, retail trade	2	18.0	0.20	−0.50	0.01	7.79	0.15
635	Metal platers	2	19.8	0.27	05.20	0.28	4.31	1.03
636	Milliners	2	46.0	0.88	02.02	0.12	5.94	0.59
640	Mine operatives, n.e.c.	2	16.5	0.15	02.13	0.14	6.06	0.56
641	Mixing operatives	2	17.6	0.18	00.92	0.06	6.44	0.43
642	Oilers and greasers, except auto	2	15.0	0.12	−0.02	0.03	8.39	0.06
643	Packers and wrappers, except meat and produce	2	18.0	0.20	−0.41	0.01	7.85	0.13
644	Painters, manufactured articles	3	18.1	0.20	02.50	0.16	6.51	0.42
645	Photographic process workers	1	42.1	0.69	05.08	0.28	4.66	0.94
650	Drill press operatives	2	21.8	0.31	02.69	0.17	3.86	0.89
651	Grinding machine operatives	3	21.9	0.31	03.22	0.20	5.15	0.81
652	Lathe and milling machine operatives	2	21.5	0.30	01.78	0.12	6.12	0.55
653	Precision machine operatives, n.e.c.	3	21.0	0.28	05.02	0.27	4.79	0.91
656	Punch and stamping press operatives	2	19.4	0.26	02.87	0.19	5.38	0.77
660	Riveters and fasteners	2	20.1	0.28	00.43	0.04	6.30	0.48
661	Sailors and deckhands	2	16.0	0.13	01.51	0.10	8.86	0.02
662	Sawyers	3	04.9	0.01	01.78	0.12	5.85	0.61
663	Sewers and stitchers	2	18.2	0.21	02.28	0.14	5.01	0.84
664	Shoemaking machine operatives	2	09.2	0.06	−0.02	0.03	6.76	0.35
665	Solderers	2	23.8	0.35	00.79	0.05	6.24	0.51
666	Stationary firemen	1	16.6	0.15	02.96	0.19	6.88	0.32
670	Carding, lapping, and combing operatives	2	03.1	0.00	01.42	0.09	6.40	0.44
671	Knitters, loopers, and toppers	2	21.0	0.28	00.97	0.07	6.97	0.29
672	Spinners, twisters, and winders	2	03.8	0.01	−0.03	0.03	6.92	0.30
673	Weavers	2	05.9	0.01	02.39	0.15	5.69	0.66
674	Textile operatives, n.e.c.	2	06.1	0.02	01.20	0.08	6.92	0.41
680	Welders and flame-cutters	1	24.0	0.36	02.78	0.18	6.87	0.32
681	Winding operatives, n.e.c.	2	19.6	0.26	01.41	0.09	6.32	0.47
690	Machine operatives, miscellaneous specified	2	19.0	0.23	02.02	0.12	6.35	0.45
692	Machine operatives, not specified	2	19.3	0.26	02.02	0.12	6.35	0.45
694	Miscellaneous operatives	2	19.2	0.25	02.02	0.12	6.35	0.45

Code and Occupation Category	1	2	3	4	5	6	7
695 Not specified operatives	2	19.2	0.25	02.02	0.12	6.35	0.45
701 Boatmen and canalmen	2	24.0	0.36	02.64	0.16	6.31	0.48
703 Bus drivers	3	24.0	0.36	06.48	0.36	2.85	2.34
704 Conductors and motormen, urban rail transit	3	32.5	0.50	06.06	0.34	4.84	0.90
705 Deliverymen and routemen	2	31.0	0.47	08.20	0.48	5.63	0.69
706 Fork lift and tow motor operatives	2	16.8	0.15	00.10	0.03	5.33	0.78
710 Motormen; mine, factory, logging camp, etcetera	2	03.0	0.00	02.88	0.19	5.36	0.77
711 Parking attendants	2	18.8	0.22	05.73	0.31	8.12	0.10
712 Railroad brakemen	3	42.0	0.69	03.29	0.21	6.27	0.50
713 Railroad switchmen	3	44.0	0.73	01.58	0.10	6.85	0.33
714 Taxicab drivers and chauffeurs	3	10.0	0.06	05.04	0.27	2.80	2.42
715 Truck drivers	2	15.1	0.13	02.09	0.13	5.41	0.76
740 Animal caretakers, except farm	2	16.9	0.16	02.47	0.16	5.79	0.63
750 Carpenters' helpers	2	07.2	0.03	-2.02	0.00	7.58	0.17
751 Construction laborers, except carpenters' helpers	2	07.1	0.03	00.53	0.05	7.38	0.20
752 Fishermen and oysterman	2	10.6	0.07	00.75	0.05	6.37	0.44
753 Freight and material handlers	2	08.7	0.05	00.99	0.07	8.17	0.09
754 Garbage collectors	2	06.0	0.01	-2.02	0.00	7.31	0.21
755 Gardeners and groundskeepers, except farm	3	10.9	0.07	01.00	0.08	6.96	0.29
760 Longshoremen and stevedores	2	11.0	0.08	00.91	0.06	7.20	0.25
761 Lumbermen, raftsmen, and woodchoppers	3	04.1	0.01	00.67	0.05	7.27	0.22
762 Stock handlers	2	16.7	0.15	02.76	0.18	7.85	0.13
763 Teamsters	2	08.0	0.04	01.62	0.11	6.74	0.36
764 Vehicle washers and equipment cleaners	2	08.6	0.05	-0.72	0.01	7.63	0.17
770 Warehousemen, n.e.c.	2	08.3	0.04	-0.09	0.02	8.19	0.08
780 Miscellaneous laborers	3	08.2	0.04	00.38	0.04	7.53	0.17
785 Not specified laborers	3	08.3	0.04	00.38	0.04	7.53	0.17
801 Farmers (owners and tenants)	1	14.0	0.12	09.29	0.63	3.25	1.82

Code	Occupation							
802	Farm managers	1	36.0	0.57	13.76	1.04	4.98	0.85
821	Farm foremen	1	20.0	0.27	13.23	0.99	0.45	5.30
822	Farm laborers, wage workers	3	06.3	0.02	01.51	0.10	6.97	0.29
823	Farm laborers, unpaid family workers	3	17.0	0.16	01.60	0.11	6.94	0.30
824	Farm service laborers, self-employed	3	22.0	0.32	05.83	0.32	8.09	0.11
901	Chambermaids and maids, except private household	3	13.4	0.11	00.85	0.06	8.17	0.09
902	Cleaners and charwomen	2	07.8	0.03	01.59	0.11	7.75	0.15
903	Janitors and sextons	3	12.7	0.11	03.00	0.19	6.44	0.44
910	Bartenders	3	19.0	0.23	08.44	0.50	8.56	0.04
911	Busboys	2	11.0	0.08	05.46	0.30	8.15	0.09
912	Cooks, except private household	1	15.0	0.12	07.87	0.44	3.72	1.41
913	Dishwashers	3	11.0	0.08	-1.97	0.01	8.24	0.08
914	Food counter and fountain workers	2	17.0	0.16	06.31	0.35	8.34	0.07
915	Waiters	2	16.0	0.13	07.93	0.45	8.53	0.05
916	Food service workers, n.e.c., except private household	3	11.0	0.08	01.20	0.08	7.97	0.12
921	Dental assistants	1	38.0	0.60	14.61	1.12	8.29	0.07
922	Health aides, except nursing	3	25.0	0.38	12.04	0.90	7.18	0.25
923	Health trainees	3	51.0	1.02	12.06	0.91	8.94	0.02
924	Lay midwives	3	37.0	0.58	06.89	0.38	7.14	0.26
925	Nursing aides, orderlies, and attendants	3	13.7	0.11	08.99	0.60	9.00	0.01
926	Practical nurses	1	22.0	0.32	12.19	0.93	8.70	0.03
931	Airline stewardesses	3	31.0	0.47	07.93	0.45	8.65	0.04
932	Attendants, recreation and amusement	3	19.1	0.25	09.81	0.73	6.66	0.38
933	Attendants personal service, n.e.c.	3	26.3	0.40	06.89	0.38	7.44	0.18
934	Baggage porters and bellhops	3	07.8	0.03	08.50	0.51	6.87	0.32
935	Barbers	1	17.0	0.16	07.37	0.40	2.09	3.30
940	Boarding and lodging housekeepers	3	30.0	0.47	16.97	1.39	3.13	2.09
941	Bootblacks	3	08.0	0.04	05.73	0.31	8.12	0.10
942	Child care workers, except private household	3	28.2	0.44	08.45	0.50	7.98	0.11
943	Elevator operators	3	10.0	0.06	07.67	0.42	6.32	0.47
944	Hairdressers and cosmetologists	1	17.0	0.16	10.45	0.76	2.21	3.12

Code and Occupation Category	1	2	3	4	5	6	7
945 Personal service apprentices	3	31.0	0.47	08.63	0.53	0.00	3.30
950 Housekeepers, except private household	1	31.0	0.47	13.93	1.07	5.56	0.72
952 School monitors	3	26.0	0.40	13.98	1.07	5.58	0.72
953 Ushers, recreation and amusement	3	25.0	0.38	06.32	0.35	7.77	0.15
954 Welfare service aides	3	11.0	0.08	18.87	1.74	4.45	1.01
960 Crossing guards and bridge tenders	3	17.9	0.19	06.71	0.37	6.83	0.33
961 Firemen, fire protection	1	37.0	0.58	05.87	0.32	7.31	0.21
962 Guards and watchmen	2	18.2	0.21	08.33	0.49	7.41	0.19
963 Marshals and constables	3	21.0	0.28	09.23	0.62	7.90	0.12
964 Policemen and detectives	3	40.5	0.66	13.63	1.03	6.05	0.57
965 Sheriffs and bailiffs	3	34.0	0.54	09.41	0.65	8.15	0.09
980 Child care workers, private household	3	07.0	0.02	07.91	0.44	8.12	0.10
981 Cooks, private household	3	07.0	0.02	08.11	0.47	5.59	0.71
982 Housekeepers, private household	3	10.7	0.07	09.20	0.62	7.26	0.23
983 Laundresses, private household	3	12.0	0.09	-0.25	0.02	8.09	0.11
984 Maids and servants, private household	3	07.0	0.02	06.28	0.35	8.52	0.05

key: 1 = Sector code, where 1 = primary-independent; 2 = primary-subordinate; 3 = secondary
2 = Duncan SEI score
3 = Exponential metric for Duncan SEI scores
4 = Substantive complexity of work scores
5 = Exponential metric for complexity scores
6 = Skill level and scope scores
7 = Exponential metric for skill scores

Indexes

Index of Authors

Alexander, Karl L., 120, 125
Almquist, Elizabeth M., 60
Althauser, Robert P., 6, 27, 28, 38, 80, 83, 96, 171
Alwin, Duane F., 120
Angrist, Shirley S., 60
Averitt, Robert T., 102

Baron, James N., 6, 25, 46, 75, 80, 84, 101, 102, 125
Beck, E.M., 102, 151, 154
Becker, Gary S., 5, 73, 84
Bendix, Reinhard, 4
Berg, Ivar, 102
Bibb, Robert, 102
Bielby, William T., 6, 19, 25, 46, 75, 80, 84, 101, 102, 125
Blau, Peter M., 5, 13, 19, 25, 73, 106, 125
Bowles, Samuel, 27, 125

Cain, Glen G., 6, 102
Cain, Pamela S., 46
Call, Vaughn R.A., 1, 9, 11, 13, 14, 19, 21, 37
Carnoy, Martin, 86, 102
Chinoy, Ely, 25, 26
Coleman, James S., 158
Collins, Randall, 52, 58
Coser, Rose Laub, 84

Datan, Nancy, 24
Davis, Kingsley, 73
Doeringer, Peter B., 6, 49, 55, 76, 102, 136
Duncan, Beverly, 106, 125
Duncan, Otis D., 5, 13, 19, 73, 106, 125, 139
Dunlop, John T., 73

Eckaus, Richard S., 19, 27, 49, 60
Ecklund, Bruce K., 120, 125

Edwards, Richard C., 6, 58, 76, 78, 79, 80, 85, 86, 87, 101, 102, 135, 136, 137

Featherman, David L., 5, 13, 19, 25, 27, 49, 60, 73, 106, 108, 121, 125, 137, 173
Fetters, William B., 120
Field, Alexander James, 84
Fligstein, Neil D., 46, 75, 87, 97, 102, 125
Form, William H., 4, 102
Freedman, Marcia K., 101
Freeman, Richard B., 101

Gaertner, Karen N., 25
Gintis, Herbert, 27, 125
Goldberg, Samuel, 158
Goldner, Fred, 60
Gordon, David M., 6
Grandjean, Burke D., 24
Granovetter, Mark, 136, 171
Griffin, Larry J., 120, 125
Groeneveld, Lyle P., 14, 157
Gross, Edward, 60

Halaby, Charles N., 158
Hall, Oswald, 4
Hall, Richard H., 170
Haller, Archibald O., 27, 106, 109, 113, 114, 120, 125, 155
Hannan, Michael T., 14, 157
Hanushek, Eric A., 142
Harbison, Frederick H., 73
Hauser, Robert M.,. 13, 18, 19, 25, 49, 60, 73, 106, 107, 108, 109, 112, 114, 120, 121, 123, 124, 125, 137, 165, 166, 173
Heckman, James J., 125
Henderson, James M., 73, 74
Hicks, Alexander, 87
Hodson, Randy, 46, 75, 102
Hogan, Dennis P., 3, 81

229

Index of Subjects

About the Authors

Kenneth I. Spenner received the Ph.D. in sociology from the University of Wisconsin-Madison in 1977. Since then he has been a postdoctoral Fellow and research associate with the Career Development Program. His research and published articles have been on social psychology and social stratification. His current research work centers on occupational characteristics, classification systems, and work careers.

Luther B. Otto is director of the Career Development Program and director of the Research Division at the Boys Town Center. He has served as acting director of the Social Research Center at Washington State University. His research interests have focused on social psychology, stratification and mobility, and the sociology of education. Dr. Otto has published widely and has presented numerous professional papers on this research on the achievement process. He is a reviewer and editorial consultant for several professional journals and publishers. He is a regular consultant to private and public agencies in the field of education and work.

Vaughn R.A. Call received the Ph.D. from Washington State University in 1977. Since then he has been a postdoctoral Fellow and research associate with the Career Development Program. Dr. Call's research interests, presentations, and published articles focus on age at marriage and other major family events as these influence and are affected by occupational, educational, and military life-course events.